Religion in the Military Worldwide

How does religion affect the lives of professional soldiers? How does religion shape militaries, their organization, procedures, and performance? This volume is the first to address these questions by comparing religious symbols and practices in nine countries: Japan, Canada, the United Kingdom, Pakistan, Israel, Iran, India, the United States, and Turkey. The contributors explore how and why soldiers pray, the role of religious rituals prior to battle, the functions that chaplains perform, the effects of religion on recruitment and unit formation, and how militaries grapple with ensuing constitutional dilemmas.

Ron E. Hassner is an associate professor in the Department of Political Science at the University of California, Berkeley. He is the codirector of Berkeley's Religion, Politics, and Globalization Program and the founder and first chair of the International Studies Association's section on Religion and International Relations. His first book, *War on Sacred Grounds* (2009), examines the causes and characteristics of disputes over sacred places around the globe and analyzes the conditions under which these conflicts can be managed. He has also published on the topic of religion and conflict in *International Security*, *Security Studies*, *Civil Wars*, *International Studies Quarterly*, *Terrorism and Political Violence*, and others journals. He has contributed chapters on similar themes to several edited volumes.

Religion in the Military Worldwide

Edited by

RON E. HASSNER
University of California, Berkeley

CAMBRIDGE
UNIVERSITY PRESS

32 Avenue of the Americas, New York, NY 10013-2473, USA

Cambridge University Press is part of the University of Cambridge.

It furthers the University's mission by disseminating knowledge in the pursuit of education, learning, and research at the highest international levels of excellence.

www.cambridge.org
Information on this title: www.cambridge.org/9781107613645

© Cambridge University Press 2014

First published 2014

Printed in the United States of America

A catalog record for this publication is available from the British Library.

Library of Congress Cataloging in Publication data
Religion in the military worldwide / [edited by] Ron E. Hassner.
    pages cm
Includes bibliographical references and index.
ISBN 978-1-107-03702-1 (hardback) – ISBN 978-1-107-61364-5 (paperback)
    1. Military chaplains – Case studies.   2. Armed Forces – Religious life – Case
studies.   3. Soldiers – Religious life – Case studies.   4. Religion and state – Case
studies.   5. War – Religious aspects – Case studies.   I. Hassner, Ron E. (Ron Eduard)
UH20.R45   2014
355.3′47–dc23   2013022229

ISBN 978-1-107-03702-1 Hardback
ISBN 978-1-107-61364-5 Paperback

Contents

Contributors

Amit Ahuja, assistant professor of political science, University of California, Santa Barbara.

Joanne Benham Rennick, assistant professor of contemporary studies, Wilfrid Laurier University.

Stuart A. Cohen, professor of politics, Ashkelon Academic College, Israel.

Martin L. Cook, professor of professional military ethics, U.S. Naval War College.

Stephen Deakin, senior lecturer, Royal Military Academy Sandhurst.

Victor Dobbin, retired chaplain general, British Army.

Gül M. Kurtoğlu Eskişar, associate professor of international relations, Dokuz Eylul University.

C. Christine Fair, assistant professor in the Center for Peace and Security Studies, Georgetown University.

Ron E. Hassner, associate professor of political science, University of California, Berkeley.

Akito Ishikawa, assistant professor in the Faculty of Letters, Hokkaido University.

Ayşegül Komsuoğlu, associate professor of political science, Istanbul University.

Pauletta Otis, professor of security studies, Marine Corps University.

Eric Patterson, Dean of the School of Government, Regent University.

Mahsa Rouhi, PhD candidate in international relations, University of Cambridge.

Aaron Skabelund, assistant professor of history, Brigham Young University.

Introduction

Religion in the Military Worldwide: Challenges and Opportunities

Ron E. Hassner

Consider the following three episodes involving religious practices in the military.[1] The first, set during the Second Kashmir War, was reported by Indian Lt. Gen. Ranjit Singh Dayal: "In 1965 we went into an objective. There we saw some cows grazing. Suddenly the shelling started. One cow got hurt by a shell and I saw a *jawan* [Indian soldier] pulling out his field dressing and applying it to the cow."[2]

The second episode occurred in Samarra, Iraq, in the spring of 2004. Sgt. Jeffrey Humphrey, of the 1st Infantry Division, noticed that his men had painted a text in giant Arabic script on the side of a Bradley armored vehicle. "'What's it mean?' asked Humphrey. 'Jesus killed Mohammed,' one of them said. The soldiers guffawed. JESUS KILLED MOHAMMED was about to cruise into the Iraqi night."[3] An Iraqi interpreter took to the roof of the vehicle, bullhorn in hand, to shout out the phrase in Arabic and English. As the soldiers drove through the streets of Samarra, their blasphemous proclamations drew live fire from the city's residents. The soldiers responded with 25-millimeter shells.[4]

The third episode took place on an Israeli military base in the spring of 1991. In preparation for Passover, observers from the Israel Defense Forces (IDF) rabbinate had arrived at the camp to supervise the ritual cleansing of the kitchen of leavened substances, such as bread crumbs, which are forbidden to observant Jews during Passover. Three intelligence analysts were excused from their regular assignments and given special kitchen duty. Although all three were nonobservant Jews, they spent the next two days immersing plates, cutlery, and cooking implements, one by one, in boiling water under the watchful eyes of the rabbinical supervisors. Occasionally, one of the supervisors would issue a corrective: a fork had not been immersed long enough, or it had accidentally touched the side of the pot and needed to be resubmerged. I was one of

Photo 1 Marine recruits pray before lights out at Parris Island. Photo copyright Shannon Stapleton/Reuters/Corbis.

the soldiers, and those two days in the kitchen, identical to procedures followed in all IDF kitchens every Passover, planted the seeds for this volume.

The three preceding episodes vary in space and time as well as in significance. The events in Lt. Gen. Dayal's dubious account had a negligible impact on the outcome of the day's battle, let alone the war.[5] My two-day stint, ritually purifying a kitchen, had little effect beyond distracting me from my professional duties. The same cannot be said of the incident in Samarra in 2004. Members of the same unit, riled up after watching a video of Mel Gibson's *The Passion of the Christ* over Easter, provoked additional outrage by spray-painting crosses on local mosques.[6]

If these incidents seem startling, it is in part because scholars of the military have yet to assemble the tools required for understanding the roots, characteristics, or consequences of religious practices in the armed forces. When international security scholars study religion, they emphasize ideas at the expense of practices. Because these religious ideas are studied as causes of conflict, the impact of religion on military organization, decision making, rhetoric, and performance before, during, and after combat has eluded scholars. At the same time, U.S. priorities in the decade since the terrorist attacks of September 11, 2001 have placed the religion of nonstate violent actors, primarily Islamist insurgents, in the spotlight. Lost in the analysis of "other people's religions" is the impact of religion on professional military forces, including U.S. troops.

Students of religion and politics have no account of the impact of Christianity, Hinduism, or Judaism (or, for that matter, moderate Islam) on conventional militaries.

This volume is the first to offer a comparative analysis of religion in militaries worldwide. Its primary goal is to turn the lens away from the religious practices of others and toward rituals, symbols, and beliefs more familiar to Western readers that affect soldiers around the world. The contributors to this volume do not purport to provide a unifying theory of religion in the military, nor do we seek to advocate for or against religion in the military. Our purpose is to initiate midlevel theorizing about the role of religion in the military by providing novel empirical and theoretical insights based on nine case studies: Japan, Canada, the United Kingdom, Pakistan, Israel, Iran, India, the United States, and Turkey.

I began this project by asking all of the contributors five questions about the role of religion in the militaries they study. These questions pertained to demography, organization, practices, religious leadership, and operations. First, how does the religious affiliation of service members reflect or distort the distribution of religious groups in society at large? Statistically speaking, which groups are underrepresented or overrepresented? Second, how does religious affiliation influence promotion and leadership positions in the armed forces? Are some units more religiously cohesive than others by design or self-selection? Third, do religious rituals and beliefs affect how soldiers are trained, armed, or led into battle? Do soldiers follow unique practices that are traceable to religious rationales and involvement, for example, the handling of weapons, the treatment of servicewomen, patterns of dress and behavior, taboos, food and drink, and recreation? Fourth, what roles do clerics play in the armed forces? What are their rights and obligations? Fifth, how does each of these variables affect military operations and the conduct of war?

In the following pages of this introduction, I briefly review existing research on the role of religion in different militaries. This includes work on civil-military relations, the literature on strategic culture, and research on military effectiveness. I then highlight the main challenges the contributors faced in responding to my prompts: the problem of expertise, the difficulty of defining religion, and the quandary of case selection. The third part of this introduction presents the unifying themes of the book: religious demographics, the impact of religion on force structure, the role of religious symbols, beliefs, and practices, the functions performed by chaplains, the effect of religion on military operations, and the prominence of constitutional issues relating to religion in the armed forces. I summarize the principal findings of the chapters by dividing the volume into four parts: chapters that emphasize religious practices (Japan, Canada, United Kingdom), chapters that highlight demographic issues (Pakistan, Israel), chapters that explore the impact of religion on operations (Iran, India), and chapters that investigate constitutional challenges (United States and Turkey).

Available Tools

Students of international security, civil-military relations, and religion in international affairs have provided little preliminary research on which contributors
to this volume could draw. Comparative analyses, along the lines offered in
this volume, are all but nonexistent.[7] Even academic research on religion in
particular militaries is sparse.[8] Extant scholarship on religion in the U.S. military, such as it is, tends to be polemical or focuses on specific constitutional
challenges.[9] The only facet of this topic that has received sustained attention is
the narrow subject of military chaplains, which is usually examined through a
historical lens.[10] Of the three academic journals most likely to address religion
in the military, the first, *Armed Forces & Society*, has published a mere six articles on the topic since its inception in 1974.[11] The second, *Review of Faith &
International Affairs*, has dedicated only nine essays to the topic, all gathered
into a single issue on military chaplains.[12] The third, *Journal of Church and
State*, has published only four articles on the military in the fifty years since its
founding.[13]

The contributors to this volume have sought to remedy this lacuna by
conducting interviews and surveys, in addition to performing field research
to provide novel empirical foundations for their chapters. Christine Fair, for
example, bases her chapter on Pakistan on a statistical analysis of an original
dataset. Mahsa Rouhi relied on Iranian government publications, archival
records, historical speeches by leading Shi'a clerics, and personal interviews
with senior Iranian officials to craft her chapter on Iran. Aaron Skabelund
and Akito Ishikawa, Ayşegül Komsuoğlu and Gül Kurtoğlu Eskişar, Joanne
Benham Rennick, and Amit Ahuja draw on interviews they conducted with
members of the Japanese, Turkish, Canadian, and Indian armed forces,
respectively.

Given the paucity of existing data on religion in the military and the absence
of low-level theories, let alone midlevel theories, the contributors to this volume have not sought to develop an all-encompassing argument about the role
of faith in the armed forces. The range of issues, actors, and levels of analyses
implied in the questions that initiated this project precludes such a unified
theory. At the same time, the chapters speak to three literatures that reflect
ongoing concerns in the study of culture and international security: the literature on civil-military relations, the study of strategic culture, and the analysis of
military effectiveness. These research programs have yet to address the topic of
religion in the military directly. Nonetheless, readers may find these frameworks
useful as lenses through which to view the arguments herein. The study of civil-
military relations, for example, can shed light on the origins and propagation
of religious organization, rules, and practices in the military. The literature on
strategic culture can clarify the effects of these variables on decision making.
Research on military effectiveness can highlight the ways in which religion
affects battlefield performance.

Civil-Military Relations

Scholars of civil-military relations have sought to understand how military institutions interact with the societies they seek to protect and with the civil authorities from which they derive their resources and legitimacy.[14] These scholars are interested in, first, the means that elites employ to promote and to curb the power of the military; second, the role of civilians in military decision making; third the influence of the military on the civilian realm; and fourth, the degree to which the military is representative of, in tension with, or integrated into society.

The authors in this volume conclude that the military reflects and replicates the contentious politics that surround religious issues in civilian society. Debates over religious freedoms and constitutional dilemmas regarding the relationship between church and state are mirrored in the military. They affect the ability of soldiers to express and act on their religious identities; to shape how religious minorities are tolerated, accommodated, or oppressed; and to influence the funding of religious institutions facilities for soldiers, such as religious instruction, state-sponsored rituals, on-base places of worship, and military chaplains.[15] Religious practices in the military, in turn, can reinforce or undermine the prevailing consensus over religion in society at large. Depending on the interconnectedness of civilian society and the military in both degree and kind, the demographics of religion in the military reflect or distort the distribution of religious groups in the larger society. This in turn may affect promotion in the ranks, determine recruitment levels and self-selection into military units, and impinge on levels of trust and cooperation between military and civilian leaders.

Strategic Culture

The literature on strategic culture has a related series of concerns.[16] Scholars of ideas, identity, and culture have sought to explain the ways in which prevailing civilian and military norms influence policy making by civilian and military leaders. A strategic culture approach to the study of religion in the military would seek to investigate how the military reproduces prevailing social norms regarding the appropriate role of religion in society. At the same time, religion itself is, among other things, a framework of ethics, ideology, and identity that can influence civilian and military decision making. Religious ideas and practices regarding appropriate and inappropriate targets, opportunities, and means for violence can shape policy. Indeed, securitization arguments imply that religion can inform the very definition of what counts as a threat, a value worth defending, a legitimate policy goal, and even the parameters of victory and defeat. Militaries can use religious ideology to recruit, mobilize, and motivate soldiers. In addition, religion can form a core or marginal aspect of a military's corporate identity and thus associate or distance the military from the identity of the state.[17]

Military Effectiveness

How the use of religion translates into success or failure on the battlefield is a core concern for scholars who study military effectiveness. Military effectiveness denotes the ability of armed forces to marshal resources to enhance power and achieve success on the battlefield.[18] Religion is one such resource. Following Risa Brooks and Elizabeth Stanley, I argue that, among the requirements for military effectiveness, two – responsiveness and skill – are particularly amenable to the influence of religion.[19] Responsiveness defines a military's ability to adapt its tactics to new information, adjusting to constraints as necessary. A responsive military tailors its doctrine to exploit enemy weaknesses while modifying its own force structure as new challenges and threats arise. Skill, in turn, measures a military's proficiency at executing doctrine to achieve a particular task. A skillful military motivates its soldiers to excel in combat by instilling a sense of commitment and initiative.[20]

Religious beliefs, practices, and institutions can play a significant role in these processes. Even religious rituals and symbols that do not have the explicit purpose of regulating or motivating combat can prove salient in times of conflict. Combatants who are also members of religious denominations may want to participate in ceremonies that honor holy days and avoid desecrating holy days by eschewing prohibited behavior. For example, consuming alcohol or refusing to take up arms in accordance with religious requirements could increase the vulnerability of combatants and enhance the capabilities of their opponents. Religious settings associated with quietism, pacifism, or concord may introduce reluctance into an actor's decision to participate in combat. On the other hand, holy days that commemorate triumphal martyrdom, holy places that represent martial deities, and religious leaders who sanction the use of force may inspire actors to engage in conflict. Religion can thus encourage or discourage participation in conflict and constrain what participants are and are not willing to do in these circumstances.

To summarize, although contemporary analyses of civil-military relations, strategic culture, and military effectiveness have yet to tackle the subject matter of religion in the military directly, readers can employ them as frameworks for examining the case studies in this volume. These frameworks in turn provide insight into the causes, characteristics, and consequences of religious practices in the military.

Primary Challenges

The contributors to this volume confronted the challenges posed by the scarcity of research on religion in the military head-on. These challenges fall into three main groups: the exceedingly interdisciplinary nature of the subject matter, the difficulty of understanding and defining religion, and the problem of case selection.

The Problem of Expertise

The analysis of religion in the military requires researchers to accumulate expertise in area studies and history, military affairs, and religion. Whereas intersections between comparative politics and military affairs, or between comparative politics and religion, are common, few academics possess a background in both religion and security studies. Yet a working knowledge of these diverging fields is particularly important in this case, given the challenge of accessing sources and obtaining reliable data. Few military organizations gather rigorous information on religious practices in the ranks, those that do tend to be reluctant to share such data with researchers, and soldiers are often disinclined to speak openly about their personal beliefs.

The authors in this volume overcame this obstacle in different ways. Several contributors, including Stuart Cohen and Joanne Benham Rennick, looked to their own academic careers, which have focused on the role of religion in particular military settings. Victor Dobbin, Martin Cook, and Pauletta Otis drew on their service experience in writing about the British and U.S. armed forces. To analyze religion in the Japanese Self-Defense Force, Aaron Skabelund, a historian of the Japanese military, joined forces with Akito Ishikawa, a scholar of religion.

Theorizing Religion

Even where researchers were able to acquire data on a particular country and military, arriving at a useful conceptualization of religion proved a formidable barrier to analysis. Variation across the cases examined in this volume and disagreements among scholars of religion as to the relative utility of competing definitions swayed us from adopting a unified theory of religion that would do justice to the Shinto, Buddhist, Sikh, Jewish, Christian, Muslim, and Hindu cases analyzed herein.

At the same time, the emphasis on religious ideas, practices, and discourses in this volume, in contrast with the narrow characterization of religion as an idea in other political science texts, suggests an eclectic and open-ended approach to religion. After all, our goal in compiling this volume was to replace the analysis of religion as an extremist, fundamentalist, and aberrant force in international security with a nuanced study of religion as a conventional and pervasive variable. The religions practiced in militaries around the world are neither confined to sacred texts nor captured in the formal theologies of religious experts. They are lived, ever present, and often informal systems of experiences and symbols.

Elsewhere, I have proposed a "thick" religion approach to the study of religion and politics, which fits well with the goals of this volume.[21] This approach requires an understanding of religious detail but also a willingness to generalize from particular religious movements, regions, or instances to arrive at broader conclusions. The analysis starts with an investigation of religion in its various manifestations: theology, hierarchy (religious organization), iconography (symbols), ceremony, and knowledge (beliefs) – hence "thick."

A thick religion analysis of religion in the military is thus anchored in answers to one or more of the following questions:

Theology: How do the tenets of particular religious movement influence military beliefs and practices?

Hierarchy: How does religion affect military organizations, and what roles do religious leaders play in the lives of soldiers?

Iconography: How do soldiers employ religious symbols, myths, images, words, or sounds?

Ceremony: How do soldiers respond to the theology, hierarchy, and iconography of their religious movements in rituals, feasts, and commemorations?

Knowledge: What do soldiers believe in? What are the foundations of their faith?

Thick religion implies an issue-area approach that focuses the analysis on a topic in which religion and international affairs interact. Instead of identifying mere correlations, this method traces a comprehensive logical chain, from the content of specific religious ideas to particular outcomes, and thus identifies causal or even constitutive relationships between religious ideas and behavior.

In this volume, several authors employ a similar approach to investigate the religious microfoundations of military practices and then construct successive layers of explanation, each more removed from the religious, until they reach the outcome to be explained. Other authors make reference to a particular approach in the sociology or philosophy of religion, be it work by Emile Durkheim, Clifford Geertz, Bruce Lincoln, and Danièle Hervieu-Léger (in the chapters on Japan and Canada); the writings of Alasdair MacIntyre and Jonathan Sacks (in the chapter on the United Kingdom); or Robert Bellah's work on "civil religion" (in Martin Cook's chapter on the United States).

In sum, rather than bemoan the burden of an interdisciplinary approach, this volume celebrates it. The contributors seek to understand religion in the military by combining insights from the sociology of religion, theology, and religious studies with lessons from politics, international security, and organizational theory.

Case Selection

The topic of religion in the military is vast, yet the number of cases that can be included in a single volume is limited. In selecting cases for inclusion, I had three goals: first, to emphasize the pervasiveness of religion in some of the most professional military forces in the world; second, to highlight the exciting variety of beliefs, symbols, and practices across religious movements that shape military behavior; and third, to explore moderate Muslim practices in the military as a counterweight to the prevailing fixation on terrorism and radical Islam.

The chapters on Japan, Canada, the United Kingdom, Israel, India, the United States, and Turkey address the first of these aspirations. These countries possess some of the most advanced, skilled, and formidable military organizations in the world, yet even here religion plays an important role. The countries examined in these chapters also demonstrate that religious traditions that are usually neglected by security scholars, such as Judaism, Shinto, Buddhism, and Hinduism, can prove as influential as Christianity, Islam, and Sikhism in affecting these military practices.

To challenge preconceptions about fundamentalist Islam and violence, I invited Christine Fair, Mahsa Rouhi, Ayşegül Komsuoğlu, and Gül Kurtoğlu Eskişar to contribute chapters on the Pakistani, Iranian, and Turkish armed forces, respectively. The chapter on Pakistan highlights the role of moderate Islam in a professional military. The chapter on religion in the Iranian armed forces during the Iran-Iraq War, the only historical case study in this book, introduces Shi'a beliefs and practices. It also brings the project full circle by examining radical Islam in a professional military setting. The Turkish case provides a provocative analysis of Islam in a military force that is viewed as a guardian of secularism.

Although the external threat faced by U.S. forces is often perceived as religiously driven, academic analyses rarely look inward to examine the role of religion in the U.S. military. Martin Cook and Pauletta Otis offer comprehensive discussions of several key themes relating to this subject, with particular emphasis on the role of chaplains, the perceived radicalization of the U.S. armed forces, and constitutional controversies surrounding the separation of church and state and religious accommodation. The inclusion of two chapters on the U.S. military permits a detailed analysis of this important yet understudied case. It also allows the two contributors to offer diverging viewpoints on these contentious issues, permitting readers to form their own opinions based on the merits of two analyses.

The ten case studies in this volume leave ample room for future work on religion in the military. Omitted are case studies from Latin America and Africa; studies of militaries in which Catholicism, Orthodox Christianity, Buddhism, and native and nature religions prevail; and arguably most important, analyses of religious practices in militaries under communist regimes. Extensions of the research project initiated here might include entries on Argentina, Brazil, China, Colombia, Egypt, Greece, Indonesia, Nigeria, North Korea, Russia, South Africa, and Vietnam.

Principal Findings

This volume is divided into four parts based on the primary theme that authors highlighted in their contributions. I begin this section by highlighting these themes and move to summarize principal findings in each section: rituals, beliefs, and practices (Japan, Canada, the United Kingdom), demographics (Pakistan, Israel), operations (Iran, India), and constitutional challenges (the United States and Turkey).

TABLE I.I. *Issue Emphasis by Chapter*

Chapter	Demographics	Force Structure	Symbols, Beliefs, Practices	Chaplains	Operations	Constitutional Issues
1. Japan			X	X		X
2. Canada	X		X	X	X	
3. United Kingdom	X		X	X	X	X
4. Pakistan	X	X				X
5. Israel	**X**	X	X	**X**	X	
6. Iran		X	X	X	**X**	X
7. India	X	X			X	X
8. United States	X			X		**X**
9. United States	X					**X**
10. Turkey	**X**	**X**	**X**	X	X	X

Note: An "X" designates an aspect of religion in the military emphasized in a particular chapter; an "**X**" designates an aspect pivotal to the chapter.

Themes and Patterns

I asked contributors to address five issues in their chapters: demography, organization, practices, religious leadership, and operations. As Table I.I illustrates, these chapters complement one another well. All authors address multiple issues and all issues receive a detailed treatment in at least two chapters. Nearly all of the authors were able to collect information on religious demographics, although few could uncover how particular denominations were distributed across military units or how this dispersal affected recruitment, retention, and promotion. More surprising, almost all of the authors chose to discuss a sixth issue, the constitutional challenges posed by religious practices in the armed forces, a topic that I had disregarded in my initial instructions.

The pattern emerging from these studies is one of disequilibrium: questions regarding the proper role of religion in the military are not confined to the armed forces but draw in, and spill over into, civilian society. None of the states examined here have yet found a way to balance religious freedoms, constitutional values, and operational requirements. In religiously homogeneous and religiously pluralistic societies, and in religious and secular states, religious practices in the military continue to fluctuate, bedevil decision makers, and provoke heated debate.

Whereas the role of military clerics proved to be a topic of interest to most contributors, fewer authors chose to describe religious symbols and rituals. The variation in both is fascinating, however, whether in the form of purification rituals in Japan, religiously grounded humanitarian ideals in Canada, religious clubs in the United Kingdom, or prayers on the battlefield in Iran.

Uncovering the effects of religious practices on contemporary battlefield performance, as did Stuart Cohen and Joanne Benham Rennick in their respective chapters on Israel and Canada, proved difficult, presumably because doing so requires unprecedented familiarity with the subject matter and access to sources. The authors who emphasized the impact of religious practices on military operations tended to do so in a historical context, reaching back decades (in the chapters on Iran and India) and even centuries (in the chapters on the United Kingdom and Turkey) for examples.

Part I: Rituals, Beliefs, and Practices

This volume begins with a study of religion in the Japanese Self-Defense Forces (SDF). The Japan case may seem an odd choice for an opening chapter in a book on religion in the military, given the highly secularized nature of Japanese society and the severe constraints that the Japanese constitution has placed both on maintaining a military force and on the comingling of church and state. Indeed, religion does not appear to affect promotion, training, gender relations, dress, diet, or many other aspects of military service in Japan. On closer examination, however, Aaron Skabelund and Akito Ishikawa find that Shinto practices proliferate in the SDF given the identification of Shinto as an essential element of Japanese national identity, martial morale, and organizational unity.

Skabelund and Ishikawa examine the historical rise of State Shinto in Japan and its interaction with the Imperial military before 1945. This controversial relationship endures to this day in visits by SDF officers to Japan's nation-protecting shrines. Although officers can visit these shrines as private citizens, they often do so in uniform and are announced by name, rank, and military branch. The practice of apotheosis, enshrining deceased personnel at these temples, has provoked additional debate. Because the SDF does not employ chaplains, soldiers routinely collect donations to fund unofficial visits by Shinto priests to SDF bases. These priests perform dedication and purification rites designed to protect military personnel from bad luck and to ensure their safety and prosperity. SDF facilities, ships, planes, and other vehicles are adorned with altars and amulets. These rituals, in turn, have strained relations between the SDF and mainstream Buddhist and Christian groups in Japan.

In Canada, on the other hand, Christianity enjoys a privileged position and a constitutionally established legacy. As Joanne Benham Rennick argues in Chapter 2, however, increasing religious diversity represents a challenge to traditional values and reflects a tendency toward religious individualism, creating uncertainty for members of the Canadian Forces (CF). Soldiers are asked to uphold "Christian" Canadian values but are unsure what this means. Despite receiving moral and ethical training from chaplains, soldiers often arrive at discordant interpretations of martial values, which can lead to impropriety and abuse, as occurred during the United Nations Observation and Peacekeeping Mission in Somalia.

The suffering witnessed by Canadian soldiers during past military operations, as well as a sense of frustration, hopelessness, and dislocation, can cause soldiers to experience confusion and trauma. Some soldiers adapt their beliefs to deal with these trying circumstances, or they consult military chaplains to help them understand their feelings. Other are driven to moral anomie. Benham Rennick concludes that religion influences values and ethical decision making in the Canadian Forces, but that lack of knowledge about religion and religious values has the potential to cause serious problems given the growing religious diversity within the CF. It could also hinder cooperation with future UN operations.

In Chapter 3, Victor Dobbin and Stephen Deakin provide a detailed account of religious institutions and practices in the British armed forces, using historical examples that include World War I, the Malayan Insurgency, and contemporary Afghanistan. Although British soldiers have always had an ambivalent relationship to their faith, religion is firmly anchored in British military laws and traditions, harking back to statutes from the seventeenth century that dictated the role of chaplains and established prayer schedules.

British military ceremonies continue to accompany the burial of the dead and acts of remembrance. Most units have dedicated churches, cemeteries, and even official prayer collections. Chaplains preach to the troops, provide pastoral care, and teach the faith as well ethical values. Soldiers participate in religious fellowships and enjoy the services of Christian welfare institutions outside the military. These traditions and institutions are now being challenged by an increasingly secularized and religiously fragmented society.

Part II: Demographics

Whereas the first three case studies emphasize rituals, beliefs, and practices in the armed forces, the next two chapters explore the distribution of religious groups in the military. In Chapter 4, Christine Fair argues that leaders in Pakistan have historically sought to employ political Islam as a unifying and mobilizing force by Islamizing the country's military institutions; encouraging orthodox teaching, practices, and rhetoric in the army; and recruiting from pious populations in urban areas. These leaders gave Islamic groups a presence in the army, and training missions in Gulf states have exposed soldiers to Wahhabism.

These developments have led decision makers in the United States to worry about the Islamization of the Pakistan Army. Fair has gathered a unique dataset on district-level officer recruitment and retirements from 1970 to 2005 to correct for the absence of empirical data on the religious affiliation of Pakistani officers. She finds that the army has grown more representative of Pakistani society at large, with officers increasingly likely to come from urban and Pashtun areas as well as from areas that are socially more liberal. These recruitment patterns may influence how officers view their militant opponents in the Pashtun belt. The data offer little support for concerns about Islamization in the ranks, but they should prompt policy makers to take national surveys to determine how the demography of military families in Pakistan differs from the rest of society.

In Chapter 5, Stuart Cohen offers an analysis of a conscript army suffused with Jewish themes and motifs. He surveys the ambivalent attitudes toward the use of force in Judaism prior to the establishment of the State of Israel and distinguishes between the prevailing attitudes toward military service among different religious sectors in Israeli society. The IDF must face the challenge of reconciling and accommodating these diverging views against a background of significant demographic change in society as a whole and declining enlistment rates among ultra-Orthodox Jews.

To enable observant Jews to serve in the military alongside their secular counterparts, the IDF has established segregated units that permit stringent conformity with Jewish law. The IDF rabbinate ensures the observance of basic Jewish standards across the military and teaches Jewish values to soldiers from all backgrounds. Unique educational arrangements allow observant soldiers to intersperse military service with study in religious academies. The graduates of these institutions tend to join homogeneous units, and they have become overrepresented in combat units. Rabbis inside and outside the military have gradually crafted a corpus of decrees designed to facilitate accommodation between traditional religious practices, such as Sabbath observance, and military requirements. Cohen dismisses concerns about heightened rabbinical influence over observant soldiers but warns of the growing social schism between national-religious and secular troops.

Part III: Operations

The third part of this volume examines the impact of religion on combat operations. In Chapter 6, Mahsa Rouhi explores how religion played a central role in the Islamic Republic of Iran Army (IRIA) in the 1980–1988 Iran-Iraq War. The transition from a secular, professional military to an ideologically trained force following the 1979 Islamic Revolution involved the creation of competing military institutions, primarily the Islamic Revolution Guards Corps and the Basij volunteer force. These radicalized organizations allowed Iran's Supreme Leader, Ayatollah Ruhollah Khomeini, and its clerical elite to expand their influence over the armed forces.

The outbreak of the Iran-Iraq War enabled these units to marginalize the IRIA and take charge of the war effort. They did so in part by implementing a doctrine of martyrdom that was executed by young volunteers. Drawing on statistics, memoirs, and interviews, Rouhi demonstrates the salience of this tactic on the battlefield and the role that religious symbols, rhetoric, and rituals – particularly those associated with the commemoration of Ashura (the ceremony observing the martyrdom of Imam Hussein) and the historical Battle of Karbala – played in motivating Iranian soldiers to become martyrs.

Amit Ahuja explores the impact of religion on combat operations in a multifaith force in which Hindus, Sikhs, Christians, Buddhists, and Muslims serve side by side. The Indian Army recruits and operates in a society characterized by religious diversity, high levels of religiosity, and intense sectarian conflict. The military thus faces the constant challenge of accommodating religious practices, subduing communal riots, and preventing interfaith conflict in the ranks. To meet this challenge, it has sought to establish the primacy of military authority so that duty trumps obligation to the faith.

The Indian Army has employed four institutional mechanisms to help it achieve this objective. First, it has organized units based on ethnicity, rather than religion, to minimize faith-based mutinies. Second, officers, who form an elite class apart from the soldiers under their command, are discouraged from open displays of piety. Third, it has institutionalized respect for all faiths through training, symbols, and rhetoric and by avoiding religious references to the enemy. Fourth, it maintains an apolitical stance. Ahuja illustrates these mechanisms at work during the 1984 counterinsurgency in Amritsar and the quelling of the subsequent Sikh mutiny.

Part IV: Constitutional Challenges

The fourth part of this book addresses the constitutional challenges posed by religion in the U.S. and Turkish militaries. In the first of two chapters on the United States, Martin Cook warns of the growing influence of Evangelical forces in the military. Dramatic increases in the number of Evangelical chaplains and the politicization of the Evangelical movement have been accompanied by proselytizing and religious worship in inappropriate military settings.

These practices, Cook argues, run counter to restrictions in the U.S. Constitution on the role of religion in the military and form part of a concerted campaign to reinterpret the Constitution and reclaim the Christian identity of the United States. The military has failed to take appropriate disciplinary action in response to this conduct. This failure could have substantial operational implications, particularly if soldiers begin to view conflicts and opponents in religious terms.

In Chapter 9, Pauletta Otis provides an alternative view of religion in the U.S. military. Otis argues that neither military practices nor military policies evidence a force unduly influenced by religion. The U.S. military does not reflect Christian beliefs nor is it entirely secular. Instead, military laws and traditions keep the values and behaviors of religious soldiers in check. With regard to religious diversity, the military roughly mirrors the distribution of denominations in the civilian population, with no apparent pattern in the recruitment of adherents to particular units. Commanders do not treat religious faith as a requirement for excellence or promotion. Christian principles have influenced the moral and ethical principles of the military, but they have not determined defense policy. The U.S. military has thus succeeded in accommodating the religious needs of individuals without compromising discipline or encouraging divisions in the ranks.

In Chapter 10, Ayşegül Komsuoğlu and Gül Kurtoğlu Eskişar analyze the Turkish armed forces, an organization that has sought to protect Turkey's secular identity and has intervened time and again in Turkish politics to block Islamist influence. Whereas Islamic symbols and practices played a central role in the Ottoman military, the secular Turkish Republic required the removal of Islam from the military's training and institutional structure. Consequently, the Turkish armed forces do not retain official chaplains, and they confine the religious practices of troops to the private sphere. At the same time, they routinely employ Islamic concepts dating back to the Ottoman Empire to boost the combat morale of their soldiers.

To defend the new state, the Turkish military struck a tentative equilibrium between secularism and religion. This balance was challenged in the 1980s when the state began incorporating Islamic values into its national ideology, and it was overturned in the 1990s when the armed forces declared their explicit opposition to Islamist political parties. This tension not only has had stark implications for officers who openly practiced their religious beliefs, but it has translated into an ever-diminishing space for religion in the Turkish military.

Conclusion

Eric Patterson concludes the volume with an evaluation of the relationship between religion and war and an assessment of the contributors' principal findings. He highlights six themes: the way that religion in the ranks mirrors the religiosity of society at large, the prevalence of civil religion in many national militaries, the role of chaplains, the differences between classical (secular) armed forces and military entities motivated by ideology or religion, debates over the appropriate balance of religion in the military, and the onset of postmodern values in Western militaries.

Patterson recommends that in future research scholars deepen the analysis of the countries examined in this volume and explore militaries in other states, particularly those with large militaries (e.g., China, the European powers, and Russia) and those in highly religious societies (e.g., Bangladesh, Brazil, and Poland). The topic of world religions training offers yet another fruitful venue for analysis. How are militaries preparing their troops for engaging in highly religious environments? Finally, future research might explore how religion influences new types of operations "other than war" in which militaries find themselves increasingly involved, such as counterterrorism and peacekeeping operations.

Religion continues to influence conflicts around the world, including operations that involve the United States and its allies. Yet Patterson finds some solace in this volume's findings. Not only have soldiers demonstrated their ability to develop cordial and professional relations with comrades from different religious backgrounds, but only rarely do militaries exhibit religiously motivated violence in the ranks. Perhaps, he concludes, the care with which militaries worldwide have treated religious differences can serve as a model for civilian society.

Notes

1 This chapter and the entire volume grew out of the "Religion in the Armed Forces" conference, organized by the Religion, Politics, and Globalization Program at the University of California, Berkeley, and sponsored by Berkeley's Institute for International Studies in December 2010. I thank the director of the institute, Pradeep Chhibber, for providing the generous funding and welcoming institutional home for this conference.

2 Mark Tully and Satish Jacob, *Amritsar: Mrs. Gandhi's Last Battle* (London: Jonathan Cape, 1985): 158.

3 Jeff Sharlet, "Jesus Killed Mohammed: The Crusade for a Christian Military," *Harpers*, May 2009: 32.

4 Ibid.

5 There are good reasons to doubt the tale's authenticity. Dayal recounted the incident in an attempt to defend the piety of India's soldiers, who had been accused of religious insensitivity and even desecration during the calamitous Golden Temple assault in 1984.

6 Sharlet, "Jesus Killed Mohammed."

7 The single exception is Hillel Frisch, "The Role of Religion in the Militaries of Egypt, Syria, and Jordan," *Orient* 43, no. 2 (2002): 207–224.

8 Stuart Cohen and Joanne Benham Rennick, both contributors to this volume, have written on religion in the Israeli and Canadian armed forces, respectively. See Stuart A. Cohen, *The Scroll or the Sword? Dilemmas of Religion and Military Service in Israel* (London: Routledge, 1997); Stuart A. Cohen, "Tensions between Military Service and Jewish Orthodoxy In Israel: Implications Imagined and Real," *Israel Studies* 12, no. 1 (Spring 2007): 103–126; Stuart A. Cohen, "From Integration to Segregation: The Role of Religion in the IDF," *Armed Forces and Society* 25, no. 3 (1999): 387–405; Joanne Benham Rennick, *Religion in the Ranks: Belief and Religious Experience in the Canadian Forces* (Toronto: University of Toronto Press, 2011); Joanne Benham Rennick, "Towards an Interfaith Ministry: Religious Adaptation and Accommodation in the Canadian Forces Chaplaincy," *Studies in Religion* 39, no. 1 (2010): 77–91; and Joanne Benham Rennick, "Canadian Military Chaplains: Bridging the Gap between Alienation and Operational Effectiveness in a Pluralistic and Multicultural Context," *Religion, State, and Society* 39, no. 1 (2011): 93–109. On Israel, see also Yohai Hakak, "From the Army of God to the Israeli Armed Forces: An Interaction between Two Cultural Models," in *Gender, Religion, and Change in the Middle East: Two Hundred Years of History*, ed. Inger

Marie Okkenhaug and Ingvild Flaskerud (London: Berg Publishers, 2005): 29–46; Elisheva Rosman-Stollman, "Mediating Structures and the Military: The Case of Religious Soldiers," *Armed Forces and Society* 34, no. 4 (2008): 615–638. On Britain, see Michael Snape, *God and the British Soldier: Religion and the British Army in the First and Second World Wars* (London: Routledge, 2005).

9 For critiques of current practices in the U.S. military, see, for example, Anne Loveland, *American Evangelicals and the U.S. Military, 1942–1993* (Baton Rouge and London: Louisiana State University Press, 1996); Michael Weinstein and Davin Sea, *With God on Our Side: One Man's War against an Evangelical Coup in America's Military* (London: Macmillan, 2008). For analyses of the constitutional ramifications of these practices, see, for example, Klaus K. Herrmann, "Some Considerations on the Constitutionality of the United States Military Chaplaincy," *American University Law Review* 14 (1964): 24–37; Albert Figinski, "Military Chaplains – A Constitutionally Permissible Accommodation between Church and State," *Maryland Law Review* 24, no. 4 (Fall 1964): 377–416; Julie B. Kaplan, "Military Mirrors on the Wall: Nonestablishment and the Military Chaplaincy," *Yale Law Journal* 95, no. 6 (May 1986): 1210–1236; David E. Fitzkee and Linell A. Letendre, "Religion in the Military: Navigating the Channel between the Religion Clauses," *Air Force Law Review* 59 (2007): 1–71; Steven K. Green, "Reconciling the Irreconcilable: Military Chaplains and the First Amendment," *West Virginia Law Review* 110, no. 1 (Fall 2007): 167–186; and Ira C. Lupu and Robert W. Tuttle, "Instruments of Accommodation: The Military Chaplaincy and the Constitution," *West Virginia Law Review* 110 (2007): 89–166.

10 See, for example, Rodger R. Ventzke, *Confidence in Battle, Inspiration in Peace: The United States Army Chaplaincy, 1945–1975* (Honolulu, HI: University Press of the Pacific, 2004); Doris L. Bergen, ed., *The Sword of the Lord: Military Chaplains from the First to the Twenty-First Century* (Notre Dame, IN: University of Notre Dame, 2004); Harvey G. Cox, ed., *Military Chaplains: From a Religious Military to a Military Religion* (New York: American Report Press, 1972); Richard M. Budd, *Serving Two Masters: The Development of American Military Chaplaincy, 1860–1920* (Lincoln: University of Nebraska Press, 2002); Gordon Zahn, *The Military Chaplaincy: A Study of Role Tension in the Royal Air Force* (Toronto: University of Toronto Press, 1969); Jacqueline Werkner, "Military Chaplaincy in International Operations: A Comparison of Two Different Traditions," *Journal of Contemporary Religion* 23, no. 1 (2008): 47–62; and the special issue on the changing role of the military chaplaincy in *Religion, State and Society* 39, no. 1 (2011).

11 These are: Kenneth Hendrickson, "Winning the Troops for Vital Religion: Female Evangelical Missionaries to the British Army, 1857–1880," *Armed Forces & Society* 23, no. 4 (Summer 1997): 615–634; Tyler V. Johnson, "To Take Up Arms against Brethren of the Same Faith: Lower Midwestern Catholic Volunteers in the Mexican-American War," *Armed Forces & Society* 32, no. 4 (July 2006): 532–548; Richard Machalek, Andrew D. Katayama, James E. Patrey, and Dana H. Born, "Suspending Routine Duty: The Sociological Significance of Military Holidays and Ceremonies," *Armed Forces & Society* 32, no. 3 (April 2006): 389–404; Ward Thomas, "ROTC and the Catholic Campus," *Armed Forces & Society* 33, no. 2 (January 2007): 224–237; Cohen, "From Integration to Segregation"; Rosman-Stollman, "Mediating Structures and the Military."

12 *Review of Faith & International Affairs* 7, no. 4 (Winter 2009).
13 These are: Paul J. Weber, "The First Amendment and the Military Chaplaincy: The Process of Reform," *Journal of Church and State* 22 (1980): 459–474; Pamela Robinson-Durso, "Chaplains in the Confederate Army," *Journal of Church and State* 33, no. 4 (1991): 747–763; Stuart A. Cohen, "The *Hesder Yeshivot* in Israel: A Church-State Military Arrangement," *Journal of Church and State* 35, no. 1 (1993): 113–130; and Etta Bick, "Rabbis and Rulings: Insubordination in the Military and Israeli Democracy," *Journal of Church and State* 49, no. 2 (2007): 305–328.
14 See, for example, Eliot Cohen, *Supreme Command: Soldiers, Statesmen, and Leadership in Wartime* (New York: Free Press, 2002); Michael Desch, *Civilian Control of the Military: The Changing Security Environment* (Baltimore: Johns Hopkins University Press, 1999); Larry Diamond and Marc Plattner, eds., *Civil-Military Relations and Democracy* (Baltimore: Johns Hopkins University Press, 1996); Peter D. Feaver and Richard H. Kohn, eds., *Soldiers and Civilians: The Civil-Military Gap and American National Security* (Cambridge, MA: MIT Press, 2001); S. E. C. Finer, *The Man on Horseback: The Role of the Military in Politics* (Boulder, CO: Westview Press, 1988); Samuel Huntington, *The Soldier and the State* (New York: Vintage Books, 1957); Ronald Krebs, "One Nation Under Arms? Military Participation Policy and the Politics of Identity," *Security Studies* 14, no. 3 (April 2005): 529–564; Ronald Krebs, *Fighting for Rights: Military Service and the Politics of Citizenship* (Ithaca, NY: Cornell University Press, 2006). For a good review of the literature, see Peter D. Feaver, "Civil-Military Relations," *Annual Review of Political Science* 2 (1999): 211–241.
15 In *The Scroll or the Sword?*, Cohen discusses the difficulties religious recruits faced in the largely secular framework of a military organization, as evidenced by correspondence between Jewish soldiers and their rabbis. In "Mediating Structures and the Military," Rosman-Stollman, reflects on the challenges of mediating between the religious needs of soldiers and their obligations to the military.
16 See, for example, Peter J. Katzenstein, ed., *The Culture of National Security* (New York: Columbia University Press, 1996); Peter J. Katzenstein, *Cultural Norms & National Security: Police and Military in Postwar Japan* (Ithaca, NY: Cornell University Press, 1996); Beth Kier, *Imagining War: French and British Military Doctrine between the Wars* (Princeton, NJ: Princeton University Press, 1997); Barry R. Posen, *Sources of Military Doctrine: France, Britain, and Germany between the World Wars* (Ithaca, NY: Cornell University Press, 1984); Jack Snyder, *The Ideology of the Offensive: Military Decision-Making and the Disasters of 1914* (Ithaca, NY: Cornell University Press, 1984).
17 On the religious identity of militaries and states in the Arab world, see Frisch, "The Role of Religion in the Militaries of Egypt, Syria, and Jordan." Frisch has argued that authoritarian Arab leaders manipulate expressions of religion in the military for instrumental reasons.
18 See, for example, Stephen Biddle, *Military Power: Explaining Victory and Defeat in Modern Battle* (Princeton, NJ: Princeton University Press, 2004); Stephen Peter Rosen, *Societies and Military Power: India and Its Armies* (Ithaca, NY: Cornell University Press, 1996); Dan Reiter and Allan Stam, *Democracies at War* (Princeton, NJ: Princeton University Press, 2002); Stephen Biddle and Robert Zirkle, "Technology, Civil-Military Relations, and Warfare in the Developing World,"

Journal of Strategic Studies 19, no. 2 (1996); Kenneth M. Pollack, *Arabs at War: Military Effectiveness, 1948–1991* (Omaha: University of Nebraska Press, 2002); Allan R. Millett and Williamson Murray, eds., *Military Effectiveness* (Boston: Allen and Unwin, 1988).

19 Risa A. Brooks and Elizabeth A. Stanley, eds., *Creating Military Power: The Sources of Military Effectiveness* (Stanford, CA: Stanford University Press, 2007): 1–26.

20 Ibid., 11–12.

21 Ron E. Hassner, "Religion and International Affairs: The State of the Art," in *Religion, Identity, and Global Governance: Ideas, Evidence and Practice*, ed. Steven Lamy and Patrick James (Toronto: University of Toronto Press, 2011): 37–56. For similar approaches, see Bruce Lincoln, *Holy Terrors: Thinking about Religion after September 11* (Chicago: University of Chicago Press, 2003): 7–18 and 73; Ernest Gellner, *Postmodernism, Reason, and Religion* (London: Routledge, 1992): 9–22.

PART I

RITUALS, BELIEFS, AND PRACTICES

I

Japan

Aaron Skabelund and Akito Ishikawa

Introduction: (Ir)religious? The Japanese Self-Defense Force's Relationship with Religion

Scholars have written much about the relationship between the postwar Japanese state and religion, but they have given little attention to interactions between the military and religion.[1] As an organ of the state, Japan's Self-Defense Force (SDF) is expected to adhere to the same constitutional and legal rules as other government bodies. The two most relevant provisions regarding the role of religion in the SDF are Articles 20 and 89. Article 20 guarantees "freedom of religion" and prohibits the state from engaging in the following activities: supporting a particular religion; compelling citizens to take "part in any religious acts, celebration, rite, or practice"; and engaging in "any other religious activity." Likewise, Article 89 stipulates that "no public money or other property shall be expended or appropriated for the use, benefit, or maintenance of any religious institution or association." Based on these constitutional provisions, and according to the organization's official policies, the SDF is required to respect the religious freedom of its personnel and not to engage in or support any religious practices.

Japan is a highly secularized society that possesses a vibrant and multifaceted religious culture. According to public opinion polls, around two-thirds of Japanese do not believe in a god or gods and do not profess a particular religious faith. Of those who do identify with a particular religion (less than a third of Japanese society), approximately 20 percent are Buddhist, nearly 6 percent are Shinto, and around 1 percent are Christian.[2] These statistics confirm that Japan is one of the most thoroughly secularized countries in the world. Nevertheless, religious practices occupy a prominent place in the lives of many Japanese, even among those who do not consider themselves religious. A significant number of Japanese take a syncretic approach to religion; in other words, as a famous saying puts it, many people are "born Shinto, die

Buddhist," get married in a Christian church, and engage in a variety of disparate religious practices over the course of their lives.

As for the role of religion in Japanese society, scholars continue to debate the following questions: Is the concept of religion, which was adopted from the West in the mid-nineteenth century, even applicable to Japan? How should one define Shinto, and can it be characterized as a religion? Shinto does not conform to a Kantian definition of religion as "the recognition of all our duties as divine commands." Rather from a sociological (Durkheimian) perspective, Shinto arguably can be understood as a religion because it has become a "unified system of beliefs and practices relative to sacred things, which unite a single moral community."[3] If one were to employ an even more "polythetic and flexible" definition of religion, as religious historian Bruce Lincoln does, then Shinto (and other Japanese faiths) exhibits elements of his four domains – discourse, practice, community, and institutions – and thus can be characterized as a religion.[4] Nevertheless, because Japan is religiously syncretic, because Shinto has long been an "ethnic religion" – that is, a faith (like Judaism and Hinduism) practiced in a particular ethnicity, culture, or country – and because of Shinto's enduring presence in Japanese culture and society, distinguishing between what is and is not religious can be difficult. This is not to say that Shinto has become completely secularized. Rather, because Shinto is syncretic and does not create expectations about how people should live their lives (unlike Buddhism, Christianity, and Islam), it is not an "ultimate concern" for Japanese, to use philosopher Paul Tillich's phrase.[5] Some Japanese, especially Christian and Buddhist pacifists, regard Shinto (or certain Shinto practices) as religious; others consider it a system of ritual or traditional charms that influences daily customs. Many Japanese visit Shinto shrines on New Year's Day to pray for happiness and a healthy year, not as a pietistic religious activity but rather in keeping with tradition. The same activity may be religious or not, depending on the circumstances or one's point of view. Thus, ambiguity is the key concept in understanding the role of religion in Japanese society and in the military.

Interestingly, Article 9 of Japan's constitution, popularly known as the "peace clause," is perhaps more important to understanding interactions between the military and religion than are Articles 20 and 89. Article 9, which was drafted along with the rest of the constitution by U.S occupation officials in 1946, "forever renounces war as a right of the nation and the threat or use of force as a means of settling international disputes." Moreover, it dictates that "land, sea, and air forces, as well as other war potential, will never be maintained."

From its battlefield victories allowing for the creation of an empire to its central role in the formation of national identity, the Imperial military played a vital role in Japan's rapid transformation into an industrialized power in the late nineteenth and early twentieth centuries. Many Japanese people held the military primarily responsible for the country's disastrous defeat in World War II and, as a result, welcomed the dissolution of the armed forces and the constitutional restrictions that contributed to the societal delegitimization of military values after 1945. With the outbreak of the Korean War in 1950, however, and in circumvention of Article 9, occupation authorities ordered the Japanese government to reconstitute an embryonic military organization, which four years later became known as the Self-Defense Force.

Nearly seven decades later, the Japanese constitution remains unchanged. Attempts by conservatives to revise Article 9 have failed in the face of deep-seated pacifist opposition and public satisfaction with the inherently contradictory nature of the status quo; that is, although Article 9 prohibits the existence of armed forces, Japan nevertheless continues to maintain a de facto military. Over the years, changing interpretations of the constitution have allowed the SDF to increase in size and power, and more recently in its ability to project considerable military might. According to the Stockholm International Peace Research Institute, Japan ranked as the world's seventh-largest military spender, expending an average of nearly $55 million annually (or 1 percent of the country's gross domestic product) for defense between 2000 and 2011. The SDF numbers 240,000 personnel – three-fifths of whom are in the Ground SDF, with the remaining two-fifths split nearly evenly between the Maritime SDF and the Air SDF. Although Japan boasts some of the world's most sophisticated "defensive" weaponry, such as surface-to-air missiles and fighter jets, it possesses neither aircraft carriers nor nuclear armaments. Constitutional constraints and public opinion prevent the SDF from taking offensive action and limit its ability to engage in collective defense. Since its inception, the SDF has performed a deputized, defensive role, backing up the nearly 40,000 American troops currently stationed on U.S. bases in the archipelago. Only in the 1990s did the SDF begin to undertake overseas deployments, joining United Nations (UN) peacekeeping operations and disaster relief missions. Under pressure from the George W. Bush administration to "show the flag," the Japanese government dispatched troops to southern Iraq from 2004 to 2006 for the purpose of "relief and reconstruction." SDF soldiers performed these tasks under extremely strict rules of engagement, which effectively required Dutch and then British troops to provide them with protection. Since its inception, the SDF has pursued a concerted strategy to gain social acceptance by concentrating on disaster relief and public service,[6] the two most prominent examples being its responses to the Great Hanshin (or Kobe) earthquake in 1995 and the triple (earthquake, tsunami, nuclear) disaster in northeast Japan in 2011. These decidedly nonmilitary missions, along with changing geopolitical dynamics – particularly real and perceived threats from North Korea and China – have indeed contributed to greater social acceptance of the military. Even so, strong resistance to the SDF becoming a "normal" military, or even to being called a "military," remains. Thus, understanding the contradictions between Article 9 and the existence of the SDF, and the long historical shadow cast by its predecessor – the Imperial military – is essential to comprehending the relationship between religion and the SDF.

Because few Japanese are religious, and because religion carries comparatively little influence – divisive or otherwise – SDF adherence to Articles 20 and 89 would seem a fairly uncomplicated task. In fact, in our initial interviews with SDF officials, we were told repeatedly that the SDF has no relationship with religion. For example, religion does not appear to influence promotion, training, gender relations, dress, diet, or many other aspects of military service. The military has never had a chaplain service, and we were informed that holding religious services or meetings on SDF bases would be unthinkable. Furthermore, although the SDF does not maintain statistics on religious affiliation, it does not appear that one faith is represented beyond its share of the population at large.

On closer examination, however, we found that the SDF in fact favors Shinto in a variety of ways, while keeping a distance from other religious belief systems, such as Buddhism and Christianity. This privileging of Shinto is motivated less by religious belief than by identification with Shinto as an essential element of Japanese national identity, martial morale, and organizational unity, and is tempered by a lingering suspicion of religious fervor of any sort, including for Shinto.[7]

This chapter examines, in two parts, the relationship between religion and the SDF. First, it briefly reviews the historical interaction between Shinto and the Imperial military until 1945 and then examines Shinto's continuing influence in the SDF. Second, it explores the SDF's relationship with other religions, including mainstream Buddhist and Christian sects as well as less-established religions that have emerged in the last few decades.

(In)separable: The State, Shinto, and the Military – Prewar and Postwar

Historical Background

August 1945 marked one of the most dramatic ruptures in Japanese history. The end of World War II and the beginning of the U.S. occupation brought an end to ultranationalism, militarism, and political oppression. It also allowed for the development of a peaceful, prosperous, and democratic Japan. The new constitution signaled the official end of state meddling in religious affairs by prohibiting the government from using Shinto as an ideological tool to unify the nation and from repressing other religious organizations and ideas. In the last couple of decades, however, a number of scholars have identified significant "transwar" continuities since 1945. Despite the momentous constitutional reforms that sought to separate the state from Shinto and other religions, some state actors – including members of the SDF – have reestablished ties with Shinto over the past six decades. Thus, in the realm of state-religion relations, continuity rather than only change characterizes the prewar/postwar continuum.

For most of its history until the mid-nineteenth century, Shinto exercised little influence on political and military matters. An exception was the fifth century, when the imperial clan marshaled its beliefs – which only much later came to be called "Shinto" – to justify its rise to power. From the start, Japan's indigenous religion, as it is often characterized, was highly localized: it "function[ed] for the most part as the communal cult of small-scale groupings," and it did not possess a comprehensive organizational structure or unified doctrines or practices.[8]

As religious studies scholar Helen Hardacre has described it, Shinto was "an ancient cult directed to native deities called *kami*, and included among these are deified emperors and heroes, spirits of nature, and deities of Japanese mythology."[9] For more than a millennium until the nineteenth century, many Japanese considered *kami* to be Buddhist gods. Indeed, Shinto had become so intertwined with Buddhism that it hardly possessed an independent identity. During the Tokugawa period (1600–1868), the ruling shogunate and the Imperial family subtly patronized Buddhism, and the shogunate used its extensive network of temples to register and maintain surveillance over the population.

The formation of Japan as a modern nation-state and Japan's rise as an industrialized military power in the second half of the nineteenth century drastically transformed Shinto and the relationship between the state and religion. During the late Tokugawa era, a movement emerged to expunge Shinto of foreign (Buddhist) elements and "restore" the Imperial household to the center of political power for the first time in more than a thousand years. The Meiji Restoration in 1868 achieved both objectives. The new regime, ostensibly led by the sixteen-year-old Emperor Meiji, dropped its support for Buddhism and adopted an expurgated form of Shinto as a sort of state religion or, more accurately, as State Shinto – a "nonreligious or suprareligious entity with the political function of establishing the spiritual unity of the populace."[10] To help accomplish this goal, the state brought all Shinto shrines under the umbrella of Ise, the shrine most closely associated with the Imperial family. Likewise, the government constructed Yasukuni Shrine in central Tokyo in 1869 and, in subsequent years, built "spirit-inviting shrines" across the country to honor soldiers who died fighting for the emperor. In 1939, the Home Ministry designated one or more of these shrines in each prefecture as "nation-protecting shrines" (*gokoku jinja*). Yasukuni became the central (or home shrine) for these regional shrines. In short, state authorities, in collaboration with Shinto priests, connected popular religious life at the local level to nationalism centered on the emperor and the glorification of soldiers who died in war on his and the nation's behalf.

State Shinto expanded in the early twentieth century, particularly after the Russo-Japanese War of 1905. The war and subsequent expansion of Japan's empire in Asia fostered a keen sense of patriotism that shrine priests supported enthusiastically. During the next four decades, priests played a key role in venerating Japan's military war dead. The emperor, politicians, military personnel, and the general populace began to observe rites at Yasukuni and its prefectural branches to celebrate the "glorious war dead." Hardacre has called this "nationwide orchestration of ritual ... an attempt at the most daring social engineering." "Here was a plan," she writes, "to use religion to unify the people in a single cult, headed by the emperor as head priest, focused upon his ancestors (and later the war dead), who had also been declared national deities."[11]

During the 1930s and 1940s, State Shinto supplied invaluable ideological support to the Imperial military as it waged war in Asia and the Pacific. Teachers taught schoolchildren to worship the emperor as a divine being in human form and told the Japanese people that they were descended from Shinto gods. They also told young men – and, by the end of the war, all Japanese subjects – that it was an unparalleled honor to die for the emperor in defense of the empire and that the spirits of the war dead would be enshrined at Yasukuni.[12] Japan's disastrous defeat and occupation in 1945 demolished such notions. As historian John Dower has aptly put it, most Japanese "embraced defeat" through widespread support of the occupation's reforms.[13] Public enthusiasm for the constitution, including support for Article 9 and to a lesser extent for the separation clauses, was fierce and deep-rooted. Other occupation reforms ended the government's financial support for shrines and declared them religious bodies similar to Buddhist temples and Christian churches. Although some Buddhist sects, such as Zen and Jōdo Shinshū (True Pure Land), actively supported the war, no religion was as discredited as Shinto, given its association with the prewar military state.[14] Needless to say, after the war, shrines struggled without state backing and with far fewer parishioners.

Despite these tremendous setbacks, Shinto survived, largely because of its symbolic links to conservative Japanese "tradition" and values. Since the 1970s, some conservative politicians have sought to tap into Shinto's source of sacred authority to bolster the state's legitimacy and their own political fortunes. During the early 1970s, lawmakers from the longtime ruling Liberal Democratic Party made four unsuccessful attempts in the Diet to declare Yasukuni a nonreligious entity dedicated to offering rites and ceremonies for the souls of war dead and to restore state funding for it. Yet because of Shinto's association with wartime militarism, the Diet rejected these attempts to permit formal public worship at Yasukuni. Indeed, public support for Article 9 – more than concern about Articles 20 and 89 – has been the primary motivator of opposition to official patronage of Shinto.

The SDF, Yasukuni, and Nation-Protecting Shrines

SDF involvement with Shinto has generated controversy for decades. The worship at shrines by SDF members and the enshrinement of the spirits of personnel killed in accidents while on duty represent the most significant connections between the SDF and Shinto. These two issues illustrate the ambiguous constitutionality of the SDF, the persistence of war memories, and conflicts over the proper relationship between religion and the state, including the armed forces.

In recent years, the more controversial of these issues has been formal visits by SDF officials to Yasukuni and nation-protecting shrines. Periodic visits by Japanese politicians to Yasukuni have generated considerable domestic and international controversy since 1985, when Nakasone Yasuhiro became the first postwar prime minister to formally worship at the shrine. Not only are 2.5 million wartime dead enshrined at Yasukuni but, since 1978, so are the spirits of fourteen top government and military leaders executed by the Allies as Class A war criminals in 1948. Critics object to such visits because they appear to condone wartime aggression, because they undermine Article 9, and because they violate the state-religion separation clauses.[15] Visits by SDF personnel have not received nearly the publicity as those by government officials. Nevertheless, they create many of the same problems, whether the location is Yasukuni or one of Japan's fifty-two regional nation-protecting shrines.

Visits by SDF personnel to these shrines have drawn media attention since at least the 1960s, but it remains difficult to determine the extent and purpose of these visits.[16] What is clear is that they occur with considerable regional variation. This variation may be in part a response to local sensitivities, but it is also a response to the SDF's lack of a unified stance on whether its personnel may make such visits on an official basis. In recent years, top uniformed defense personnel have not made public visits to Yasukuni, probably to prevent the SDF – whose historic lack of legitimacy has already made it vulnerable to charges of religious engagement – from becoming entangled in political controversy.[17] Instead, top commanders have been represented by the chairperson of the Staff Officers' Committee dressed in civilian attire.[18]

Outside Tokyo, individual prerogative rather than local concerns appears to determine whether SDF personnel visit Japan's nation-protecting shrines. In Kumamoto, for example, on the southern island of Kyushu – a region known for its unrivaled prewar and postwar support for the military – the current commander does not attend the annual nation-protecting shrine spring and fall festivals (*reitaisai*), during which priests perform rites of propitiation to pacify and venerate apotheosized war dead. One young priest complained that one of the only times he saw SDF personnel visit the shrine was when a unit was out jogging.[19] But in Asahikawa, on the northern island of Hokkaido, another "base town" since prewar days, SDF commanders have worshipped at the spring festival of the Hokkaido Nation-Protecting Shrine for at least several decades, despite considerable criticism from local pacifists and unfavorable national attention. On June 5, 2010, regional and local base commanders representing each of the services appeared in full dress uniform to honor the spirits of the shrine's war dead (see Photo 2). During the ceremony, the SDF officers sat next to representatives of war veterans and families that lost loved ones in battle. Meanwhile, in the inner chamber of the shrine, priests made offerings and female dancers clad in exquisite kimonos entertained the spirits of the war dead. After being introduced, the officers and other invited guests paid their respects to the enshrined dead. Like many other *gokoku jinja*, the

Photo 2 Self-Defense Force (SDF) commanders, following a Boy Scout leader, entering the Hokkaido Nation-Protecting Shrine in Asahikawa for a ceremony to honor military war dead, June 5, 2010. Photo by Aaron Skabelund.

location of the Hokkaido Nation-Protecting Shrine speaks volumes about the shrine's special relationship with the military: constructed in 1902, it stands adjacent to the main base of the Northern Army's Second Division, which until 1945 was the headquarters of the Imperial Army's Seventh Division.

Although the SDF appears keen to avoid controversy, some commanders and conservative politicians visit regional nation-protecting shrines to obtain increased support from conservative groups. In the face of mounting criticism, the commanders have adopted some of the same strategies that politicians have used to deflect criticism; for example, they claim they are worshipping as private citizens, not as government officials, and insist their donations come from their own pockets rather than from public coffers.

Two factors challenge such claims. First, priests at shrine festivals announce the presence of visiting SDF commanders, stating their names, ranks, and military branches. Such introductions undermine the pretense that SDF officers are acting as private citizens rather than as government officials. Elected officials face the same problem. Unlike politicians, however, SDF officers face a second difficulty: their military dress weakens any claims that they are off duty and visiting in a private capacity. The appearance of even rank-and-file SDF personnel in uniform at Yasukuni has elicited criticism from progressive journalists and critics.[20]

The other significant connection between the SDF and Shinto is the apotheosis or enshrinement of deceased SDF personnel at nation-protecting shrines. As is the case with worship by SDF personnel at such shrines, the enshrinement of the spirits of SDF personnel killed while on duty occurs on a regional basis and is not officially sanctioned by the SDF. Between 1950 and June 1988, when the Supreme Court ruled on a case challenging the practice of enshrinement, SDF officials in fifteen western prefectures helped facilitate the apotheosis of some 465 souls, often with the assistance of prefectural veterans' associations (Taiyūkai).[21] These prefectures, of which Kumamoto is one, have been known for their robust support of the military, both before and since 1945. The rites of apotheosis for SDF personnel who die on duty are the same as for those conducted for war dead, although the spirits are categorized in a slightly different way. Priests conduct these rites as part of elaborate ceremonies in which they place "slips of paper inscribed with the names of the dead" on an elevated altar in the innermost chamber of the shrine. The ritual results in the "transformation of the ... dead from spirits of undefined status into *kami*," gods "no longer to be mourned" but celebrated "like *kami* everywhere" during the seasonal shrine festivals.[22]

Although at least three lawsuits had already been brought against prefectural veterans' associations over the practice of enshrinement, it took a case filed by a Christian, Nakaya Yasuko, to capture the attention of the Japanese people. Nakaya's husband, Takafumi, was killed in a traffic accident while on duty in 1968. In line with her beliefs, she entrusted his remains to her local Christian church in Yamaguchi Prefecture, in southern Honshu. Several years later, Veterans' Association officials in Yamaguchi approached her to obtain documents so they could arrange for an apotheosis ceremony at the local nation-protecting shrine. Nakaya refused to provide the documents and declined to give permission for the enshrinement. Over her protests, the association carried out the apotheosis using information obtained from a local SDF base. In 1973, Nakaya sued the SDF for violating her right to religious freedom through its cooperation with the Veterans' Association. A lower court ruled in Nakaya's favor and awarded her the sum of one million yen; this ruling was upheld on appeal. The state filed another appeal.

On June 1, 1988, the Supreme Court ruled in favor of the state, although one justice dissented. The majority opinion found that the SDF's assistance of the Veterans' Association had not violated the constitutional provision of separation of religion and state because the association had acted alone. The court ruled that whether the SDF had cooperated with the association or not, its actions were not religious – the SDF's intention was not to promote a particular religion but to raise its prestige by promoting a martial spirit. The Court decreed that even if the state or one of its organs had engaged in unconstitutional activities, these activities did not violate the religious rights of individuals unless they either coerced them to perform or limited religious activity. The Court's decree implied that Yasukuni and its constellation of nation-protecting shrines could apotheosize the souls of SDF personnel (and just about anyone else) without having to worry whether such actions might be challenged in the courts on the basis of religious freedom.

The importance of the Nakaya suit cannot be overstated. Because the nation-protecting shrines performed the same rites as the Yasukuni Shrine, the case had important implications for future litigation against the shrine, the preeminent symbol of Shinto's intimate ties with the state. As Hardacre has observed, "a judicial finding that the rite of apotheosis is religious in character would bear on the constitutionality of state patronage of the shrine, since the apotheosis of the war dead is the shrine's principal raison d'etre."[23]

Although the Nakaya case seemed to dismantle legal barriers, it was up to individual nation-protecting shrines to decide how to respond to the ruling. Just as there is no unity of opinion within the SDF about how the organization should interact with Yasukuni and the regional *gokoku jinja*, the shrines themselves differ on how to deal with the SDF. Certainly at Yamaguchi and other nation-protecting shrines in western Japan, the practice of enshrining SDF personnel continues, and it may have spread to other *gokoku jinja* shrines in other prefectures. Our attempts to confirm the proliferation of SDF apotheosis with the national Veterans' Association went unfulfilled. If the stance of a top-ranking priest at the Asahikawa Shrine in Hokkaido is any indication, however, the Nakaya ruling probably did not set a precedent at all regional *gokoku* shrines. The priest adamantly stated that the enshrinement of SDF members will be performed at his shrine *only* if Japan is at war. Needless to say, he hoped that such ceremonies would never be necessary.[24]

The question of how to honor SDF members who die while on duty but not at war (which of course to date has always been the case) is of great concern for the government and the SDF. As early as 1962, the SDF constructed a memorial on the grounds of its headquarters in Ichigaya in central Tokyo for military personnel who died in work-related accidents. In 1980, in response to families' requests for a monument worthy of the sacrifice of their loved ones, the SDF refurbished the memorial. More recently, it completed extensive renovations and a beautification project of the area. These efforts may represent an attempt to create an alternative site for honoring SDF dead. For some, however, the memorial is inadequate for personnel who perished while on duty. The cenotaph, built of black granite and white stone, is not nearly as imposing as the broad, rustic wooden structures of Yasukuni and the regional *gokoku* shrines, which can only be approached under a massive *torii* gate and are usually surrounded by cherry trees and well-tended gardens. Whether the memorial is sufficient to honor SDF war dead is even more doubtful. Fortunately, no personnel have died while participating in UN missions or in southern Iraq. If, however, a soldier should die in a future mission, clash, or full-blown conflict, it is hard to imagine that the memorial could compete with the grandeur and tradition – invented as it is – of Yasukuni and the nation-protecting shrines.

Other SDF-Shinto Interactions

Many more SDF personnel, both officers and rank-and-file members – whether or not they are religious or affiliated with a religion other than Shinto – engage in practices that nevertheless privilege Shinto. Many of these practices appeal to Shinto gods for safety and prosperity and may be performed by Shinto priests on SDF bases during "unofficial" visits to shrines. In some cases, Shinto priests place Shinto altars and amulets within SDF facilities as well as on ships, planes, and other vehicles. Our interviews with officers and enlisted personnel representing all three branches of the SDF, as well as with Shinto priests, revealed that despite little organizational or geographic uniformity, such actions are commonplace. SDF personnel do not generally regard these practices as religious or political, and those who object to state efforts to restore ties with Shinto have rarely challenged them. Nevertheless, such practices – many of which are an amalgam of folk magico-religious Shinto rites in which a large number of Japanese engage – strengthen cultural connections between the SDF and Shinto institutions, such as Yasukuni and the nation-protecting shrines. Thus, they may indirectly lend support to the reestablishment of official ties between the armed forces and Shinto.

Shrine priests regularly perform ceremonies at SDF bases to entreat Shinto gods to protect military personnel. These events are best described as dedication ceremonies. Maritime SDF and Air SDF officers explained that it is standard procedure for a priest to perform so-called safety ceremonies (*kigansai*) when a new ship or airplane arrives on base. During these ceremonies, as service members stand at attention, a priest performs purification rites by waving a wand over the object to be purified and then transferring spirits into the object, providing it and its occupants with protection. In addition, priests regularly conduct decommissioning ceremonies when a ship or plane – and its protective spirits – is removed from service. The priests employed for these rituals typically come either from a nearby shrine (perhaps a nation-protecting shrine) or from a shrine that has a connection to the ship or plane. For example, many new ships are named after Imperial Navy vessels, such as the *Hyūga*, *Kirishima*, and *Myōkō*, all of which derive their appellations from place names. In such cases, a priest from a shrine in that area might conduct the rites. According to our interviewees, these ceremonies are generally not official and attendance is not mandatory.[25]

Some SDF units routinely summon priests to conduct safety ceremonies before the commencement of training exercises, especially at the beginning of the year. For example, it is common practice for a priest from the nearby Toyosaka Shrine to visit the Eniwa Ground SDF base on Hokkaido in early January. In another example, a series of accidents could prompt the base commander to ask a priest to perform a special safety ceremony at any time during the year.[26]

For similar reasons, groups or entire units of SDF personnel visit local shrines, or shrines with a special connection, to entreat a god for protection.

Maritime SDF crews based in Yokosuka, for example, frequently visit Tōgō
Shrine in Tokyo before departing for extended tours of duty. The shrine is
dedicated to the spirit of Adm. Tōgō Heihachirō (1847–1934), a hero of the
Russo-Japanese War. Such visits are ostensibly voluntary and usually made by
off-duty service members, but the unofficial nature of these visits is undercut
by the fact that uniformed service members often visit shrines in groups or
as entire units, not as individuals. For example, sailors who visit Tōgō Shrine
wear formal dress whites. Shrine staff have confirmed that these excursions are
scheduled by officials at the Ministry of Defense. Such visits are just one way
that SDF personnel interact with Shinto shrines.

Members of the SDF routinely provide support for local shrine festivals as
part of the SDF's public outreach program. Since its establishment, the SDF
has been heavily involved in public service projects, including building public
roads, grading school grounds, harvesting crops, and helping out with sporting
events. These efforts are designed to generate friendly interactions with, and
support from, particular segments of society – in the case of local shrine festivals, Shinto priests and community members who participate in the festivals.
These festivals usually involve carrying a portable shrine known as a *mikoshi*,
an ornate palanquin-like structure that rests on two long horizontal poles, in
the area around the shrine. The purpose is to spread the divine protection and
blessings of the deity enshrined in the *mikoshi*. SDF personnel and community
members may be found carrying *mikoshi* on their shoulders as the procession
weaves its way through surrounding streets.[27]

Entreaties to the gods for protection and good fortune do not end with visits to or support for shrines. They continue on an individual and a collective
level through the placement of Shinto talismans inside SDF buildings, ships,
and some types of airplanes. The most prominent talisman is *kamidana* (literally, god-shelves), or small wooden shelves that hold tiny houses in which a
god dwells. They can be found in base command rooms and in the wardrooms
or bridges of ships. Items such as candles and offerings of food are expected
to be placed in a *kamidana* on a daily basis. If there is a mishap, personnel
sometimes might suggest half-jokingly that it was because the god had been
neglected. *Kamidana* can be found on many bases. A Ground SDF member
reported that, at the East Chitose Base in Hokkaido, commanders installed
kamidana in nearly every billet after soldiers said they had seen ghosts of personnel who had died during training exercises.[28]

In spaces too small to accommodate *kamidana*, SDF personnel have been
known to substitute *o-fuda*, an amulet inscribed with the name of a *kami* or the
name of a Shinto shrine on a strip of paper, wood, cloth, or metal. This talisman
transfers part of the god into the object on which it is attached, thereby providing divine protection. SDF personnel, often acting on behalf of their unit or
squadron, make annual purchases of *o-fuda* at shrines, placing them in planes
and other vehicles (see Photo 3). Instead of *o-fuda*, personnel at the Ground
SDF base in Eniwa place *shimekazari*, a Shinto New Year's decoration made of

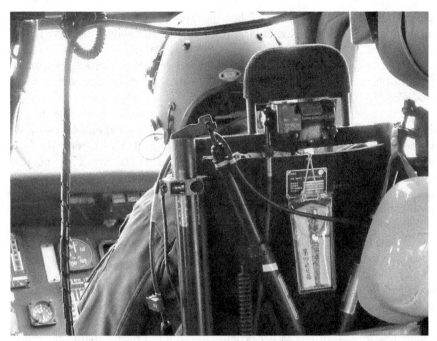

Photo 3 An *o-fuda* on the back of a Maritime SDF helicopter pilot's seat at an open-base-day event at the Okadama Ground SDF Base in Sapporo, June 2010. These talismans transfer part of the god into the object on which they are placed and thereby provide divine protection. Photo by Akito Ishikawa.

rope, festoons, and other adornments such as oranges, ferns, and folded fans, on the front of tanks for a week or two at the start of the year.[29] Throughout Japan, people hang *shimekazari* on cars and in front of houses to mark them as sacred spaces and to prevent misfortune or evil spirits from entering. Compared to *kamidana* and *o-fuda*, *shimekazari* have a more secularized meaning, akin to Christmas wreaths, and can be purchased at supermarkets as well as shrines.

Many SDF members carry *o-mamori*, a personal protection amulet that contains the spirit of a god. One of our interviewees, an Air SDF officer, carries a credit card–sized *o-mamori* from the Hikō (Flying) Shrine in Kyoto Prefecture, whose god protects those who fly.[30] Such individual expressions are entirely outside the realm of the SDF as a government organization and are perhaps comparable to wearing a cross or carrying a small Bible. Similar to *kamidana* and *o-fuda*, *o-mamori* indicate a connection with a particular Shinto shrine.

None of these practices – the performance of rites of divine protection by Shinto priests both on and off base, participation in Shinto festivals, and the placement of sacred amulets – is explicitly prohibited by Japan's constitution or other legal codes. An examination of the context in which Article 20 was drafted, however, confirms that these practices (except perhaps for *o-mamori* because of their personal nature) violate the intent of the law. The placement of *kamidana* and *o-fuda* are particularly problematic; the Shinto directive issued by U.S. occupation authorities in December 1945 dictated that "god-shelves and all other physical symbols of State Shinto in any office, school, institution, organization, or structure supported wholly or in part by public funds are prohibited."[31]

SDF commanders generally avoid violating Article 89's prohibition against using public funds for religious purposes by paying for expenses from their own pocket or by soliciting voluntary donations from unit members. Yet, how voluntary can such contributions be in this environment? Likewise, although participation in events such as dedication ceremonies is ostensibly not mandatory, attendance is expected of on-duty soldiers. Suzuki Kenji, a Christian and former Ground SDF member who was stationed at the East Chitose Base for four years, recalled that the only way he could avoid participating in the annual New Year's consecration ceremonies performed by a visiting priest was to take the day off. Suzuki claimed that any objection to the ceremonies would not have been taken seriously. He also asserted that although the SDF maintains the appearance of respect for the separation of religion and the state and of religious tolerance, in practice this was not the case.[32] Other Christian SDF personnel we interviewed, including at least one from the same sect as Suzuki, did not express qualms about participating in such rituals, either because they did not regard them as religious or because they did not view them as infringing on their beliefs.

Although liberal critics frequently object to military visits to Yasukuni and other nation-protecting shrines and the enshrinement of SDF personnel, there have been almost no public objections to such ceremonies or practices. Perhaps one reason is that they take place in the hidden confines of SDF bases, making them invisible to the wider population. Unlike visits by top officers to shrine festivals, visits to shrines do not take place as part of public events. Probably the most compelling explanation for the lack of complaints – from either inside or outside the SDF – is that such practices pervade Japanese society, and that many people who engage in them either do not consider them religious acts or because they are unbothered by their religious nature. Many Japanese, regardless of their beliefs, periodically visit shrines, whether to ask priests to perform safety rites on newly acquired automobiles or to make wishes for health, love, and success at school or work. Companies routinely place *kamidana* at their headquarters, and individuals hang *o-fuda* from their car mirrors.

If someone were to object to such practices, it is doubtful their case would be successful given legal precedent established by the Supreme Court. Since the 1970s, the high court has offered contradictory interpretations of Articles 20 and 89. In 1977, for example, it ruled in the Tsu Grounds Purification Case that state involvement in religion was forbidden only if it went "beyond an appropriate level." The meaning of "appropriate" was to be determined by both the "object" and the "effect" of the state's actions. In another case, the Court concluded that a Shinto dedication ceremony was "entirely secular" and in accordance with "general social customs" – a familiar argument. Declaring Shinto rites to be nonreligious was in keeping with what the pre-1945 state mandated and what conservative politicians failed to achieve in the Diet during the early 1970s. It is also an argument that some SDF officers use today to dismiss questions about visits to and enshrinement practices at the nation-protecting shrines. In contrast, the Court ruled in the 1990s that a governor's use of public funds to make contributions to Yasukuni and a local nation-protecting shrine was unconstitutional because its object and effect was to "assist, aid, and promote" a specific religion.[33] Thus, the legal line between religion and the state and whether Shinto ceremonies are secular or religious remains in dispute.

Some SDF commanders appear unwilling to adhere strictly to the letter of the law against engaging in religious activities – although the constitutional grounds are admittedly unclear – but do not want the organization's actions becoming a source of controversy. A planned regimental visit to the Osaka Nation-Protecting Shrine in early January 2010 offers one such example, although the public did not seem to have noticed. Ironically, these internal concerns were generated by the *Sankei shinbun*, a nationwide daily newspaper famous for its support of conservative causes in Japan, including the dismantlement of Article 9. On December 24, 2009, the newspaper reported that the regimental commander at the Shinodayama Base was planning to march his unit of 800 soldiers, dressed in camouflage, 18.5 kilometers to Suminoe Park as part of the regiment's first day of training the next year. The article did not mention the commonly known fact that the park is also the location of the Osaka Nation-Protecting Shrine.[34] According to a local SDF public affairs official, when top Central Army staff learned that the *Sankei* had reported the planned march and discovered that it was the commander's intent to have all of his soldiers pay their respects at the shrine, they became concerned that the sight of SDF soldiers, dressed in battle fatigues and worshipping at a nation-protecting shrine, might create controversy. They ordered the commander to exercise caution, and ultimately the unit marched to the park to perform so-called public service by picking up trash. Soldiers then "voluntarily" visited the shrine during a break. This approach avoided the appearance that the march was made for the express purpose of visiting the shrine and that worship at the shrine was performed while the soldiers were on duty or that their participation was mandatory.[35] The public affairs officer disclosed that top Central Army brass were relieved that the media did not even mention the march after it had taken place. It probably would have been forgotten except for a video posted on YouTube, which, to the accompaniment of rousing military march music, provides a photographic slide show of the day's events. As of June 2013, the video had been viewed only 4,700 times and had elicited just a handful of comments, all of which praise the SDF.[36]

Although SDF officials do not want these informal interactions with Shinto to create the kind of controversy that the more public visits and enshrinements do, the scrutiny they invite may be having an effect on the SDF's relationship to Shinto. Take a case in the city of Asahikawa, for example. For a number of years, the Ground SDF has supported another local shrine on the occasion of its annual summer festival held each year on July 21. On that day, Seventh Division vehicles driven by base personnel carry priests and a portable *mikoshi* from the Kawakami Shrine as the procession parades through neighborhoods adjacent to the shrine. In 2009, local activists, who are often affiliated with Christian churches and have objected to the public worship of top officers at the Hokkaido Nation-Protecting Shrine since at least 1980, raised concerns about the SDF's support for the parade. In response, base commanders made a partial retreat by providing vehicles for only the second half of the procession, which did not include the portable shrine. To justify the continuing participation of the SDF, the commanders relied on a familiar trope: they were providing "public service" to the community.[37] To what community and for what purpose, they did not say.

(In)tolerant, and If So, Who? The SDF and Buddhism, Christianity, and Other Religions

Unlike the public and private interactions between the SDF and Shinto, relations between the SDF and mainstream Buddhism and Christian sects and less-established religious movements have been strained. The SDF's uncomfortable relationship with other religions is not determined primarily by its special connection to Shinto but rather by the attitude and actions of these other religious groups. For its part, the SDF deals with these other religions in a neutral manner, following Articles 20 and 89. Except for privileging Shinto, the SDF neither favors nor discriminates against these other religions or personnel affiliated with them. Some Christians, for example, have risen high within the ranks of the SDF. The SDF, however, maintains a list of religious organizations, such as Jehovah's Witnesses and other groups, whose pacifist, ultranationalist, or apocalyptic beliefs, it believes, might compromise its service members' obligation to protect the country against military threats.[38] Such concerns became public after the 1995 Tokyo subway sarin gas attack by Aum Shinrikyo. Aum was a new religious group that had won some converts within the SDF who leaked internal information during the government's investigation following the attack. As a result, unit commanders periodically ask their subordinates about their religious affiliation in an attempt to guard against such problems. Officially, however, they do so under the pretext of needing this information in the event the service member dies while on duty.[39] For their part, many mainstream Buddhist and Christian organizations have long regarded the very existence of the SDF as a violation of Article 9. They object to the SDF's unofficial patronage of Shinto, but they are motivated less by the separation clauses than by the peace clause. Indeed, many Buddhists and Christians view Article 9 with a kind of religious reverence – an attitude that has translated into antipathy for members of the SDF. Some Christian SDF personnel claim that they rarely experience discrimination at work because of their religion, yet they often experience intolerance in church from clergy and other parishioners because of their military affiliation. To understand this issue, it is again useful to look to the past.

Even as the government sought to use State Shinto to achieve spiritual unity in the late nineteenth century, Christian missionaries were making inroads into the imperial military. One of the first missionaries to reach out to soldiers was Estella Finch, a twenty-four-year-old American who arrived in Japan in 1893. Six years later, she and a minister, Kuroda Korenobu, founded the Army and Navy Mission Club and devoted their lives to spreading Protestant Christianity to servicemen.[40] Based at the port of Yokosuka, Kuroda and Finch (who became a Japanese citizen and changed her name to Hoshida Mitsuyo in 1909) had more influence with naval officers – who, thanks to their travels, were more cosmopolitan –than with army officers, who tended to be more conservative.

Despite the upsurge in Shinto-fueled nationalism following Japan's victory over Russia in 1905, the Imperial military granted Christian missionaries and servicemen a remarkable degree of toleration. An indication of their new status was the invitation in 1912 of Finch by the naval engineering school to attend its graduation ceremony as a special guest. Later, in 1923, the Imperial Navy invited the well-known minister Uemura Masahisa to speak about Christianity at a naval base assembly hall in Hiroshima.[41] In addition, the navy and army promoted a number of Christian officers to top-ranking positions. Still, in an atmosphere in which many felt the need to reaffirm the "Japanese spirit" in what had become a highly Westernized society, it was not unusual for other soldiers to denigrate Christians who expressed belief in a Western God. Thus, openness came at a cost. During the first half of the twentieth century, when Japan's nationalist spirit had become particularly intense, many Christians and Buddhists – both in and outside the military – may have compensated for doubts expressed by others about their "Japaneseness" and loyalty to Japan by becoming overzealous jingoists.[42]

In contrast, for decades SDF personnel have had to deal less with internal suspicions about their loyalties than with the distrust of Buddhists and Christians, who themselves were probably trying to compensate for their support of or lack of resistance to Japan's militarist state during the 1930s and 1940s. For example, the United Church of Christ, the largest Japanese Protestant denomination, issued "The Confession of Responsibility for World War II" in 1967.[43] The statement pledged to never again let Japan go to war and reiterated the church's unwavering support for Article 9, which in the eyes of many Christian and Buddhist pacifists had almost become scripture. Not surprisingly, such vows tended to foment antipathy toward the SDF and its personnel. For many people, pacifism equaled "anti-SDFism," and many Christians thought it was impossible to be both a follower of Christ and a member of the SDF.

For the most part, tensions between the SDF and religions other than Shinto have manifested themselves privately, but periodically they have broken out into the open – for example, on the pages of United Church of Christ publications in the early 1970s. In 1971, an SDF major, Yatabe Minoru, contributed an essay titled "A Major's Wish" to a monthly church bulletin.[44] Yatabe was a member of the Cornelius Group, a network of Christian SDF officers, enlisted personnel, National Defense Academy students, and family members who met privately to study the Bible and build faith and solidarity. Founded in 1959, the group derived its name from the devout Roman military officer whose vision led Peter to begin preaching the gospel to the Gentiles.[45] In his essay, Yatabe described his faith and expressed the wish of Christian personnel for religious leaders who would provide spiritual sustenance while respecting their occupation. In response, a church minister, Iwamoto Jirō, wrote several indignant letters to the editor of another church publication, claiming that Yatabe's essay was nothing but an expression of militarism and was at odds with the church's commitment to peace.[46] Iwamoto accused SDF personnel of living a life of sin by earning their livelihoods through violent aggression. Iwamoto's stance dismayed Yatabe and other Christian SDF personnel, although such reactions by ministers have not been unusual.[47] Many pacifist Christians then and even some today view SDF personnel as little more than an embodiment of a violation of Article 9.

Since the 1990s, however, the number of ministers who support Christian personnel in the SDF has increased. Recently, one chairperson of the United Church of Christ provided support for military Christian groups, such as the Cornelius Group. Within the wider society, the SDF has achieved much greater acceptance since the end of the Cold War. In the last two decades, a more multipolar world, growing tensions with North Korea and China, and the specter of terrorism have led many Japanese citizens to support a more assertive international role for their country and for the SDF. Currently, the public is about evenly divided on proposals to revise the constitution. Although antimilitary sentiments remain deeply rooted in Japanese society, the SDF's disaster relief work and other public service projects at home – in addition to participation in UN operations abroad – have greatly improved its image. Still, some Christian churches staunchly support Article 9, and this seems inevitably to engender an aversion to the SDF and its personnel. In some quarters, pacifism remains a quasi-religion or nonreligious religion with devoted adherents who join forces to defend and spread Article 9's gospel of peace. The unwillingness of mainstream Buddhists and Christians to welcome military personnel and address their spiritual needs may have contributed to the success of Aum and other new religious groups in recruiting followers among SDF personnel. Deep-rooted pacifism, as much as the principle of separation of politics and religion, has deterred clergy from calling for the introduction of a chaplaincy within the SDF. In sum, the established Buddhist and Christian sects have resisted involvement with the SDF because they regret their past collaboration with the military and fear being complicit in another war.

Conclusion

This chapter examines some of the ways in which the SDF privileges Shinto while treating other mainstream religious belief systems in a fairly neutral manner. The special treatment of Shinto is a legacy of the tight relationship forged between the state and Shinto – a relationship that in the first half of the twentieth century fostered a tremendous sense of nationalism among the Japanese people. Today, some SDF commanders and conservative political leaders use Shinto to heighten national loyalty, military morale, and organizational cohesion, but some pacifists object to such practices because of Shinto's support for World War II. Thus, the past continues to complicate the present for the SDF's interactions with religion and Japanese society.

In 2013, the resurgent ruling Liberal Democratic Party, which returned to power the previous year, issued a new proposal to revise the constitution. The proposal calls for the retention of Article 9's commitment to the renunciation of both war and "the threat or use of force as a means of settling international disputes," but it eliminates the existing constitutional prohibition on the maintenance of "war potential" through the use of "land, sea, and air forces," and recognizes the "exercise of self-defence." Furthermore, it calls for changing the name of the Self-Defence Force (Jiei-tai) to the National Defence Force (Kokubō-gun). In English, this new designation may not sound like a significant change, but in Japanese the organization would be called a "military" (*gun*) for the first time, a term the government has avoided since the end of World War II. Other than this dramatic symbolic shift, the other changes would essentially confirm the current interpretation of the constitution, but would likely provide for interpretations that would allow the government greater strategic flexibility, such as entering into a collective-defence arrangement with the United States, and increase the possibility of Japan going to war. The proposal maintains Article 20's guarantee of the "freedom of religion" and the prohibitions on the state supporting any particular religion, compelling citizens to take part in religious activities, and engaging in "any other religious activity," but it adds a clause stating that "social rites" and "customary acts" are constitutional. This addition makes it possible for the government to openly patronize Yasukuni and the nation-protecting shrines – precisely what the Diet failed to accomplish in the early 1970s. Needless to say, these proposed changes would drastically change the relationship between religion and the state, including the armed forces. Even though support appears to be gradually increasing for constitutional reform, change in this suggested form is not inevitable. One can easily imagine, however, that further geopolitical shifts – even greater friction with China, an unpredictable North Korea, and a reworking of the U.S.-Japan alliance that created and made Article 9 viable at least in spirit – might lead to a greater sense of nationalism and nativism and enough public support for constitutional revision that would allow Japan's military to legitimate and formalize its relationship with Shinto.

Notes

1   The authors would like to acknowledge the cooperation of more than a dozen interviewees, including active and former Self-Defense Force (SDF) personnel and religious leaders. They are also grateful for the assistance of Kawano Hitoshi of the National Defense Academy, Philip Seaton of Hokkaido University, and Konno Yōji, each of whom provided invaluable introductions. Aaron Skabelund acknowledges the support of the Japan Foundation, which provided a fellowship that funded this research. Throughout this chapter, Japanese personal names appear surname (family name) first followed by personal name except in the case of Japanese scholars who publish in English.

2   Ishii Kenji, *Gendai Nihonjin no shūkyō* [Contemporary Japanese religion] (Tokyo: Shinyōsha, 2007): 4–5, 54–59.

3   Emile Durkheim, *The Elementary Forms of the Religious Life*, trans. J. W. Swain (London: Allen and Unwin, 1915): 47; Immanuel Kant, *Kritik der praktischen Vernunft* [Critique of Practical Reason], ed. Karl Vorleander (Hamburg: Felix MeinerVerlag, 1990 [1788]): 148.

4   Bruce Lincoln, *Holy Terrors: Thinking about Religion after September 11* (Chicago: University of Chicago Press, 2003): 5–7. Likewise, Shinto comports Danièle Hervieu-Léger's definition of religion as a shared community of memory. Danièle Hervieu-Léger, *Religion as a Chain of Memory*, trans. Simon Lee (New Brunswick, NJ: Rutgers University Press, 1993).

5   Paul Tillich, *Systematic Theology*, vol. 1 (Chicago: University of Chicago Press, 1951).

6   For an analysis of public outreach performed by the SDF during the early 1960s, see Aaron Skabelund, "Public Service/Public Relations: The Mobilization of the Self-Defense Force for the Tokyo Olympic Games," in *The East Asian Olympiads, 1934–2008: Building Bodies and Nations in Japan, Korea, and China*, ed. Michael Baskett and William M. Tsutsui (Lieden: Global Oriental, 2011): 63–76. For more recent efforts by the SDF to address its problematic relationship with society since the end of the Cold War, see Sabine Frühstück and Eyal Ben-Ari, "'Now We Show It All!' Normalization and the Management of Violence in Japan's Armed Forces," *Journal of Japanese Studies* 28, no. 1 (Winter 2002): 1–39.

7   We arrived at these conclusions through surveying primary and secondary sources related to the SDF and, most important, by conducting more than a dozen research interviews throughout Japan with active and former SDF personnel, as well as with religious leaders, during mid-2010. Because at the time we were both affiliated with Hokkaido University in Sapporo on the northern island of Hokkaido, our initial interviews were with public affairs officials of the Northern Army in Sapporo and Asahikawa. Using contacts and introductions within the SDF and through local shrines and churches, we located a number of active and former personnel who agreed to speak with us, although finding them proved to be a challenge,

because few Japanese, either within or outside the SDF, identify themselves as religious or affiliated with a particular religion. Gradually, we extended our interviews to Tokyo and Osaka, on the main island of Honshu, and to Kumamoto, on the southern island of Kyushu. While recognizing regional disparities and differences in individual experience and perception, we gained a fairly representative and comprehensive view of the relationship between religion and the armed forces in Japan today and in the past.

8 Helen Hardacre, *Shintō and the State, 1868–1988* (Princeton, NJ: Princeton University Press, 1989): 10.

9 Ibid., (italics added).

10 Ibid., 22.

11 Ibid., 32–33.

12 For the way in which radical Shinto ideology contributed to the drive to imperial expansion and war, see Walter A. Skya, *Japan's Holy War: The Ideology of Radical Shintō Ultranationalism* (Durham, NC: Duke University Press, 2009).

13 John Dower, *Embracing Defeat: Japan in the Wake of World War II* (New York: W. W. Norton, 1999).

14 For an account of Zen Buddhism's support for the war, see Brian Daizen Victoria, *Zen at War* (Lanham, MD: Rowman and Littlefield, 2006).

15 For an overview of the political debate over Yasukuni, see Franziska Seraphim, *War Memory and Social Politics in Japan, 1945–2005* (Cambridge, MA: Harvard University Asia Center, 2006), especially chapter 8.

16 "Kanzen busō de 'Yasukuni' sanpai" [Worshipping at 'Yasukuni' fully armed], *Asahi shinbun* [Asahi newspaper], 21 June 1966.

17 Sabine Frühstück, *Uneasy Warriors: Gender, Memory, and Popular Culture in the Japanese Army* (Berkeley: University of California Press, 2007): 151.

18 John Breen, "The Dead and the Living in the Land of Peace: A Sociology of the Yasukuni Shrine," *Mortality* 9, no. 1 (February 2004): 85.

19 Interview, Kumamoto, 11 May 2010.

20 See, for example, "Seifuku sugata no jieikan dōdō Yasukuni sanpai" [SDF officers in uniform unashamedly worship at Yasukuni], *Shūkan Kinyōbi* [Weekly Friday], no. 378 (7 September 2001): 24–27.

21 Hardacre, *Shintō and the State*, 154.

22 Breen, "The Dead and the Living," 80–81 (italics added for consistency).

23 Hardacre, *Shintō and the State*, 154.

24 Interview, Hokaido, 13 April 2010.

25 Interview, Yokosuka, 26 April 2010.

26 Interview, Sapporo, 9 May 2010.

27 For an example of such support, see "Kamakura Ishigami jinja reisai ni kyōryoku" [Cooperation for the Kamakura Ishigami shrine festival], *Asagumo shinbun* [Asagumo newspaper], 19 September 2010. At this festival, which coincided with a national holiday celebrating Japan's close relationship with the ocean – Marine Day (*Umi no hi*) – personnel and community members carried the *mikoshi* through the waves to give beachgoers protection. The *Asagumo* weekly newspaper, which is the SDF equivalent of the *Stars and Stripes* that caters to U.S. military personnel, probably reported on the festival because of its unique nature.

28 Interview, Sapporo, 9 May 2010.

29 Ibid.

30 Interview, Yokosuka, 26 May 2010.
31 For a complete version of the directive, see Hardacre, *Shintō and the State*, 167–170.
32 Interview, Sapporo, 16 May 2010. Suzuki Kenji is a pseudonym.
33 For an overview of these and more recent cases, see David M. O'Brien with Yasuo Ohkoshi, *To Dream of Dreams: Religious Freedom and Constitutional Politics in Postwar Japan* (Honolulu: University of Hawaii Press, 1996); and John Breen, "'Conventional Wisdom' and the Politics of Shinto in Postwar Japan," *Politics and Religion* 9, no. 1 (Spring 2010): 68–81.
34 "Rikuji 'Kunren hajime' hatsu no hakuchū – ippan doro 'gyōgun' Osaka, buki keikō sezu" ['Training start' of Ground SDF, first in daylight – a 'military march' on regular roads in Osaka without carrying weapons], *Sankei shinbun* [Sankei newspaper], 24 December 2009.
35 Interview, Itami, 15 July 2010.
36 YouTube video, "Rikuji Shinodayama chūtonchi kunren hajime 2010 'kōgun'" [Training start, a 'march,' from Ground SDF's Shinodayama base], http://www.youtube.com/watch?v=KZoghoDFDKg, accessed 13 December 2012.
37 Interview with Yui Hisashi, Asahikawa, 5 June 2010.
38 "Rikujō jieitai ga gokuhi ni sakusei shita shūkyō dantai risuto [List of religious groups secretly compiled by Ground SDF]," *Sandē mainichi* [Sunday daily], 15 April 2001, 152–157.
39 Interview, Yokosukua, 26 May 2010.
40 Minesaki Yasutada, *Gunjin dendō ni kansuru kenkyū* [Research related to missionary work among soldiers], (Fukuoka: Yorudan sha, 1980).
41 "Dendō gikai no hataraki" [The works of Dendō gikai], *Kirisuto shinbun* [Newspaper of Christ], 4 September 1992; Minesaki Yasutada, *Gunjin dendō ni kansuru kenkyū: Nihon OCU no genryū* [Research on missionary work among soldiers: The origins of Japan OCU] (Tokyo: Yorudansha, 1980): 44–45.
42 Ogawara Masamichi, *Kindai Nihon no sensō to shūkyō* [War and religion in modern Japan], (Tokyo: Kodansha, 2010): 177.
43 See http://www.uccj.or.jp/english/war.html, accessed on 21 July 2010.
44 Yatabe Minoru, "Aru santō rikusa no negai" [A major's wish], *Kokoro no tomo* [A heart's friend], 1 November 1971.
45 Acts 10. The group, which now also refers to itself as the Japan Military Christian Fellowship, has around 250 members.
46 Iwamoto Jirō, "'Kokoro no tomo' ni tazuneru" [A question for 'Kokoro no tomo'], *Kyōdan shinpō* [Kyōdan news], no. 3683 (1971); "Rentai yori mo kyozetsu o" [Rejection, not solidarity], *Kyōdan shinpō* [Kyōdan news], no. 3687 (1972); "Sengo Kirisuto-kyō wa kyomō ka" [Is postwar Christianity an illusion?] *Kyōdan shinpō* [Kyōdan news], no. 3694 (1972); "Mondai o sorasanai de!" [Don't distract attention from the issue], *Kyōdan shinpō* [Kyōdan news], no. 3710 (1972).
47 Interview with Yatabe Minoru, Chiba, 28 May 2010.

2

Canada

Joanne Benham Rennick

Historically, Christianity has enjoyed a privileged position in shaping Canadian social values through the work of churches and shared Christian ideals.[1] Today, Canada is experiencing the tension between a historical legacy of constitutionally established Christian traditions[2] and the Canadian Charter of Rights and Freedoms' guarantee of protection and endorsement of religious diversity and freedom. This tension is heightened with increasing secularization, greater religious pluralism as a result of increased immigration, and highly individualized and subjective ways of interpreting meaning. In fact, numerous influences apart from established religious authorities now affect the way Canadians find meaning and form their values. For many people, religious identity, personal values, and one's sense of purpose in the world are largely diffuse and unrefined notions.

For institutions such as the Canadian Forces (CF), where group cohesion and shared purpose are paramount, differences in values or uncertain values can be problematic on a number of levels. Although military socialization is important for teaching values, some scholars argue that the values people bring with them to the military are far more significant for determining how fully they will embrace the military ethos.[3] As a result, while individuals must commit themselves to upholding "Canadian values" embedded in the Canadian Forces' codes of conduct and statements of military ethos, they may not always be certain about what this entails and how to do so appropriately.[4]

This chapter explores the relationship between the changing nature of religion in Canada and the values that people bring to the Canadian Forces. It provides insights into the continuing significance of religion as an influence on values and ethical decision making. It points to the growing significance of subjective interpretations of meaning and diffuse forms of spirituality in undermining group cohesion and shared notions of purpose. Finally, it highlights religion, in its diverse forms, as a resource that can help influence moral and ethical behavior and address moral anomie.

Methods

Since 2004, I have conducted formal and informal interviews with military personnel about the role of religion and personal spirituality in their lives.[5] I have interviewed male and female members from all ranks and services and from as wide a variety of belief systems as possible. Some of those people are active members of formal faith traditions. Others are atheists who employ practices typically associated with religious beliefs such as yoga, meditation, or visualization. Still others have diffuse beliefs but continue to ask existential questions about meaning, purpose, and morality. In addition to interviews, I examined Web sites dedicated to specific religious groups within the CF, news reports about religion in the CF, and relied on ombudsman reports, government documents, and Department of National Defence newsletters. I also examined the little existing research and documentation that address the role of religion in the Canadian Forces (mainly historical works on the chaplaincy).

Most of this research formed the basis of *Religion in the Ranks*.[6] During research presentations and in peer reviews of the manuscript, however, military sociologists struggling with how best to consider religion in the military expressed interest in seeing how religion in Canada relates to the values that military personnel bring with them into the CF. This chapter is an attempt to engage some of these concerns.

Recent efforts by U.S., Australian, and Dutch military policy makers to promote "cultural intelligence" among military personnel are garnering some attention to religion as an aspect of culture.[7] Although these projects note the importance of training military members in aspects of the culture in the regions to which they are deployed, they relegate religion and religious identity to one small component within the notion of culture rather than recognizing it as a significant force for shaping and informing culture. Despite the familiarity of the term, "religion" remains an elusive and challenging concept to define – perhaps even more so in Canada where many have rejected traditional institutional forms of religion and where the forces of immigration, secularization, and individualism offer myriad alternative approaches to spiritual ways of being, such as paganism, holistic healing, and various religious syncretisms (e.g., Catholics who practice yoga and meditation). Consequently, when looking at religion in the Canadian Forces, one must look at all of its aspects, whether formal and traditional or private and subjective, expressed primarily with regard to practices or ideas, or highly adaptable communities and symbols connected to spiritual ideas and interests.

Although scholars have attempted to describe the essence of religion, there is no undisputed standard. Emile Durkheim (and numerous others following him) understood religion as a product of society necessary to ensure "social cohesion" rather than a supernaturally inspired reality. He argued that all religious beliefs have in common a division of the world into the categories of sacred (things "set apart and forbidden") and profane (everything else).[8] Anthropologist Clifford Geertz viewed religion as a powerful "cultural system" capable of motivating people and establishing a "general order of existence."[9] Interest in social cohesion and cultural systems continues in ongoing discussions of organizational culture,[10] and it becomes increasingly relevant in multicultural and pluralistic contexts such as military forces.

More recent attempts to define religion help account for new and diffuse forms of religion. French sociologist Danièle Hervieu-Léger, for example, follows Durkheim's reasoning but, in recognition of secularizing trends and other changes affecting religion in modernity, includes not only organized religion but also invisible, or private, forms.[11] She argues that religion can be defined as an "ideological, practical and symbolic system" from which individuals and groups that share in the associated traditions and memories gain a sense of belonging.[12] Hervieu-Léger links her ideas about "remembered beliefs" with Durkheim's theory of social cohesion to describe religion as a tradition-based social construct that generates a sense of belonging and establishes social norms for its members. In this sense, unlike in anthropological models where religion is one element of culture, religion *is* culture – it is who we are, where we come from, how we act, and what matters most. Roger O'Toole, in keeping with Hervieu-Léger's position, states that, despite decreasing numbers of participants in Canadian religious congregations, "a sense of belonging, albeit derived, in many cases, from a passive, perceived identification with a particular organization, appears to be important in the Canadian context."[13]

This modern twist makes religious belief somewhat more difficult to examine than simply relying on statistical information, because, as Robert Wuthnow states, the highly individualized state of modern spirituality means that it is typically hidden from view "except insofar as it is talked about or revealed through personal interviews or indirectly in public behavior."[14] This is an excellent reason for scholars to attend to both public and private views about religion; to consider, as Bruce Lincoln does, the beliefs, practices, community, and institutions; and to recognize that some views are based in tradition but have taken on a private form and interpretation.[15] As I show in this chapter, spiritual and religious thinking in the late modern era is contingent on one's personal experience as well as dependent on underlying aspects of the established social norms (rules and guidelines for behavior) and values (things considered to have value) of Canadian and military society. It is one means by which individuals define and understand themselves, establish their worldview, and develop a sense of purpose in life, as well as relate their personal interests to their military careers. Where people participate in a particular religious institution, as in the case of military chaplains, I use the term "formal religion." Where people identify with a formal religious tradition but do not participate in an organized community, I use the term "private religion." Where people describe a vaguely defined sense of a power or force beyond themselves or reject the term "religion" or "religious," I use the term "personal spirituality."

Religious Demographics in the Canadian Forces

So what does the religious makeup of Canada's military forces look like today? Amazingly, given recent concerns relating to religion in Canada, the Canadian Forces does not compile statistics on the religious demography of its members. Although the data are collected, stamped on identification tags, and provided to commanding officers and chaplains they are not collected and compiled as a whole. This surprising lack of data is all the more significant given both the changing demographics of broader Canadian society as a result of increasing immigration and that reality that values are often inherited from one's family of origin.[16] For example, Statistics Canada notes that by 2017 as much as 10 percent of the Canadian population will comprise people from non-Christian traditions, with the Muslim, Hindu, and Sikh religions growing most rapidly. In fact, these religious traditions could see their memberships increase by 145 percent, 92 percent, and 72 percent, respectively.[17] Already these changes are being felt in the largest reserve units based in multicultural urban centers such as Toronto, Vancouver, and Montreal.[18]

Despite CF efforts to incorporate greater numbers of minority personnel and the lack of evidence to show otherwise, National Defence and the Canadian Forces continue to posit that religious affiliation in the forces is similar to that of broader Canadian society. According to this reasoning, the CF should be predominantly Christian with a small secondary population of Muslims and small numbers of other minority groups.[19] Without valid data on religion, however, it is difficult to say what the majority of CF personnel believe. Analysis of the statistical data that are available implies that most Canadian military personnel are young Caucasian males from provinces that report Christian denominations as the primary religion. The situation in Québec, however, highlights the problematic nature of relying on these numbers without going deeper. Although statistics show that the largest majority of Québécois identify as Roman Catholic, other research indicates that Roman Catholicism in Québec has more to do with culture and heritage than with active participation. Furthermore, one could easily speculate that religious groups with strong military traditions such as Sikhs and Aboriginals (First Nations Peoples) join the CF in larger numbers than are present in civilian society.[20]

These examples indicate a need to test the assumption that religion in military society is similar to that of Canadian society. Without knowledge about the religious makeup and the spiritual beliefs of Canadian Forces personnel, it will be increasingly difficult to identify differences in values and worldview that could undermine group cohesion or interfere with military objectives.[21] Moreover, a lack of knowledge about the values that people bring with them to the forces makes it impossible for policy makers to know which values should be expressly stated and emphasized for all members to embrace and uphold.[22] Finally, without this knowledge, it will be impossible to prepare and equip leaders to manage diversity within their units.

Practice: Diffuse Religion, Individualism, Personal Experience

In addition to growing religious diversity, the new social realities of the so-called postmodern era are influencing the way people establish their values. The concept of postmodernity is both ambiguous and contentious because, among other things, highly individual and subjectivized interpretations of thought and experience (as opposed to imposed authority and meaning handed down from social elites) reveal endless forms of relativism that make it impossible to draw any meaningful conclusions about human experience. In fact, individualism and subjectivization have become catch phrases indicative of human experience in late modernity.[23] Limitations of space and time prevent a full discussion of this category of analysis. For my purposes here, however, I employ Hervieu-Léger's term "late modernity" to describe the present milieu. In addition, I follow Hervieu-Léger and Anthony Giddens, who argue that the present social context in the Global North retains much of what was established during the industrialized era (e.g., scientific rationalism, progress, and bureaucratic efficiency) within a social context now dominated by globalized interests, scientific and technological advances, greater information exchange, and a more relativistic – at times even cynical – outlook toward any one claim to "the truth."[24]

An example of the late modern discomfort with traditional forms of meaning and authority is evident in the way interview participants expressed their discomfort with the term "religious" (as associated with a formal institution), generally preferring instead to use the word "spiritual." When I asked individuals why they were uncomfortable using the term "religion," they made comments such as, "Well, I don't go to church," and "Religion is about rules," and "My spirituality is my own – it's not something someone else made up and then forced on me." Being religious implied an association and acceptance of a formal, institutional, communal creed and formula, whereas being spiritual implied reliance on internal and self-directed exploration of existential and transcendent issues.

In clarifying the differences between these two labels, Robert Fuller states that spirituality and religion are essentially the same because they connote a belief in and a desire to connect with a Higher Power or reach a higher state of being.[25] Confusion regarding these terms comes from the gradual association of the word "spiritual" with "the private realm of thought and experience while the word 'religious' is associated more with the public realm of membership in religious institutions, participation in formal rituals, and adherence to official denominational doctrines."[26] Fuller argues that people who call themselves "spiritual but not religious" reject formal religious organizations in favor of "individualized spirituality that includes picking and choosing from a wide range of alternative religious philosophies."[27]

This new religious individualism is not exclusive to those outside formal religious traditions. In fact, there is widespread evidence of the focus on individualized spirituality even within organized religious communities.[28] Even when people who consider themselves spiritual but not religious belong to a particular religious tradition, they insist that as individuals they have the final interpretive authority on religious doctrines that they consider relevant to them. For example, Roman Catholic teachings place attendance at Mass and participation in the Eucharist as central to Catholicism, whereas many Québécois understand themselves Catholic simply because they were baptized as infants and attended Catholic schools.[29] Similarly, within identifiable religious groups such as Buddhism and New Religious Movements, practices and beliefs vary depending on ethnic identity or the focus of a particular subgroup.[30]

Despite accommodations for special dietary requirements, clothing, or time for prayer, religious personnel who want to practice their faith in the military have learned to adapt their needs to their conditions in various ways, including shaving part of their beard to comply with health and safety regulations regarding oxygen masks,[31] praying whenever and wherever possible, and adapting their values to the ones most in evidence in the unit. For example, one Muslim solider explained that although his religious beliefs help him in his duties, they also create a value conflict that sets him apart from his colleagues. He says:

Islam really helps me in my duties because the disciplines of the religion carry over into the work ethic in the CF. Islam has taught me to do well under pressure and stress, it has helped me appreciate fellowship and community and all of those are also present in the CF. It helps with everything – it gives a sense of purpose and direction to everything I do. I'm working and challenging myself as a Muslim as much as I'm working and challenging myself as a soldier. Some people are just here for the money, some are here for the experience and the community – all of this is also part of my experience too, but I also have a reason and foundation for my work that comes from my religious beliefs. ... It's not the job that makes it hard being a Muslim – it's more that there are aspects of the informal culture that are opposed to Islamic values.

As a response to this reality, individuals learn to adapt their values while still honoring the internal traditions such as the Muslim who, on being promoted, instead of buying the traditional round of beer, bought everyone pizza as a way to respect the tradition without abandoning his values. The willingness of believers to modify and adapt their beliefs to meet military obligations points to the individualized and subjective nature of religious identities in late modernity. The same is true for values and ethics they adopt from those traditions.

Whereas strictly modern rational thinking might dismiss religious beliefs as impossible to test, prove, or quantify through scientific means, the late modern appreciation for personal interpretation based on experience causes people to apply both a rational and a subjective lens to matters of belief, meaning, morality, and values. Not surprisingly, then, the values and worldview people take from these traditions are also highly individualized and, as such, common denominators of belief – even within a specific tradition – cannot be assumed.

This commingling of modern tendencies to apply scientific reasoning and late modern tendencies to elevate personal interpretive authority above traditional authority offers striking insights into the way religion is remade in late modernity and has significant implications for military culture where conformity, collaboration, and shared values are aspired-to ideals for operational effectiveness. The implication is that, in late modern global society, there can be no such thing as a truly shared set of values; instead, people may share purpose, resolve, or ideals. The values they carry, however, are largely informed by personal religious or spiritual beliefs (including the antireligious), as these are informed by ethnicity, language, culture, gender (and other aspects of identity), and most importantly, personal experiences in light of these. This makes crucial the need for greater training about religion, spirituality, and values for all military personnel. It also requires that purposeful attention be ascribed to helping personnel interpret and negotiate the in-group differences that are increasingly likely to be the norm within their units. Indeed, religious leaders within the CF and in other forces around the world are frequently being called on for this very purpose.

Clerics: Religious Leadership as a Moral Resource

Even as religious identity becomes more individualized, it appears that a place still exists for religious leadership to contribute to the moral development of personnel, clarify which values personnel must uphold, and provide leadership about how this should be done. As of May 2012, the Canadian Forces Chaplain Branch (regular forces) included 222 chaplains and had 14 in training. It was made up chiefly of males (81.3 percent) from Protestant traditions (63.2 percent). The historical predominance of Anglicans, Roman Catholics, and those from groups that form what is now the United Church continues today. Roman Catholic chaplains constitute approximately 34.7 percent of the branch.[32] Anglican priests account for about 17.3 percent of all Protestants (2010 estimates on Anglican military personnel were placed at 12 percent of the CF), and United Church ministers make up the next largest group at nearly 11.4 percent (personnel estimates were slightly more than 10 percent). The next largest groups include Baptists (9.7 percent) and the Christian Evangelical Fellowship of Canada (8.4 percent). Remaining members come from other Protestant groups and include three imams, one rabbi, and one Orthodox priest.[33]

Chaplains are recruited based on an identified need for a representative from a particular denomination or faith group. The Interfaith Committee on Canadian Military Chaplaincy (ICCMC), a subcommittee of the Canadian Council of Churches, then works in consultation with the chaplain general to identify and retain qualified candidates.[34]

Although non-Christian religious leaders are now being invited to join the chaplaincy, their appointment remains subject to approval and recognition by the Canadian Council of Churches. Potential candidates from groups not recognized by the Canadian Council of Churches (e.g., pagans, Wiccans, and other such loosely affiliated groups and associations) are not eligible to serve as military chaplains. The rationale for this type of exclusivity is to ensure adequate pastoral training and standard entry requirements for all chaplains.[35]

Military personnel commit themselves to protecting and upholding Canadian values as they are described in the Canadian Forces document *Duty with Honour: The Profession of Arms in Canada*. As this document states,

The very legitimacy of the profession of arms in Canada demands that the military embody the same fundamental values and beliefs as those of the society it defends. ... The *Constitution Act* of 1982, the *Charter of Rights and Freedoms* and other foundational legislation all reflect the value Canadians place on the democratic ideal, the rule of law, and the concept of peace, order and good government.[36]

In addition to the legal "Canadian values," *Duty with Honour* identifies a place for martial values, or "fighting spirit" as well. In some cases, this is effective for helping people perform their roles well; without proper leadership, however, it has the potential to become an excuse for self-destructive behavior. For example, one young member of an infantry unit with a reputation for being very tough told me:

We might meet a guy who's an alcoholic and a chain smoker, who's divorced and is totally screwed up. But he's been in Afghanistan and on other missions and, to us, that guy's a hero because he has given himself body and soul to the CF – to support the missions, to fight and protect – to uphold Canadian values. He is tougher and harder than other people – he's a survivor.

Both the Canadian and martial values are evident in this description, although they are clearly being interpreted subjectively based on this young man's notions of heroism. An Aboriginal (First Nations) officer I interviewed had an entirely different interpretation of these same values. He said,

I am a warrior. We are all warriors. All Aboriginals raised in Aboriginal spirituality are warriors. To be a warrior is to be someone who picks you up when you fall down, who lends a shoulder for you to cry on, who brings people up when they're down. You don't have to be a soldier to be a warrior – you are a warrior in everyday life.

These seemingly insignificant examples of discordant interpretations of Canadian and martial values have the potential to become highly problematic when adequate leadership is not in place to encourage critical reflection and redirection. A poignant example of this occurred in 1991 when the First Canadian Airborne Regiment served on the UN Observation and Peacekeeping Mission in Somalia (UNOSOM II). A number of improprieties and abuses occurred during this mission, including the murder of a Somali teenager and the refusal of members to cooperate with the inquiry.[37] One of the many controversies arising from the Somalia affair was the discovery by the media of a number of "trophy photos" of captive Somalis taken by members of the squadron. Among the photos eventually released to the media was one of Padre Mark Sargent standing behind five bound and blindfolded young boys being held for attempting to steal garbage from the Canadian compound at Belet Huen. Although the photograph implied complicity in the boys' mistreatment, what is not immediately obvious is that the chaplain is speaking to a local leader, who stands half-concealed behind a billboard (his feet and elbow are evident in the picture). Reports exonerating Sargent argue that, speaking through a translator to local leaders, the padre was able to intervene and stop the boys from being beaten and further abused. Sargent was issued a commendation for his "commendable performance" in Somalia.[38] Following this tour of duty, the Canadian Airborne Regiment was disbanded, and a full investigation was mandated to discover the cause of the failure of the mission.[39] One result of the inquiry noted a lack of effective leadership as well as uncertainty about the values (and therefore the values that should have been on display) of the mission.[40]

The incident in Somalia made it clear that military personnel need moral leadership and encouragement to think and act in ways that accord with Canadian and mission values. Since then, moral and ethical training has taken a more prominent place in pre-tour work-up training, and, interestingly, chaplains are now frequently relied on to act as moral leaders who draw attention to the lapses between desired and actual values. The Canadian Forces Chaplain Branch calls on padres to "provide ethical advice and counsel ... [and] deliver ethical training to units as required. The chaplain is called to ... [challenge members] to exhibit the highest possible ethical standards in the conduct of peacekeeping and humanitarian operations as well as in theatres of war or regional conflict. The chaplain must be the moral conscience of the unit."[41]

A similar response to moral lapses has been employed in the Russian military where, in 1997, in response to numerous instances of aggressive hazing, Orthodox priests were employed to encourage moral behavior among the enlisted personnel. Since that time, statistics demonstrate that instances of hazing and suicide in the Russian military have dropped "significantly."[42]

In Canada, military chaplains believe that their presence can help guide moral behavior because, even as personnel are obliged to uphold Canadian values, they are not always clear about what those values are. One chaplain said, "There are very few opportunities for young soldiers to ask questions and talk about things. The CF is very much about proficiencies, but there are few opportunities to talk about the purpose behind missions and that type of thing. Soldiers should always [have the] opportunity to ask, 'Am I doing the right thing?'"

A navy chaplain said, "They want to uphold Canadian values, and there seems to be enormous reflection on *how* they're supporting those values." He added that members depend on us to tell them when they're going astray. They're willing, as soldiers, to let others lead. They have a very high sense of honor and shame, and they want to do their job well. They want to do a good job for a good cause, but they're not always reflecting on the bigger picture. Chaplains need to clarify for soldiers and COs [commanding officers] when the activities are no longer representing [Canadian] values. We need to clarify for them what they're doing and relay that information – especially if there's a disconnect between the goals of the mission and the behavior that's occurring – up the chain.

One Francophone chaplain who had served in Afghanistan described the importance of being a moral adviser for personnel.[43] He said:

In the CF, we anticipate a higher level of consciousness from most of our soldiers. If you just obey because you are afraid, there is a problem. A lot of our people are limited by peer pressure to conform – Somalia was an example of that – because you live and breathe with a small group that controls the whole game and puts a lot of pressure on you. It is very easy to give in to that. What is "right" and what is "wrong" is determined by the group; it shouldn't be like that.

Another Francophone chaplain stated:

My biggest job is to help people find their place in the organization ... when individuals don't have a lot of power ... it's easy for them to be coerced into 'groupthink' because they think that's just how it is in the military. Somalia is the perfect example of that. Lots of little unchecked actions resulted first in individuals and then the whole group going over to the dark side.

He continued:

In real life the "bad guys" are not always so easy to identify. When you're in theater, there can be a real cognitive dissonance between what you expected or what's supposed to be happening and what's really going on around you. The people you're supposed to protect might appear as bad as the "bad guys." So you start to lose perspective about right and wrong, good and bad. You need someone outside of that situation to give that perspective back and identify and clarify what's going on. Your spouse isn't there, and your friends are all dealing with the same thing, so it falls to the padre to help you work through the cognitive dissonance that is happening in the field.

Cognitive dissonance is an unfortunate hazard of military service in virtually any type of theater, from humanitarian aid and disaster relief to combat, because it results from abnormal or unfamiliar situations that threaten to overwhelm one's moral worldview and values. As with helping people reflect on their moral obligations in the context of a mission, military chaplains can also be an important resource for helping individual members deal with the psychoemotional challenges they face within the mission environment.

Religion, Values, and Understanding the Theater of Operations

A clash, or perceived absence, of values can be a source of moral anomie. Durkheim describes anomie as a response to conditions where norms and values are unclear or absent and argues that this state of moral confusion can be a source of deviance and alienation with the real potential for harm.[44] Although those in authority can sometimes address some of these concerns by clarifying the goals of the mission, priority is given to tactical and strategic issues, and leaders may be struggling with their own moral and ethical concerns. In these cases, Canadian personnel may go to chaplains for help in sorting out ethical dilemmas and clarifying which values and ethics they should be supporting (or resisting) during the mission.

This was certainly true during the UN Assistance Mission for Rwanda (UNAMIR). In the face of genocide, an act utterly opposed to Canadian values to protect human life and appreciate differences, it fell to the chaplains to help personnel find meaning in the chaos that surrounded them. A unit padre, David Melanson, "found himself listening to an endless flow of stories and emotional outpourings" from personnel on the mission.[45]

On deployments that take personnel to unstable regions where they face the suffering of local people experiencing famine, the aftereffects of a natural disaster, injury and loss of life, as well as civil and military unrest, their sense of dislocation, culture shock, and anomie can be significant. A counselor at an operational trauma center explained the confusion of the mission environment as follows:

Here [in Canada] we don't have a clue of what war is really like. Canada is such a clean, sterile country and then these soldiers get sent into a place where people are killing each other and being left there – that never leaves you. You can really lose faith in humanity. I have people asking me, "How could they do that? How can people do that to one another?"

A Francophone infantry member who had served in Afghanistan explained:

You give something as basic as a water bottle to a little child, and hundreds of them will jump on him and beat him up to get it. I gave [one child] a package of gum, and there was a fight because they all came and jumped on him. ... But these people are in survival mode. They are threatened. ... War is beyond language, beyond words – it's an experience.

The lack of control over the chaos inherent in the mission environment can result in a sense of helplessness and frustration that leads to extreme mental stress, which can have a profound effect on personnel. As one army major explained:

I think anybody who goes into a situation that is different than what they have normally seen will be changed. In the military we go off on tours, we come back different. You're affected by the environment. One of the major contributors is the feeling of helplessness. I remember when I was in Bosnia, it was during the Kosovo bombing, and I remember a trucker coming back to camp just weeping because they had driven by a convoy of maybe five hundred people – women and children out in the rain, out in the cold. He came back crying because, what could we do for those women and children who are suffering and didn't ask for this?" ... "Well, there wasn't much we could do. It wasn't our role to be doing a humanitarian task. The UN had people there taking care of that so our role was to bring stability to the country. But we're not used to that; we don't come from a country where there are wars, and you don't see people who are abandoned along [the] side of the road. You're in those countries and a woman's on the side of the road giving birth on the side of the road. What do you do? You stop, you put her in the back of the truck and you allow her to give birth in the back of the truck. But you're not trained for that! You're trying to assist out of human interest – you do the best you can. What happens if the baby dies? That would be traumatic! Is that your fault? No, but it's a traumatic event because it doesn't happen here.

A chaplain serving with a Francophone unit said:

Soldiers go through an emotional trauma because of a value judgment they make about the event. For example, what is wrong with a child being killed unless there is a value associated with it? The event is filtered through our ethical and moral value system. I have had a lot of people telling me stories where they were so hopeless and they were so upset because somewhere somehow they felt they should have been able to control the event.

A number of recent reports demonstrate how, in some cases, the profound sense of anomie that a person experiences during a mission because of a severe clash of values can produce extreme emotional, psychological, and spiritual stresses that can lead to serious stress injuries. Canadian Lt. Gen. (ret.) Roméo Dallaire, in both his book and many of his public speaking engagements about the Rwandan genocide, relates his extreme frustration in not having been able to intervene and stop the imminent slaughter.[46] A report by the Canadian Forces Ombudsman on the experiences of Cpl. Christian McEachern indicates frustration at not being "able to make a difference" as a source of his post-traumatic stress disorder. He described being witness to the rape of a woman outside the Canadian compound during his duties as a member of the UN Observer Mission to Uganda in 1993. He states:

While we're over there, there were a number of incidents that happened where we weren't allowed to do anything about it 'cause we weren't in Uganda to do anything. ... I think the one that bothered me the most was the night the woman got raped right beside our compound, we could see the whole thing and hear her screaming. I called in about three times and asked if I could interfere, fire a shot or do something and I wasn't allowed to do anything because security for the division compound could not be compromised, so ... we just had to stand there and watch. That bugged me, that was probably the worst. ... The act was pretty bad but not being able to do anything. ... You trained hard to go over there and be able to make a difference and then they tie your hands like that.[47]

Members of the failed mission to Somalia describe the hopelessness of their assignment and their feelings of being unable to make any positive contributions to the region. In part this led to the anger and resentment they felt toward the Somali people.[48] Individual reports and transcripts from the Somalia Commission of Inquiry offer vivid examples of personnel dealing with culture shock, a frustrating and uncertain mission, as well as a serious lack of understanding of the Somali culture and value system.[49] In fact, one analysis of the abuses that occurred in Somalia suggests that lack of knowledge about the culture and values at work in the region led personnel to "dehumanize" the Somalis.[50] A female air force member I interviewed who had been posted to the Middle East and Bosnia said:

We really noticed the cultural differences. We'd have to stand back and watch when the locals were being cruel to animals or hitting their wives. You're not allowed to get involved and that can be very upsetting. I think that has something to do with being Canadian – but not being able to intervene adds a lot of stress to a mission. The women in Bosnia saw their kids being attacked by wild dogs, but we had to continue to stand guard and we couldn't help. That was terrible.

In these cases, it is not just a conflict of values that causes moral anomie, but also the ensuing feelings of guilt, responsibility, and anxiety that come from not having upheld one's values coupled with the inability to put the situation into a broader framework of understanding.

Personal values are a filter through which many military personnel on deployments where lawlessness is the norm are able to "make sense" of the situation. In instances where the violation of personal values leads to a serious inner conflict, CF members should be encouraged to seek opportunities that can help restore meaning and order.[51] In some cases, even though they are prohibited from intervening to stop the violation of these values, military personnel seek alternative ways to make a difference and uphold Canadian values. I know of numerous examples where deployed personnel contacted their families and home communities to collect sports equipment, warm clothes, and school, medical, and other supplies to be distributed by military personnel. Other initiatives included personnel using their free time to initiate or participate in projects to rebuild schools, orphanages, hospitals, and libraries that would improve the day-to-day conditions of local people, again reflecting the social values of Canadian society. Although in some cases personnel initiated these projects independently, in many cases religious leaders proposed these projects as a means for personnel to have a positive experience during a difficult mission. A retired chaplain, Al Fowler, gives the example of personnel in Rwanda going into an orphanage that housed about 500 displaced children of all ages. Most were sick, with diseases ranging from scabies to cholera. The soldiers, especially those who had children at home, were deeply moved and spent a lot of their off-duty time trying to help the orphans. Eventually, the regiment was supporting 2,300 children in six orphanages.[52]

In fact, the objective of "doing good" is a frequent refrain in my interviews with military personnel, and many of them (such as former lt. gen. Roméo Dallaire) use religious and value-laden language to describe their experiences in the CF. One person described his job as "fighting evil," another saw it as "improving conditions for civilians," and someone else explained that they hoped to be able to "make something good come out of a bad situation." Consider the religious language in these quotes from two different officers.

From an air force major: "They see themselves as an ally with God for fighting pain and evil in this world. I can tell you when we were [in Afghanistan], we did our best to fight evil. I couldn't explain it but I lived it, and I acted on it and I responded to it ... so that's at least one of the steps that people can take [to overcome stress] ... the idea that they are helping to fight evil."

From an army captain: "The stuff we do in the post–Cold War era is more on the side of the angels than not. Accounts from young people coming back from Afghanistan are positive – that we're there helping create democracy and tolerance. This unit is trained for combat, but they're not in there to kill the enemy. They're there because civilians need protection."

For many personnel, the moral and ethical concerns that arise in the course of their duties raise questions about existential issues, the meaning of suffering and hardship, and ideas about right and wrong and good and evil. Helping people and "making a difference in others' lives are a way for members to fight evil, do good, and avoid being part of the problem." A Canadian general I spoke with said that this type of thinking along with projects that do good are also important for their capacity to protect personnel from some of the stresses and strains of military experience. He says:

If you're fighting to protect people there's a certain level of satisfaction in that but you may still be doing some pretty horrible stuff. But if you're building a bridge [that helps people get to a clean water supply], you're into a whole new dimension of providing support. These projects should be made essential parts of a soldier's normal routine for these guys to be able to sustain their ability to handle the incredible trauma they can face – these are routes that give immediate consolation. These different projects can be a high point they can look back to and say, "It wasn't all bad. We weren't able to intervene here and people were killed, but we were able to build that or do this and that did help some." ... The veterans of these missions will want to talk, to laugh, and to cry – it's absolutely important that they be able to do that. If they only have things to cry about, things that bring out pain and anger, then there will be no comfort for them. They will remain bitter and broken.

The values that service members carry with them in theater have an impact on their experience and on their capacity to influence the success of the mission. Although many military personnel turn to chaplains and other traditional religious resources to help them deal with these concerns, the thinking, discussions, value judgments, and questions that result from them can be considered religious in their own right according to late modern notions of religion as subjective, quest based, and spiritual but not institutionally bound.

Impact on the Conduct of War

Although different values stemming from different religious beliefs can set individuals apart from their peers, sometimes it is the lack of religious knowledge within a group that has the greater potential for harm. Studies show that Canadian attempts to remove religion from the public sphere – which resulted from the legal establishment of French Roman Catholic and English Anglican traditions at the founding of the nation as well as from rights ensured by the Canadian Charter of Rights and Freedoms – have ensured that the majority of Canadian young people know very little about world religions.[53] Religious minorities within the CF point to lack of religious knowledge as a source for conflict and misunderstanding, and ignorance about religion can be a serious problem when Canadian military members are deployed to work with personnel from international forces and also with civilian populations that do not share Canadian "Christian" values. In this sense, the main problem that the CF faces is not too much religion, but too little – particularly in the context of understanding differences within units and in the mission environment.

Different groups often face conflict and misunderstanding of one type or another, but the potential for confusion increases when individuals lack sufficient knowledge to engage in useful dialogue or to develop a framework of reference about the relevant issues. Among minority personnel in the Canadian Forces, there is an evident lack of knowledge about world religions. A Muslim told me that

very few people ask about my religion. I think most of them are embarrassed to ask "stupid questions" because when people *do* ask me things they always frame it that way: "Is this a stupid question? I don't mean to be stupid but. ..." I think they're interested, they just don't know how to ask. I think it's good when they ask, it shows that they're trying to understand.

An Aboriginal describing discrimination from coworkers explained that, although she was hurt by comments made about her, "I believe what was said was out of ignorance and lack of education." Similarly, two Sikh reservists from the Toronto region stated that others have little knowledge about their religion. As one notes, "I have not come across any blatant discrimination or harassment. In fact, what I have come across is positive curiosity, understanding, and acceptance." Another Sikh from the same region mentions that curiosity about his religious identity is common among those with whom he works. He states that almost all of the people he has met "have shown an earnest interest in the turban and Sikhism." These examples suggest that ignorance about religion is a reality in the CF even when personnel do not experience discrimination as a result.

A lack of knowledge and an unwillingness to ask questions that could lead to greater understanding, however, have the potential to create conflict both within a unit and beyond. A Muslim gave this example of religious ignorance from a unit member during a training session:

One time we were waiting to hand in weapons and it was time to pray, so I started to pray and another soldier thought I was having a breakdown, and he came over to me and said, "Hey are you alright?" and tried to help me. Of course I couldn't answer him because I was praying! So I finished my prayers and then I explained what I had been doing.

On the other hand, there are examples where religious difference can imply collusion with the enemy. As a convert to Islam explained:

I think there's also a strong sense of "us" and "them" mentality. For example, the army is a very Canadian institution, and then you've got all these Western military forces engaged in the so-called war on terror that in many ways translates to war on Islam. Some of our most recent engagements have been in Muslim nations – Bosnia, Somalia, Afghanistan – there's a real sense of uneasiness in this regard. A lot of Muslims are uncomfortable with Canada's roles in those theaters and also there's a sense of betraying other Muslims. So there's this sense of being on the outside. This is one of the biggest drawbacks. I'd prefer to go in on a humanitarian mission, but if they asked me to go as a rifleman, would I go? Yeah, I'd go. It's not my first choice but there's such a strong humanitarian and nation-building aspect to that operation [Afghanistan] that I'd go. The Taliban is not an Islam I know, so I don't consider it a conflict with my beliefs. In fact, my religious beliefs are more of a motivation to go and be part of a project that helps people out of that kind of situation.

Despite his willingness to fulfill his duties as a soldier, and without opportunities for education and discussion, this person's values may appear to be in conflict with military objectives and potentially ostracize him from his peers while also subjecting him to undue scrutiny from his superiors.

Although religious illiteracy and lack of understanding about associated religious values may simply embarrass colleagues, they have the dangerous potential to create anger and resentment in a theater of operations. A scenario described by a member of a mission in the Golan Heights offers insight into why clarification about religion and values is important for every operational theater and how something seemingly mundane has the potential to create a serious incident. He explained how one of the men in his unit, a nonpracticing Muslim, became angry because "we were using prayer mats as carpets. We had them beside our beds to keep our feet warm. They had pictures of Mecca on them, and he was annoyed because we were standing on them." Clearly the lack of religious knowledge evident in this example has the capacity to create conflict within the unit; on a larger spectrum, however, this kind of ignorant behavior could lead to unnecessarily negative interactions for troops working in regions where religion is central to the culture. Such ignorance about religion and values has the potential to put both military and civilian lives in danger as well as undermine the goals of the mission.

Conclusion

Although the majority of Canadians continue to self-identify as Christians, most young people in Canada interpret their values and religious beliefs primarily from an individual perspective, filtered through religious meaning systems and aligned with sociocultural norms and values, rather than according to the doctrines of a single moral authority. Whether diffuse or particular, personal beliefs continue to inform right and wrong behavior. Furthermore, when a member's sense of right and wrong clashes with the values on display in the mission environment, or when members are prohibited from intervening to establish what they believe are good values, they may experience a profound sense of moral anomie that leaves them in emotional, spiritual, and psychological chaos. Under these conditions, even personnel who have little value for religion and religious authorities may seek moral guidance, consolation, and courage. Furthermore, lack of knowledge about religion and religious values has the potential to cause serious problems both within units – as I have shown in numerous examples given here – and externally during operations that occur in regions where religion is central to the culture and when Canadian Forces must work with UN troops from other parts of the world. This was true of the Canada's mission to Somalia (UNOSOM II), where Canadian soldiers were held responsible for the deadly beating of a Somali teenager because of a "lack of moral leadership" and for "dehumanizing" the Somali people, and during the UNAMIR mission (Rwanda) where religious leaders encouraged and participated in the genocide, causing greater confusion for those appointed to intervene.

As religious identity in Canada becomes increasingly diverse, military policy makers must attune themselves to the reality that traditional shared values (i.e., those espoused by the Christian churches that helped shape Canadian society) may not be understood or even recognized by all service members. In fact, as people increasingly rely on individual and subjective interpretations of meaning and values, military leaders must reexamine any assumptions of shared values and explicitly name, define, and enforce the values they expect members to uphold. Moreover, they must recognize the likelihood that personal, religious, and institutional values may conflict and be prepared to address those differences in ways that do not undermine social cohesion or military objectives. Too much religion can also be a problem, as in the case of the Evangelical Christian who told me that women do not belong in fighting forces, homosexuals are an "abomination," and members of other religious groups are "inspired by demons."[54] Finally, leaders must establish forums for teaching and learning about world religions and religious diversity in Canada, including individualized forms, so that personnel are attuned to and informed about the potential differences in values and beliefs. Without a commitment to education and ongoing discussion about religious identities, the CF will face continuing challenges to establish cohesion within the ranks and develop effective civil-military relations in theater.

Notes

1   I gratefully acknowledge the Social Sciences and Humanities Research Council and the University of Waterloo for their financial support of my research. An earlier

version of this chapter appeared in *Armed Forces and Society* (Published online before print April 26, 2012, doi: 10.1177/0095327X12441326 *Armed Forces & Society July 2013 vol. 39 no. 3 511–530*).

2   The role of religion in New France and British North America was sufficiently integrated into all aspects of state and society, so when French and later British colonizers established their authority over a region, they naturally imposed their religious values on the cultural, political, economic, and social institutions that developed therein. As a result, from the 1700s to the late 1800s, early institutions were clearly defined by the Christian values of those in authority. In regions under French control, Catholicism dominated; in English territories, the Church of England was granted state-sanctioned authority that lasted until the mid-1800s. Terrence Murphy, "The English-Speaking Colonies to 1854," in *A Concise History of Christianity in Canada*, ed. Robert Perrin and Terrence Murphy (Toronto: Oxford University Press, 1996): 113, 184–188. Ultimately, however, established church rule in Canada failed because, unlike in the home countries of France and Britain, church authority in the new territories suffered from lack of resources, competition from one another and other smaller sects, as well as having to struggle against the problems of a widely dispersed population that was not always warmly inclined to church governance of their frontier lifestyles S. D. Clark, *Church and Sect in Canada* (Toronto: Toronto University Press, 1948).

3   David Bercuson, *Significant Incident: Canada's Army, the Airborne, and the Murder in Somalia* (Toronto: McLelland and Stewart): 108–109. See also Jerald G. Bachman et al., "Distinctive Attitudes among US Enlistees 1976–1997: Self-Selection versus Socialization," *Armed Forces and Society* 26, no. 4 (Summer 2000): 561–585; Diana C. Pheysey, *Organizational Cultures: Types and Transformations* (London: Routledge, 1993).

4   Although it is important to recognize that the stated values of an organization are not always the same as those operating in its everyday practices. See Jesper Pedersen and Jesper S. Sorensen, *Organisational Cultures in Theory and Practice* (Aldershot, UK: Avebury Press, 1989); C. Cotton, "A Canadian Military Ethos," *Canadian Defence Quarterly* 12, no. 3 (Winter 1982/1983): 10–18; Paul Johnston, "Doctrine Is Not Enough: The Effect of Doctrine on the Behaviour of Armies" *Parameters* 30, no. 3 (Autumn 2000): 30–39. In fact, Cotton, the inspiration behind the current Canadian Forces Ethos Statement, argued that a military ethos should propose the aspired-to values rather than the actual values in a military environment. A recent example of this can be found in Yagil Levy, "The Right to Fight: A Conceptual Framework for the Analysis of Recruitment Policy toward Gays and Lesbians," in *Armed Forces & Society* 33, no. 2 (January 2007): 186–202.

5   Interview material contained in this chapter is presented in such a way as to protect the identity of those who participated – an express stipulation of both the University of Waterloo's Office of Human Research Ethics and the Canadian Forces Directorate of Human Resources Research and Evaluation. The Canadian Forces are both insular and highly integrated. The principle of universality of service means that military members can be posted anywhere the CF needs them. This means that personnel are posted to a variety of locations and work with others from across the country. As a result, many people in the CF know one another and could easily identify another member with only a few key pieces of information, such as rank, location, or service. This is particularly true for women, homosexuals,

visible and religious minorities, as well as chaplains (who number fewer than 200 in the regular forces). To avoid exposing participants' identities, where it does not confuse or distort the data, I have changed or obscured the location of an interview, unit, mission, or rank. For example, instead of identifying someone as a lieutenant colonel, I might refer to him or her as a senior officer. A few of the people I interviewed stand out in such a way in the forces that is with great difficulty that I can refer to them at all without making their identity obvious. In the cases where I provide a name or other information about personnel, that information is available publicly elsewhere, and I have cited the source.

6 Joanne Benham Rennick, *Religion in the Ranks: Belief and Religious Experience in the Canadian Forces* (Toronto: University of Toronto Press, 2011).

7 Elizabeth Bledsoe, "The Use of Culture in Operational Planning," master's of military art and science, Army Command and General Staff College, 2005; Barack A. Salmoni, "Beyond Hearts and Minds: Culture Matters," *US Naval Institute Proceedings* 130, no. 11 (November 2004): 54–58; Barack A. Salmoni, "Advances in Predeployment Culture Training: The U.S. Marine Corps Approach," *Military Review* 86 (November–December 2004): 79–88; Brian R. Selmeski, "Military Cross-Cultural Competence: Core Concepts and Individual Development" (Kingston: Royal Military College of Canada, Centre for Security, Armed Forces & Society, 2008), unpublished paper.

8 Emile Durkheim, *Elementary Forms of the Religious Life* (New York: Free Press, 1965 [1912]): 34.

9 Clifford Geertz, *The Interpretation of Cultures* (New York: Basic Books, 1973): 90.

10 Gary Johns, *Organizational Behavior* (Boston: Pearson Scott Foresman, 1988); Pedersen and Sorensen, *Organisational Cultures*; Pheysey, *Organizational Cultures*; Edgar H. Schein, *Organizational Culture and Leadership* (San Francisco: Jossey-Bass, 1992).

11 Danièle Hervieu-Léger, *Religion as a Chain of Memory* (New Brunswick, NJ: Rutgers University Press), 81.

12 Ibid., 82.

13 Roger O'Toole, "Canadian Religion: Heritage and Project," in *Rethinking Church, State, and Modernity: Canada between Europe and America*, ed. David Lyon and Marguerite Van Die (Toronto: University of Toronto Press, 2000): 46.

14 Robert Wuthnow, *After Heaven: Spirituality in America since the 1950s* (Los Angeles: University of California Press, 1998): vii–viii.

15 Bruce Lincoln provides a helpful definition for examining religion in late modernity by suggesting than any definition be "polythetic and flexible" and comprise "discourse, practices, community and institutions." Bruce Lincoln, *Holy Terrors: Thinking about Religion after September 11* (Chicago: University of Chicago Press, 2003): 6–7.

16 In fact, Charles Kammer suggests that experience, values, norms, and socialization are central components in establishing a "moral landscape" to guide one's behavior. C. Kammer, *Ethics and Liberation: An Introduction* (New York: Orbis Books, 1988): 18–19.

17 Alain Bélanger, L. Martel, and E. Caron-Malenfant, "Population Projections of Visible Minority Groups, Canada, Provinces, and Regions, 2001–2017," in *Population Projections of Visible Minority Groups, Canada, Provinces and*

Regions, 2001–2017. (Ottawa: Statistics Canada, Ministry of Industry, 2005), http://www.statcan.ca/english/freepub/91-541-XIE/91-541-XIE2005001.pdf. The report attributes the growth in Muslim, Hindu, and Sikh religions to increased immigration from regions where those are the majority religions. In addition, the authors observe that high fertility rates among Muslim Canadians may further contribute to growth of that population.

18 Jack Jedwab, "Interview with David Pratt: Minister of National Defence," *Canadian Diversity/Diversité canadienne* 3, no. 2 (Spring 2004): 9–10.

19 Statistics Canada places the percentage of Christians in Canada at more than 70 percent, with the majority of those being Roman Catholic (43.2 percent) and the remainder (29 percent) consisting mainly of mainline Protestant denominations. The largest denominational percentages outside of Roman Catholicism are the United Church of Canada at 9.6 percent and the Anglican Church of Canada at 6.9 percent. Statistics Canada, "Overview: Canada Still Predominantly Roman Catholic and Protestant," http://www12.statcan.ca/english/census01/Products/Analytic/companion/rel/canada.cfm#growth. Following the Christian majority, 16 percent of Canadians report "no religion." Muslims represent the fastest growing minority group and presently represent 2 percent of the population. Jews follow them at 1.1 percent, and Hindus, Sikhs, and Buddhists account for 1 percent each. Ibid. Ontario hosts 61 percent of all Muslims in Canada. Québec is home to the next largest group with 20 percent. The remaining Muslims in Canada are distributed throughout British Columbia (10 percent), Alberta (8 percent), and the remaining provinces (2 percent). Statistics Canada, "Provincial and Territorial Highlights," http://www12.statcan.ca/english/census01/Products/Analytic/companion/rel/provs.cfm.

20 Canadian Aboriginals have a long history of military service. John MacFarlane and John Moses, "Different Drummers: Aboriginal Culture and the Canadian Armed Forces, 1939–2002," *Canadian Military Journal* 6, no. 1 (Spring 2005): 25–32. Differences of culture and problems with discrimination, however, have resulted in poor recruitment and retention rates for Aboriginals in the past three decades. As a result, the CF has designed a number of programs aimed at recruiting and retaining Aboriginals in the forces. John Moses, Donald Graves, and Warren Sinclair, *A Sketch Account of Aboriginal Peoples in the Canadian Military* (Ottawa: Department of National Defence, 2004); C. Vance White, "CF Making Progress Recruiting Aboriginal Canadians," *Canadian Forces Personnel Newsletter* (Borden, ON: Department of National Defence, 2000); Marie-Chantale Bergeron, "Respect and Honour: Values Shared by the Aboriginal Peoples and the CF," *The Maple Leaf/La Feuille d'Érable* 9, no. 22 (July 2006): 16; Henry McCue, *Strengthening Relationships between the Canadian Forces and Aboriginal People* (Ottawa: Department of National Defence, 2000). The Department of Defence uses the term "Aboriginal" to include First Nations, Métis, and Inuit peoples – that is how it has been used throughout this chapter.

21 Leal points to value differences between cultural and gender groups in the United States on issues of militarism. David Leal, "American Public Opinion toward the Military: Differences by Race, Gender, and Class?" *Armed Forces & Society* 32, no. 1 (October 2005): 123–138. It is logical to assume that, in addition to culture and gender, religion plays a role in the formation of these value differences among groups.

22 For an interesting analysis of value differences between Japanese and American cadets, see Eloise Malone and Chie Matsuzawa Paik, "Value Priorities of Japanese and American Service Academy Students," *Armed Forces & Society* 33, no. 2 (January 2007): 169–185.

23 James A. Beckford, "Religion Modernity and Post-Modernity," in *Religion: Contemporary Issues*, ed. B. R. Wilson (London: Bellew Press, 1992): 11–23; Hervieu-Léger, *Religion as a Chain*; Roger O'Toole, "Canadian Religion"; Wade Clark Roof, *Spiritual Marketplace: Baby Boomers and the Remaking of America* (Princeton, NJ: Princeton University Press, 1999); Robert Wuthnow, *After Heaven*.

24 Hervieu-Léger, *Religion as a Chain*; Anthony Giddens, *Modernity and Self-Identity: Self and Society in the Late Modern Age* (Stanford, CA: Stanford University Press, 1991).

25 Roger C. Fuller, "Fresh Takes on a Classic: William James's Varieties Approaches Its Centennial," *Religious Studies Review* 26 (April 2000): 151.

26 Roger C. Fuller, *Spiritual But Not Religious: Understanding Unchurched America* (New York: Oxford University Press, 2001): 5.

27 Ibid., 6.

28 Robert N. Bellah et al., *Habits of the Heart* (Berkeley: University of California Press, 1985); Peter Beyer, "Modern Forms of the Religious Life," in *Rethinking Church, State, and Modernity*; Reginald Bibby, *Restless Gods: The Renaissance of Religion in Canada* (Toronto: Stoddart Publishing, 2002); Fuller, *Spiritual But Not Religious*; Roof, *Spiritual Marketplace*; Rodney Stark and Roger Finke, *Acts of Faith: Explaining the Human Side of Religion* (Berkeley: University of California Press, 2000); Robert Wuthnow, *The Restructuring of American Religion: Society and Faith since World War II* (Princeton, NJ: Princeton University Press, 1988).

29 Bibby, *Restless Gods*; Raymond Lemieux and Jean-Paul Montminy, *Le Catholicisme Québécois* (Québec: Les Presses de l'université Laval, 2000).

30 Lorne Dawson, *Comprehending Cults: The Sociology of New Religious Movements* (New York: Oxford University Press, 1998); Janet McLellan, *Many Petals of the Lotus: Five Asian Buddhist Communities in Toronto* (Toronto: University of Toronto Press, 1999).

31 Many religious groups, including some Muslims, Jews, Christians, Hindus, Buddhists, and Rastafarians, favor beards for men as indicators of orthodoxy.

32 Roman Catholic personnel are estimated at almost 49 percent of the military population, but the Canadian Forces does not compile statistics on the religious affiliation of its members, so these data are lacking. Statistics show, however, that 79 percent of enlisted personnel come from the regions of Canada that have predominantly Christian populations. Statistics Canada, "Military Personnel and Pay," ed. Statistics Canada Tables (Ottawa: Statistics Canada, 2007). Thirty-five percent of enlisted personnel come from Ontario, Québec contributes 21 percent, Nova Scotia is responsible for 12 percent, Alberta 11 percent, British Columbia 8 percent, and the remaining provinces 7 percent combined (the final 6 percent come from outside Canada). In Ontario, 66 percent of the population is either Roman Catholic or Protestant (33 percent each), while in Québec, 83 percent of the population identifies as Roman Catholic. In Nova Scotia, 86 percent of the population belongs to Christian denominations (49 percent Protestant and 37 percent Roman Catholic), and in Alberta, 65 percent are Christian (39 percent

Protestant and 26 percent Roman Catholic). For further statistics on military personnel by province, see the Statistics Canada table "Military Personnel and Pay," http://www40.statcan.ca/lo1/cst01/govt16a.htm. The leadership gap results from the shortage of Roman Catholic priests in Canada, but increasing numbers of pastoral associates are filling the need.

33 The reserve forces chaplains include an additional 133 members; all but one (a rabbi) are from Christian denominations. Note that the data on chaplains are in regular flux given ongoing recruitment and attrition – these percentages include the current chaplains in training (fourteen) and were provided to me in May 2012 by the director of Chaplain Services section of the Canadian Forces.

34 Until 2007, the ICCMC, which remains a subcommittee of the Canadian Council of Churches, was composed entirely of Christian members, including a Roman Catholic, a Presbyterian, a Lutheran, an Anglican, members of the United Church of Canada, and members of the Churches of the Evangelical Fellowship of Canada. At that time, new representatives of non-Christian traditions were invited to sit on the council. One of the hurdles that the ICCMC has faced in becoming an interfaith group is in identifying individuals who can adequately represent religious traditions that are very diverse, such as First Nations and Muslim groups. Further, while there are growing numbers of new religious movements in Canada, such as Wicca, these frequently lack the continuity of belief, structure, and leadership of an established religious tradition, making it extremely difficult to fairly represent them as a group and, as with Muslims and Aboriginals, appoint a representative who can speak on behalf of all members.

35 Joanne Benham Rennick, "Towards an Interfaith Ministry: Religious Adaptation and Accommodation in the Canadian Forces Chaplaincy," *Studies in Religion* 39, no. 1 (March 2010): 77–91. For more on this aspect of the Canadian Forces Chaplaincy, see the full article.

36 Canadian Defence Academy/Canadian Forces Leadership Institute, *Duty with Honour: The Profession of Arms in Canada* (Ottawa: Department of National Defence, 2003): 15.

37 Commission of Inquiry into the Deployment of Canadian Forces to Somalia, "Report of the Somalia Commission of Inquiry," in *Report of the Somalia Commission of Inquiry* (Ottawa: Minister of Public Works and Government Services Canada, 1997).

38 See Allan Thompson, "Chaplain in Somali Affair Keeps Job," *Toronto Star*, 30 August 1999; Simon Tuck, "Military Ombudsman Supports 'Trophy Photo' Chaplain on Staff," *Globe and Mail*, 30 August 1999. Nonetheless, Sargent declined to be interviewed.

39 There is extensive literature on the events that occurred in Somalia. See, for example, Bercuson, *Significant Incident*; Sherene H. Razack, "From the 'Clean Snows of Petawawa': The Violence of Canadian Peacekeepers in Somalia," *Cultural Anthropology* 15, no. 1 (Spring 2000): 127–163; Sandra Whitworth, "Militarized Masculinities and the Politics of Peacekeeping: The Canadian Case," in *Critical Security Studies and World Politics*, ed. Ken Booth (Boulder, CO: Lynne Rienner Publishers, 2005); Donna Winslow, "The Canadian Airborne Regiment in Somalia: A Socio-Cultural Inquiry," in *The Canadian Airborne Regiment in Somalia: A Socio-Cultural Inquiry* (Ottawa: Minster of Public Works and Government Services Canada, 1997).

40   Indeed, the complexities and challenges of that mission continue to be debated, but uncertain goals, values, and leadership were significant contributors.

41   Department of National Defence, *Canadian Forces Chaplain Branch Manual* (Ottawa: Chief of Defence Staff, Department of National Defence, 2003): 6.4.

42   Robert Parsons, *Russia: Muslims Oppose Bill to Add Chaplains to Army*, Radio Free Europe, 17 March 2006 (cited 30 December 2008), http://www.rferl.org/content/Article/1066820.html.

43   A Francophone is a person for whom French is his or her primary language. The use of Francophones and Anglophones indicates language preference without implying allegiance to a foreign nation (either England or France). The French-English language and culture debate is a prominent one in Canadian history and is tied closely to political and religious (Roman Catholic and Protestant) differences.

44   Emile Durkheim, *Suicide: A Study in Sociology* (London: Routledge, 1952).

45   Albert G. Fowler, *Peacetime Padres: Canadian Protestant Military Chaplains, 1945–1995* (St. Catharine's, Ontario: Vanwell Publishing Limited, 1996): 258–259.

46   CBC News, *The Ghosts of Rwanda*, CBC Digital Archives Web site, 16 May 2005 (cited 11 July 2007), http://archives.cbc.ca/IDC-1-71-1686-11622/conflict_war/romeo_dallaire/clip1; Roméo Dallaire, "A Good Man in Hell: Roméo Dallaire and the Rwandan Genocide," United States Holocaust Memorial Museum (2002); R. Dallaire, *Shake Hands with the Devil: The Failure of Humanity in Rwanda* (Toronto: Random House, 2003).

47   DND, Systemic Treatment of CF Members with PTSD Complainant: Christian McEachern (Ottawa: National Defence and Canadian Forces Ombudsman, 2002).

48   Commando.org, *The Canadian Airborne Regiment in Somalia: A Soldier's Journals*, commando.org, 15 June 2004 (accessed 15 June 2007), http://www.commando.org/somalia.php; Sherene Razack, *Dark Threats and White Nights: The Somalia Affair, Peacekeeping, and the New Imperialism* (Toronto: University of Toronto Press, 2004); Winslow, "The Canadian Airborne Regiment in Somalia."

49   Commission of Inquiry into the Deployment of Canadian Forces to Somalia, "Report of the Somalia Commission of Inquiry," *Report of the Somalia Commission of Inquiry*; Commando.org, *The Canadian Airborne Regiment in Somalia*.

50   Whitworth, "Militarized Masculinities and the Politics of Peacekeeping."

51   In the case of Rwanda, many members faced additional trauma because of the role of religious leaders in encouraging and sustaining the genocide. Benham Rennick, *Religion in the Ranks*, 59.

52   Fowler, *Peacetime Padres*, 259.

53   David Seljak, "Education, Multiculturalism, and Religion," in *Religion and Ethnicity in Canada*, ed. Paul Bramadat and David Seljak (Toronto: Pearson Longman, 2005): 178–200; David Seljak, Joanne Benham Rennick, et al., *Religion and Multiculturalism in Canada: The Challenge of Religious Intolerance and Discrimination, Final Report* (Ottawa: Multiculturalism and Human Rights Program at the Department of Canadian Heritage, 2007); Lois Sweet, *God in the Classroom: The Controversial Issue of Religion in Canada's Schools* (Toronto: McClelland & Stewart, 1997).

54   Benham Rennick, *Religion in the Ranks*, 95, 118, 250.

3

United Kingdom

Victor Dobbin and Stephen Deakin

The role religion plays in the British armed forces is a function of the close relationship between the monarch, the government, the Church of England, and the British armed forces as well as the complex role religion performs in modern British society. The Church of England, also known as the Anglican Church, is the officially established Church in England (hereafter "the Church"), whose supreme governor is the British monarch.[1] Twenty-six bishops of the Church, known as the Lords Spiritual, hold seats in the Upper House of Parliament, the House of Lords. In addition to taking part in the debates in the Upper House, the bishops read Christian prayers at the start of each daily meeting. The British monarch, the British Parliament, and the British armed forces have enjoyed important historical and legal links.[2] Because the Queen, as head of state, is nominally head of the armed forces, they are often referred to as "Her Majesty's Armed Forces." Officers, soldiers, marines, and airmen all swear their allegiance to the Queen.[3] In practice, however, executive authority over the military is vested in the office of the prime minister and his cabinet.

Statistics regarding patterns of belief in British society and in the British armed forces paint a deceptively simple picture. In the 2001 official census, 72 percent of citizens in the United Kingdom – or 42 million individuals – registered as Christians. Only 15.5 percent indicated that they had no religion. These figures, together with the presence of beautiful churches in practically every country village – not to mention numerous churches representing different Christian denominations in most towns as well as large, impressive cathedrals centrally located in most cities – would suggest that Christianity plays an important part in the life of the nation. Similarly, records from April 2010 show 85.8 percent of the British armed forces registered as Christians. This figure represented 162,140 personnel, a reduction of some 7,900 from April 2007. In addition, the number of regular forces personnel citing "no religion" increased from 17,980 in the year 2007 to 23,770 in the year 2010.

Personnel registered as being from other major faith groups numbered 1,930, and 870 personnel registered as belonging to "other religions."[4]

The large numbers of people registered as Christians on official census forms and armed forces documents do not accurately reflect the role of religion in Britain or its military. A closer examination of the facts shows rapidly declining levels of involvement with organized Christian religion in the United Kingdom. In the mid-nineteenth century, more than half of the adult population of England and Wales attended services on any given Sunday. By the close of the twentieth century, the fraction attending in a typical week was less than one-twelfth.[5] Research carried out by Tear Fund in 2006 discovered that 66 percent of the adult population in the United Kingdom had no connection with the Church, and only 15 percent claimed to attend church once a month. An additional study carried out by Tear Fund in 2007 discovered that nearly half of all adults in the United Kingdom prayed, including 41 percent of those who never attended church.[6] Grace Davie has offered one possible explanation for these apparent contradictions, which she refers to as "Believing without Belonging." The author points out that "more and more people within British society are, it appears, wanting to believe but without putting this belief into practice."[7]

Michael Snape, writing about the Christian religion within the British Army in World Wars I and II, concludes: "This prevalent, if somewhat elusive form of belief, is perhaps best described as an ethically-based and non-dogmatic form of Christianity, one which derived its currency from a sense of religious social utility and from an almost universal (if generally limited) measure of religious education."[8] Snape quotes John Drewett, a clergyman from Sheffield, who in 1942 wrote:

The diffused Christianity of the Ruling class is not without its effect in many departments of our social life. Without it there could hardly be an Established Church or Bishops sitting in the House of Lords. It is the religion of many of our judges, executive and civil service chiefs, and of high officers in the services. It ensures that Christian opinion will receive, at any rate, a courteous hearing in the affairs of state. It means, in general, that this country may in some sense be called Christian, and that up to now no rival philosophy has been accepted as the basis of our national life.[9]

Diffused Christianity proved to be insufficiently strong to withstand the assault from a rival philosophy of secularism that emerged strongly in Britain in the 1960s. The battle between the two belief systems is still being fought in British life today – for example, in controversy about whether Christians should be allowed to wear symbolic jewelry, such as a crucifix, in the workplace. In more traditional social areas, such as divorce, abortion, and euthanasia, secular principles largely hold sway. Secularism, not diffuse Christianity, is now the dominant "religion" in Britain. The military has had to accommodate itself to these changes, and some service members may now favor secular beliefs or have unconsciously syncretized the two belief systems. As this chapter argues, this practice makes it difficult to identify and evaluate the impact of religion in the British military.

We begin this chapter with a study of religion's role in the armed forces during the First World War. In the next section, we trace this role to its origins in British military law and traditions. We explore several religious practices, including the function performed by chapels, cemeteries, and ceremonies. Subsequently, we discuss the various responsibilities that chaplains have assumed, including their role as preachers, pastors, and teachers to the armed forces. After considering several religious organizations associated with the military, we explore the faith of individual soldiers. We conclude with an assessment of current changes and challenges faced by the military.

Religion in the Great War

A publication in 1919 on religion and army life during World War I, *The Army and Religion*, reflected some of the ambiguities discussed earlier. The report concurred with an observation made by an officer in a Scottish regiment who described the religion of 90 percent of the soldiers as "not distinctively Christian, but a religion of patriotism and of valour, tinged with chivalry and, at best, merely coloured with sentiment and emotion borrowed from Christianity."[10] The Reverend Doctor David Cairns, a Scottish Presbyterian academic and lead author of the report, commented as follows:

My feeling is that the Churches need to have brought before them the real state of matters, viz. that they have lost, or are in danger of losing the faith of the nation, and that they have got to look deeply into the matter and set their hearts and minds to the problem of how the situation may, by God's grace, be retrieved before it is too late.[11]

These concerns reflected what so many chaplains had discovered in the course of their ministries during the years of the war. At the same time, the trauma of the war may have created a tendency to blame Christian churches for the perceived spiritual state of the nation.

Julian Bickersteth wrote in his diary in July 1916, "Never has the failure of the Church of England been more apparent than it has been to the chaplains at the front: man after man with no knowledge of the Faith of his Fathers, man after man to whom religion is simply a name and has never touched either his heart or mind."[12] Similarly, Neville Talbot, who served as a chaplain in World War I, acknowledged that "indifference to organised religion was widespread among officers and men and that he sometimes felt he was peddling 'unmarketable Church of England goods.'"[13]

Despite the perceived absence of much liturgical and general understanding of the Christian religion, there was a less dogmatic form of religion reflected in the soldiers' attitudes and behavior. The *Army and Religion* report noted that during the war, the soldiers displayed virtues such as unselfishness, cheerfulness, sense of duty, courage, sincerity, and humility. One chaplain in a Scottish regiment expressed his surprise at these qualities, stating: "Unredeemed human nature is infinitely nobler than I had dreamed."[14] In *Thoughts on Religion at the Front*, the Reverend Neville Talbot wrote: "There is no great revival of the Christian religion at the front. Yet I am eager to acclaim the wonderful quality of spirit which men of our race display in this war, and to claim it as Christian and God-inspired. Deep in their hearts is a great trust and faith in God. It is an inarticulate faith expressed in deeds."[15] A. M. Perkins, serving within the Young Men's Christian Association (YMCA), recorded how soldiers waiting for the train at a

"siding one wet Sunday night" during the time of the battle for Passchendaele in 1917 began to sing, and it was not "Tipperary" but "Lead, Kindly Light."... Then followed "Rock of Ages" and other well-known hymns. ... The eyes of the Y.M.C.A. workers were filled with tears as the voices of men going into battle rang out: The night is dark, and I am far from home, Lead Thou me on.[16]

Was this a World War I example of "Believing without Belonging?" There are many accounts of similar incidents.

In 2006, Gen. Sir Richard Dannatt, chief of the General Staff, summarized the unique role that religion plays in the British armed forces:

Our society has always been embedded in Christian values; once you have pulled the anchor up there is a danger that our society moves with the prevailing wind. ... There is an element of the moral compass spinning. I am responsible for the Army, to make sure that its moral compass is well aligned and that we live by what we believe in. It is said we live in a post-Christian society. I think that is a great shame. The Judaic-Christian tradition has underpinned British society. It underpins the British Army.[17]

Religion in British Military Law and Tradition

British military codes and practices illustrate the integral role of Christianity in the armed forces. Throughout British history, these laws and traditions have emphasized the importance of Christian belief and prayer and the teaching of Christian ethical behavior.

Military law and practice therefore has allotted a significant role to military chaplains. For example, Article 13 of the Articles of War of 1639 stated: "For the better Government of His Majesties Army Royall. ... No enterprise shall be taken in hand, but the company that are to execute the same shall first commend themselves to God, and pray to Him to grant them good successe."[18] Article 1 of the Articles of War of 1641 made it a duty for the military to "diligently frequent Divine Service and sermon."[19] Only in 1847 was this article moved from its prominent position to another part of the military code.

The Articles of War from 1662 to 1663 listed the duties of every chaplain this way: "The Chaplains to the Troops of Guards and others in Regiments shall every day read the Common Prayers of the Church of England to the Soldiers respectively under their charge, and to preach to them as often with convenience shall be thought fit."[20] Standing Order RB 1801 read, "Every Officer and soldier who professes himself to be a Christian should be taught to know that true religious fortitude generally makes the best men, and consequently the best soldiers. A man without religion is generally a disobedient, a drunken, a cowardly and of course a cruel man, and the soldier who acknowledges not his Creator is not very likely to care much for the commands of any officer or other superior on earth."[21] A powerful original article that was included in the revision of the Naval Discipline Act of 1886 punished sailors found "guilty of any profane oath, cursing, execration, drunkenness, uncleanness or other scandalous action in derogation of God's honour and corruption of good manners."[22]

Worship of God has also been at the heart of naval military law. Article 1 of the Naval Discipline Act of 1661 stated that "all Comanders, Captaines and other Officers at Sea shall cause the publique Worshipp of Almighty God according to the Liturgy of the Church of England established by Law ... to be performed in theire respective Ships and that prayers and preachings by the respective Chaplaines in holy Orders be performed diligently and that the Lord's Day be observed according to Law."[23] The Church of England's *Book of Common Prayer* from 1662 contained a chapter entitled "Forms of Prayer to Be Used at Sea," which stated that morning and evening services were to be said daily at sea accompanied by special daily naval prayers.

The importance of religion has continued to be emphasized over the years. In 1957, Royal Navy administrative regulations stated, for example, that "the British way of life is founded on the Christian faith and in the Royal Navy life is conducted according to Christian principles. Religious faith where it exists is the strongest and greatest activating force there is. Officers and men are strongly urged to have a religious faith and practise it. It is the duty of officers to see that the spiritual needs of their subordinates are met."[24]

By the 1970s, the Queen's Regulations, which applied across all three services, gave clear guidelines in relation to chaplaincy: "Chaplains are commissioned by Her Majesty The Queen to provide for the spiritual well being of Service personnel and their families. They are to be given every assistance to fulfil their ministry."[25] In addition, it stated, "Commanding Officers [COs] have the primary responsibility for encouraging religious observance by those under command, but it is important that all who exercise authority should set a good example in order to lead others to an intelligent acceptance of Christian principles in the life of the Armed Forces."[26] The Regulations also gave special attention to places of education within the armed services, directing commanding officers "to ensure that the curricula of training and educational establishments provide for appropriate religious instruction to young personnel."[27]

As a result, military academies for officers – including Dartmouth for the Royal Navy, Sandhurst for the British Army, and Cranwell for the Royal Air

Force – emphasize Christian leadership, as do all training bases in all three services. At Sandhurst the motto is "Serve to Lead," echoing the servant leadership of Christ, who "did not come to be served, but to serve, and to give his life."[28]

Military Chapels, Cemeteries, and Ceremonies

As church buildings are signs and symbols of the Christian tradition within the armed forces, so too are a number of military ceremonies. These include the burial of the dead, acts of remembrance, and the presentation of new Regimental Colors. The writing of "collects" (official prayers) for all regiments, corps, and services also underline the importance of the Christian religion within the services.

Each of the three military academies has a Christian chapel, as do most training depots. In addition, the British Army and the Royal Air Force each have a large, almost cathedral-like church in the City of London, as did the Royal Navy until 1998. The histories of these church buildings – and all military churches – are themselves testimonies to the adoption of the Christian religion within the armed forces in both the past and the present. The Guards Chapel, which was formerly known as the Royal Military Chapel, Saint James's Park, was first opened in 1838. Destroyed during World War II, it was rebuilt and rededicated in 1963. Similarly, the church now called Saint Clement Danes was destroyed during the war and rededicated in 1958 as a memorial to all those in the Royal Air Force as well as to those of the Allied Air Forces who gave their lives during World War II.

The military also oversees its own Christian cemeteries. At the Royal Military Academy Sandhurst, students and staff have a cemetery for their exclusive use. In naval ports such as Portsmouth, there are dedicated naval cemeteries, as at Gosport. The National Memorial Arboretum in Staffordshire, consisting of 150 acres of memorials and 50,000 trees, offers a place of peace and memory to the families and friends of those who have made the ultimate sacrifice for their country. The Millennium Chapel of Peace and Forgiveness, a Christian chapel located within the Arboretum, was dedicated on November 2, 2000, and is the only place within the United Kingdom where the act of remembrance is observed every day of the year.

The Christian religion is particularly in evidence when service personnel are buried and in remembrances of the dead. Many naval sailors, wrapped in a shroud and covered in a Union Jack, were buried at sea. Special prayers from the Church of England's *Book of Common Prayer* from 1662 were said for the dead sailors. If the ship did not carry a chaplain, the captain would conduct the service. Military funerals on land have also carried their own strong Christian symbolism. The three rifle volleys represent the Christian Trinity of Father, Son, and Holy Spirit.[29] The carrying of rifles in the reversed position acknowledges the shame of killing, while the Union Jack is laid on the body to show that "he died in the Service of the State and that the State takes responsibility for what it ordered him to do as a soldier."[30] According to Rear Adm. Gerard Wells, author of *Naval Customs and Traditions*, even the bugle calls accompanying a soldier's funeral can carry symbolic significance: "The Last Post is the *Nunc Dimittis* of the dead soldier. It is the last bugle call ... but it gives promise of reveille ... of the great reveille which ultimately the Archangel Gabriel will blow."[31]

After World War I, the Commonwealth War Graves Commission provided Christian burials or remembrance memorials for most of the war's dead. The war raised considerable debate about the architecture of the new cemeteries and memorials and the extent of religious symbolism that they should express. Winston Churchill, for example, wrote to the archbishop of Canterbury, "I am very anxious indeed ... to do everything that is possible to emphasize the distinctively Christian and religious character of these memorials."[32] In the event, the symbols of the commission's memorials were solidly Christian with crosses on individual tombstones and frequent biblical inscriptions in the cemeteries. The commission agreed on a simple monument in the form of a stone Christian cross with a symbolic sword on its face, which became known as the "Cross of Sacrifice." For the dead who could not be identified, the committee adopted the following words: "A soldier of the Great War. ... Known unto God."[33] The memorial tablet to the Unknown Soldier in Westminster Abbey begins, "To the Glory of God and to the memory of one million dead of the British Empire who fell in the Great War 1914–1918." Christian memorial services were performed to honor the military dead.

Official prayers furnish additional examples for the prevalence of religious practices in the military. The chaplain general offers one such prayer whenever colors are presented to a regiment. Traditionally, infantry regiments in the British Army carry two colors when they participate in official parades. One of these is known as the "Queen's Color"; it represents the military's loyalty to the queen. The other is the "Regimental Color," on which are embroidered the regiment's battle honors. The equivalent for the armored and cavalry regiments are the standard and the guidon. These emblems are normally presented to the regiment by a member of the royal family and are consecrated by the chaplain general or his deputy. The prayers offered by the chaplain general on such an occasion include the following words:

O Lord, who rulest over all things, accept, we beseech Thee, our service this day. Bless what we have blessed in Thy Name. Let Thy gracious favour rest on those who shall follow the Colours now about to be committed to their Trust. Give them courage, and may their courage ever rest on their sure confidence in Thee. May they show self-control in the hour of success, patience in time of adversity; and may their honour lie in seeking the honour and glory of Thy great Name. Guide the counsels of those who shall lead them, and sustain them by Thy help in the time of need. Grant that they may all so faithfully serve Thee in this life, that they fail not finally to obtain an entrance into Thy heavenly Kingdom, through the merits of Thy Blessed Son, Jesus Christ our Lord. Amen.

All regiments and corps of the British Army, the Royal Navy, and the Royal Air Force have their own short regimental prayers, known as collects. Many of these were composed by Reverend Matthew Tobias in his *Collects for the British Army* in 1930. In 1976, the chaplain general published an updated version of the *Collects*, consolidating all those collects issued from his office over the years. The reorganization of the British Army in the early 1990s and all subsequent changes necessitated new collects and provided the opportunity to amend existing ones. A process now ensures that all new regiments have their own prayer, reflecting once again the presence of Christianity in the British armed forces.

The collect of the Royal Marines reads:

O Eternal Lord God, who through many generations has united and inspired the members of our Corps, grant thy blessing, we beseech thee, on Royal Marines serving all round the globe. Bestow thy crown of righteousness upon all our efforts and endeavours, and may our laurels be those of gallantry and honour, loyalty and courage. We ask these things in the name of him whose courage never failed, our Redeemer Jesus Christ. Amen.

The collect for the Corps of Royal Engineers reads:

O God, whose righteousness is exceeding glorious, may it please Thee to send out Thy light and Thy truth so to lead us Thy servants of the Corps of Royal Engineers that everywhere we may be enabled to do our duty, and so may glorify Thee our Father in Heaven, for the sake of Jesus Christ our Lord. Amen.

The collect of the Royal Air Force Regiment reads:

Almighty God, Lord of heaven and earth, whose son Jesus Christ showed us the path of duty, we beseech thee to bless all who serve in the Royal Air Force Regiment. Help us to do our duty with courage and dedication. Of thy goodness be our strength in times of danger, watch over our loved ones when we are separated, and make us a sure defence to those we serve. We ask this in the name of Jesus Christ our Lord. Amen.

Today, British armed forces personnel serving in Afghanistan are encouraged by their chaplains to learn their collect, which is included as part of any religious service. Brig. Justin Maciejewski, commander of the 12th Mechanized Brigade, in his delivery of the Niblett Memorial Lecture in 2010, recalled how, at the end of an operational tour in Iraq, his soldiers knew the regimental collect and the Lord's Prayer by heart.[34]

Chaplains in the British Armed Forces

The British armed forces have long recognized the important contribution that chaplains have made to the moral and spiritual welfare of their personnel. These chaplains provide evidence for the significant role of Christianity in the British

Photo 4 British soldiers receiving communion from 16 Air Assault Brigade's chaplain, Padre Andrew Totten, at Patrol Base Kuday Noor in the Nad-e-Ali district of Helmand Province, Afghanistan, during Operation Herrick 13, October 10, 2010. Photo by Andrew Totten.

military. Many commanders have continued to put a high premium on spiritual values and have supported the work of chaplains. Bernard Montgomery, First Viscount Montgomery of Alamein, once said:

The British soldier responds to leadership in a most remarkable way; once you have won his heart he will follow you anywhere. I do not believe that today a commander can inspire great armies or single units, or even individual men, and lead them to achieve great victories, unless he has a proper sense of religious truth; he must be prepared to acknowledge it and to lead his troops in the light of that truth. He must always keep his finger on the spiritual pulse of his armies; he must be sure that the spiritual purpose which inspires them is right and true.[35]

Montgomery is also reported to have said, "The most important people in the army are the nursing sisters and the padres: the sisters because they tell the men they matter to us and the padres because they tell the men they matter to God".[36]

When one studies the presence of chaplains and their ministry within the British armed forces, it is important to appreciate that it is not only the history of three separate organizations – the Naval Chaplaincy Service, the Royal Army Chaplains Department, and the Royal Air Force Chaplains Branch as well as that of each individual chaplain – but that it is primarily the story of the ministry of the Christian churches to the British armed forces. In some respects, the armed forces became another diocese of the Church of England, with a bishop who acts as pastor and overseer of all Church of England chaplains and service personnel. As far back as 1639, the Church of Scotland, with its Presbyterian form of church government, appointed Kirk Sessions with ordained elders within a number of Scottish battalions, thus associating the regiment with that of any normal parish. In addition, the Roman Catholic Church, similar to the Church of England, continues to appoint a bishop to the British armed forces. The bishop's role is primarily as pastor to their respective chaplain and their congregation. The bishop has no executive authority within the military, as the administrative responsibilities for chaplains and their ministry is given to the respective principal chaplains.

Such arrangements, when viewed within the traditional network of church, monarchy, state, and armed forces, underline the importance placed on the Christian religion. Chaplains are ordained ministers and priests of their own denominations. They are men and women set apart to preach the Word of God and administer the sacraments of the Christian Church. Because theirs is the ministry of their specific church, they remain under the jurisdiction of that church in relation to their calling as priest or minister, but they also come under the jurisdiction of the military in relation to their military duties. It is through carrying out their duties as Christian priests and ministers that the Christian religion is made available to individual members of the armed forces. Moreover, the respective chaplaincy services minister to the Royal Navy, the British Army, and Royal Air Force as institutions.

British chaplains serve three roles: a preaching/liturgical role, a pastoral/caring role, and a teaching role.

Chaplains as Preachers

During military operations, services of worship are organized whenever possible. Thomas Jones, a chaplain during the fateful Gallipoli campaign at the height of World War I, described the following moving communion service:

Services are not easily arranged on the peninsula, as being constantly within range of shell fire, the congregating of large companies of men is too risky. Still, we managed to hold services and at times if well sheltered there with large numbers attending and all show interest in singing and in the Gospel message. One Sunday evening recently our gathering was not more than 150, but all felt the presence of the Prince of Peace in spite of such tumult of war. At the close we distributed several gifts from Scotland, and every recipient was most grateful. Then the Lord's Supper was observed, and a season of real spiritual blessing experienced, as under the beams of the pale cold moon on the shore of the Aegean Sea we remembered Him who laid down His life for His friends, and we prayed for loved ones far away in the homeland, for our comrades in battle, and for ourselves. There was something very impressive in the sight of those brave fellows, as with bowed heads they remembered their Lord's death, perhaps for the last time on earth.[37]

Examples of how chaplains used their experience to convey a spiritual truth include a report from the Reverend J. C. Gunn, a chaplain attached to the 1st Battalion Gordon Highlanders at the battle El Alamein in World War II. He writes:

As we gathered round the C.O. prior to marching into battle, his spirit of calm determination could be felt. ... One felt terribly naked sometimes when the shelling was at its fiercest: one could remember the lines of the hymn, "naked come to thee for dress." ... We had no sooner gone to ground than all sorts of stuff flew over us, artillery air bursts, the terrible crack of anti-tank guns, stukas' dive bombing machine guns etc. We had no corrugated sheeting over our trenches. As I lay looking up into the clear night a white vapour appeared: one expected some new horror, but instead it was a pure white cloud sailing calmly and slowly across the sky making me feel how weak and small all the tumult and noise around really were compared to the solemnity and calm of the eternal things. Frequently some great passage of scripture would come to me like this white cloud bringing assurance of well being that goes deeper than the tumult of strife. I spoke of this in my sermon. One Company Commander wanted some references so that he could have some of these passages in mind and another Lieutenant mentioned how he had also been uplifted by words of scripture.[38]

In 2006, at the end of a six-month tour of duty in Afghanistan in which thirty-two British personnel had been killed, the Reverend Father Daren Brown shared some thoughts with his unit. Entries from his journal read:

Jesus said "blessed are they who mourn. ..." 32 UK personnel have been killed since April. We have certainly collectively mourned our comrades who gave their lives. Jesus said "blessed are they who hunger and thirst for righteousness." Isn't that why we are here, to give the Afghan people opportunity to build a society together, and not be denied the choice by the few? Jesus said "blessed are the merciful." In our hospital we have shown mercy to those who have come in with injuries after having tried to kill our soldiers on the ground. We've shown them how to treat their fellow humans with respect and dignity. Jesus said "blessed are the peacemakers." Our efforts, although sometimes with measured violence, are to bring peace to this land and into families so they can live without fear of others who wish to do them harm.[39]

Chaplains as Pastors

During World War I, chaplains discovered that the best way to demonstrate God's undifferentiating love and concern toward the officers and men was to be on the front line. Initially chaplains were forbidden by the army to go to the front lines and were advised instead to locate at the forward dressing station. Nevertheless, within a relatively short period of time, Roman Catholic chaplains began visiting the front line to administer the sacrament to their members, a gesture greatly appreciated by the troops. In May 1916, orders were issued that encouraged all chaplains with frontline units to visit their soldiers in the trenches.

One source of inspiration for this style of ministry was the Reverend Studdert Kennedy, known by soldiers as Woodbine Willie. In a meeting with

Padre Theodore Bayley Hardy, newly arrived on the western front in December 1916, Studdert-Kennedy gave advice that unwittingly became the basis for the British Army's chaplaincy model:

Live with the men. Go wherever they go. Make up your mind to share all their risks and more if you can do any good. You can take it that the best place for a Padre ... is where there is most danger of death. Our first job is to go beyond the men in self-sacrifice and reckless devotion. ... The more padres die in battle doing Christ-like deeds, the better for the Church. ... Take a box of fags in your haversack and a great deal of love in your heart. ... Laugh with them, joke with them: you can pray with them sometimes, but pray for them always.[40]

Bayley Hardy went on to become the most decorated noncombatant of the war, winning the Victoria Cross, the Distinguished Service Order, and the Military Cross before being killed in October 1918. His example demonstrates how seriously Studdert-Kennedy's advice was taken and followed as a model for effective chaplaincy work.

Years later in the Malayan jungle, a chaplain expressed a similar model of chaplaincy: "Four or five days dirt, discomfort and wetness shared, of fear mutually experienced, can achieve more for Christ than all the sermons in the world." The task of the chaplain, he wrote, was "to help the soldier to appreciate and understand the ever-present reality of the Christ as an element, the element, in the midst of their normality, to help each man to realise that he is a child of God and so to live."[41]

This same principle was articulated in a study carried out in 1999 by Brig. Ian McGill CBE entitled "An Investigation into the Need for Spiritual Values in the Army." McGill emphasized that the British Army's values, standards, and ethos are founded on a shared Christian history, culture, and civilization. Chaplains are a crucial resource for commanders and soldiers, he argued, and their efforts should be focused on the front line.[42]

Chaplains as Teachers

The term "Padre's Hour" originates in the work of the Reverend John Hodgins, a chaplain who served with the Airborne Division. In 1942, he began to hold teaching sessions with soldiers. During these sessions, he provided formal teaching and discussions on numerous subjects related to the Christian faith. Often the chaplain chose the topics for discussion, but increasingly the soldiers assumed this responsibility based on what interested them. The scheme proved to be a great success, partly because it allowed the soldiers to discuss topics relevant to their own experience and to express their own thoughts and opinions.

These Padres' Hours were less formal than official church services, and over the years they became an important part of every chaplain's ministry. As early as 1944, the Royal Air Force called these sessions Moral Leadership Courses. Today, chaplains in all three services contribute to the teaching of the core values of their services. In the Royal Navy and the Royal Air Force, this component is entitled "Beliefs and Values." In the British Army, the chaplains' input is now part of the overall Values and Standards program of training.

These training sessions have undergone considerable development since their inception. Chaplains have received training and equipment to reinforce their roles as professional teachers, and the instruction has become mandatory in all initial chaplain training programs. The success of secularism in becoming the dominant religious belief system in Britain has, of course, placed the Christian element of such teaching under pressure. The response from individual chaplains varies, but the formal content of these sessions now places increasing emphasis on secular philosophical ethics rather than on Christian ethics as the main source underpinning core military values.

Unless the two belief systems can be accommodated together, this development must in the long term undermine the impact of Christianity within the British military. The army's 1989 Character Training program provides some evidence for such an accommodation. The program, designed to be taught by chaplains during Padres' Hours, concentrated on three values: service, courage, and discipline. In the introduction to the program, the chaplain general wrote,

It is recognised that [these values] are the safeguard for all ranks against any forms of unacceptable behaviour either on or off duty. However, I believe it must be understood that they cannot exist in a vacuum and that they are not self-generating. Also, it must be stated clearly that the Christian faith and tradition has fundamental and relevant things to say on each of them as essential ingredients of our way of life. Moreover, it claims to provide the foundation which underpins these qualities of service, courage and discipline and which enables them to endure.[43]

Today, the foreword to the Values and Standards training program within the British Army does not directly refer to the Christian tradition, and army chaplains play a much smaller role in providing the training. In both the Royal Navy and the Royal Air Force, however, the Christian religion is still regarded as the principal foundation for the core values of their services. The Royal Navy's current Beliefs and Values program states that it "is designed to give both the Officers and Ratings a growing sense of not only what Chaplaincy and our values are about, but also to see that the values and beliefs that the Royal Navy holds are based within a Christian Ethos." The Beliefs and Values program for the Royal Air Force makes no specific reference to the Christian religion, but it is still provided primarily by chaplains.[44]

Christianity by Other Means

A number of voluntary welfare agencies provide services to the Royal Navy, the British Army, and the Royal Air Force on the basis of the Christian religion. Many of these organizations maintain the same objectives they did at their founding in the late nineteenth century.

The founders of two such organizations, Miss Daniell's Homes and SANDES – formed in the latter half of the nineteenth century – were women: Louisa Daniell and Elise Sandes. The former began her work in Aldershot, England, the latter in Ireland. Both shared a concern for the soldiers and hoped to provide them with a real home, not just a club or a canteen. Sandes outlined her vision as follows:

My experience has been that, under God, the secret of success in Soldiers' Homes is to make them true substitutes for the homes these men have left, and to have those in them who can really take the places of their mothers and sisters. ... I believe no human influences move the heart so powerfully for good as memories of a good home and pure women's love, and that such memories put the right kind of grit into our men when they are called upon to fight for their country. ... What a soldier values is not a fine building or a well-regulated reading room, but a HOMELY HOME, with a warm, motherly heart in it that cares for him. Therefore I try to make my Homes not merely institutes or clubs, or mission halls, but in the truest sense of the word "homes."[45]

Daniell and Sandes believed their efforts would make better soldiers, but they also believed those soldiers needed to understand the love of God as revealed in the life, death, and resurrection of Jesus Christ. Today, these homes are still operating as two of a number of Christian voluntary organizations active within the British military.

The Naval, Military & Air Force Bible Society, the oldest active Bible society in the world, provides another example of religion-based welfare in the armed services. Founded in 1779 as the Bible Society, it became the Naval, Military & Air Force Bible Society in 1961. The society's aim was recorded on November 8, 1779. It read, "For purchasing Bibles to be distributed among British soldiers and seamen of the Navy, to spread abroad (by the blessing of God) Christian knowledge and reformation of manners." The society continues to be busy, and in 2009 distributed more than 6,000 Bibles and 25,000 New Testaments.

The presence of these and similar charities working within army barracks, air stations, and naval bases signifies the importance of the Christian religion in the traditions of the British armed forces. Other charities include the Catholic Women's League; Church Army; Church of England Soldiers', Sailors', and Airmens' Clubs; Methodist Church Forces' Centers; Mission to Military Garrisons; Royal Sailors' Rest; Salvation Army Red Shield Services; Soldiers' and Airmen's Scripture Readers Association; and the YMCA and YWCA.

The Faith of Individual Service Members

Individual Christian servicepeople have sought to share their faith with others through their own work and have tried to influence policy relating to their services. Many of these Christians enjoy fellowship within a Christian Union. One such organization is the Armed Forces Christian Union, which draws it membership from across the three services. Its focus is on prayer for members of the armed forces and their families, Christian fellowship, and evangelism.

One story that captures the importance of personal faith on the battlefield is told by Lt. Col. Chris Keeble DSO. When his commanding officer was killed during the Battle for Goose Green in May 1982 during the Falklands War, Keeble suddenly found himself in charge of the battalion. He writes,

My heart beat faster. It was an immense responsibility. ... We had been fighting for forty hours and we were very tired. It was bitterly cold. One in six of us was either injured or killed, and we had no reinforcements. I went back to my group of leaders and it was quite clear they were looking to me for solutions. ... We were in a perilous position, and the responsibility for getting us out of it lay with me. I had no idea what to do. I walked up a gully to be alone for a moment to try and think. I put my hands into my pockets and my fingernails caught on a piece of plastic. It was a prayer which I had typed out and had laminated as a kind of deal with God, you know, "I'll carry this prayer if you will look after me" stuff.

Keeble knelt in the gorse and, although he found it hard, he prayed the prayer written by the desert mystic Charles de Foucault: "My Father, I abandon myself to you. Do with me as you will. Whatever you may do with me I thank you, provided your will is fulfilled in me. I ask for nothing more." Keeble concludes, "To my amazement I went through a real transformation. Instead of feeling frightened, uncertain, cold, miserable, confused, I suddenly felt joyful, happy, warm." He returned to his fellow officers and told them that he was going to offer the Argentineans the opportunity to surrender. Two Argentine prisoners of war were sent to their commanders with the offer and returned shortly with the news that they would be willing to talk. The result was that approximately 1,500 Argentine troops surrendered to 450 British paratroopers with no further loss of life.[46]

The importance of prayer is also reflected in a poem written on a scrap of paper by an anonymous soldier hidden in a foxhole in North Africa during World War II. The poem was found by another soldier while sheltering in the same hole:

> Stay with me, God. The night is dark,
> The night is cold: my little spark
> Of courage dies. The night is long;
> Be with me, God, and make me strong ...
> Help me, O God, when Death is near
> To mock the haggard face of fear,
> That when I fall – if fall I must –
> My soul may triumph in the Dust.[47]

Changes and Challenges Facing the British Armed Forces

Since the Enlightenment, Western society has undergone many changes. As Jonathan Sacks writes, "For centuries Western civilisation had been based on a Judaeo-Christian ethic. That was now being abandoned, systematically, ideologically, and with meticulous thoroughness."[48] The moral fabric of British society, he claimed, reveals many holes: "We have tolerated the collapse of the family. ... We have dissolved the bonds of community. ... We have given children no framework within which to learn civic virtue and responsibility."[49] Philosophers such as Alasdair MacIntyre have suggested that one way to escape the severity of this fragmentation and move forward is to create moral communities. In the 1990s, Iain Torrance, the current dean of Princeton Theological Seminary, suggested during a series of lectures to senior officers in the British Army that it could become one such moral community.[50] This suggestion raises the difficult question of whether it is the task of the military to form a Christian Church–style moral community separate from the society it serves.

Yet the British armed forces are recruiting their personnel from a society that, from a Christian perspective, is experiencing moral fragmentation and is evolving into a multicultural and multifaith society. If there is a Christian revival in Britain, as recent trends in church attendance suggest, the situation will change radically.[51] Nevertheless, Britain has become a society in which secularism and spiritual and ethical relativism have become widely accepted. This development poses a problem for the British military. Regardless of the level of personal commitment of individuals in the military, Christianity has provided a spiritual and moral basis for military organizational life. A 1999 study of the need for spiritual values in the British Army recognized that significant changes had taken place within British society, noting that "a moral code in the United Kingdom based on Christianity can no longer be taken for granted and the attitudes of people joining the Army today are different from previous generations."[52] Yet the report also recognized that "the British Army's standards, values and ethos are founded on our Christian history, culture and civilisation."[53]

As Britain becomes a multiethnic, multiracial society, the British Army must address the spiritual needs of non-Christian and Christian personnel alike. Although the share of ethnic minorities is still relatively small – approximately 1 percent of total armed forces personnel – provisions have now been made to cater to their moral and spiritual well-being through the appointment in 2005 of four nonuniformed chaplains: a Hindu chaplain, a Muslim chaplain, a Sikh chaplain, and a Buddhist chaplain. It is important to note, however, that multifaith chaplaincy is not new within the British armed forces. Jewish chaplains have been active in the forces since 1892 in lay positions, apart from times of war, when they wore uniforms. Military personnel with a religion other than Christianity are small in number in the British military. This is true even though the military has gone to great lengths to avoid discrimination on racial or religious grounds and has long abided by government legislation regarding race relations. There are many possible reasons for the low number of people from non-Christian backgrounds in the military. At its simplest, people from other denominations may simply be uninterested in joining the British military.

As long as recruitment practices are fair, there is no reason why racial or religious communities should be mathematically represented in the military. Gurkas, who are mainly Hindu or Buddhist, have long served with distinction in the British military. Some more recent recruits are from a Christian background; the British Army has 2,000 Fijian soldiers, many of whom are Christians.[54]

In view of the changes taking place within British society, the British Army published a paper in 2000 entitled "Values and Standards."[55] This document is the army's primary source on ethics. In addition to a discussion of core values, it contains a "service test" that is to be administered when considering possible cases of misconduct to determine whether the army has a duty to intervene in the personal lives of soldiers. The relevant text reads as follows: "Have the actions or behaviour of an individual adversely impacted or are likely to impact on the efficiency or operational effectiveness of the Army?" This service test lies at the heart of the Armed Forces Code of Social Conduct and is equally applicable to all forms of conduct.[56]

On close examination, this service test deviates significantly from the traditional Christian principles that have played such a major role in the life of the British armed forces. The adoption of this service test reveals the power of secularism in shaping British military ethics. Its focus is on operational effectiveness rather than, ostensibly, on moral behavior. Although this seems to be a way of avoiding any discussion of ethics, in reality, separating operational effectiveness from ethics can be difficult. Notwithstanding this change of emphasis, "Values and Standards" does make use of recognizably Christian virtues: selfless commitment, courage, discipline, and respect for others. It also employs the concept of "military covenant," a term with positive Christian overtones that implies a binding commitment between officers and soldiers and between armed forces and nation. "Values and Standards" is another example of the syncretized ethics of secularism and Christianity at play in the current British military.

Although the attitude and values of military personnel reflect, to a large degree, the values of the society from which they are recruited, Christianity continues to affect the armed forces in ways that differ from its impact on society in general. Approximately 178,750 armed forces personnel are ministered to by 281 chaplains, which means that there is a chaplain for every 636 personnel. This level of provision means that practically every member of the armed forces knows about the work of the chaplain. At the start of their military careers, they will meet him or her in the latter's capacity as pastor, preacher, or teacher, and they will continue to meet for years to come. Such a level of spiritual care and support would be difficult to replicate throughout society generally. It would be fair to conclude that in Britain the military and military culture are more "Christianized" than civilians.

It is difficult to measure the impact that religion has on the British armed forces or on their operational effectiveness. For example, how can one measure the effect of a soldier's encouraging friendly chat with a chaplain? What can be measured is the systematic creation of a Christian military structure, akin in many ways to a diocese of the Church of England, and the evidence for this in military churches, military legislation, the role of chaplains and Christian worship, and the like. War and conflict confront service members with many challenges. Soldiers undergo experiences they may be unable to articulate or even understand later. The Reverend David Cooper, a British Army chaplain during the Falklands War in 1982, later reflected on his experience, stating: "The past 25 years have convinced me that those humans who have undergone a particularly harrowing experience, that involves the premature death of friends or colleagues and the same threat to themselves, are separated from the rest of humanity by their experience and their inability to communicate the full depth of its impact."[57]

The Christian faith has played an integral part in the life of the British armed forces for centuries. Today, its influence can be identified in all aspects of service life. In addition to providing for the moral and spiritual needs of all personnel, the British armed forces continue to recognize the importance of the Christian religion as an essential component of their military ethos. At the same time, the British military has accommodated secular humanist beliefs into its ethics, producing a syncretic ethical mix for both religious believers and nonbelievers.

Notes

1 The Anglican Church is not the established Church in Wales, Ireland, or Scotland. In 1920, the Church in Wales, which is the Anglican Church in Wales, was disestablished but remains part of the Anglican communion. Similarly, the Church of Ireland, also part of the Anglican communion, was disestablished in 1871. The Church of Scotland, however, is an established church but lies within the Reformed tradition and is not part of the Anglican communion.

2 In this chapter, we use the terms "British armed forces" to refer to the armed forces of the United Kingdom, comprising both Britain (England, Wales, and Scotland) and Northern Ireland.

3 For historical reasons, Royal Navy personnel are not required to swear allegiance to the monarch. During the English Civil War, the army usurped the power of Parliament, but the navy took no part in this usurpation. As a result, it exists by royal prerogative: naval personnel do not take an oath of loyalty because their loyalty was never in doubt. This distinction is also reflected in the Church of England's *Book of Common Prayer* from 1662, which includes "Forms of Prayer to Be Used at Sea," two of which were to be used in Her Majesty's Navy every day. No such prayers are included for the British Army.

4 The latter category includes Druid, Pagan, Rastafarian, Spiritualist, Zoroastrian (Parsee), Wicca, and Baha'i. *UK Defence Statistics* (London: Defence Analytical Services Agency, 2010), chapter 2, table 2.13.

5 Alasdair Crockett and David Voas, "Generations of Decline: Religious Change in 20th Century Britain," *Journal for the Scientific Study of Religion* 45, no. 4 (November 2006): 568.

6   Jacinta Ashworth and Ian Farthing, "Churchgoing in the UK" (London: Tearfund, April 2007): 1.

7   Grace Davie, *Religion in Britain since 1945* (London: Blackwell, 1994): 463.

8   Michael Snape, *God and the British Soldier* (London: Routledge, 2005): 22.

9   Ibid., 23.

10 David S. Cairns, *The Army and Religion: An Enquiry and Its Bearing upon the Religious Life of the Nation* (London: Macmillan, 1919): 10; Alan Robinson, "British Chaplains in the First World War," unpublished manuscript: 34.

11 Snape, *God and the British Soldier*, 2.

12 John Bickersteth, *The Bickersteth Diaries* (London: Leo Cooper, 1995): 78.

13 Edward Madigan, "'The Life Lived' versus 'Balaam's Ass's Ears,'" *Royal Army Chaplains' Department Journal* 47 (2008): 17.

14 Cited in Robinson, "British Chaplains in the First World War," 35.

15 Madigan, "'The Life Lived' versus 'Balaam's Ass's Ears,'" 17.

16 Neil E. Allison, "Baptist Military Chaplaincy during the Great War 1914–1918," master's thesis, University of Wales, 2006: 113.

17 Sarah Sands, "Sir Richard Dannatt: A Very Honest General," *Daily Mail*, 12 October 2006.

18 Clifford Walton, *History of the British Standing Army* (London: Harrison, 1849): 339.

19 Ibid., 809.

20 Ibid.

21 Rifle Brigade Standing Order 1801.

22 Naval Discipline Act (1886), as cited in Stephen Deakin, "British Military Ethos and Christianity," *British Army Review*, no. 138 (Winter 2005): 101.

23 Naval Discipline Act (1661), as cited in ibid.

24 Officers Christian Union, *Military Leadership and Christian Faith* (Edinburgh: Pentland Press, 1998).

25 *Queens Regulations*, JS261 (London: Her Majesty's Stationery Office, 1975).

26 *Queens Regulations*, JS1427, 1971.

27 Ibid.

28 Bible, Matthew's Gospel chapter 20: 28.

29 Rear Adm. Gerard Wells, *Naval Customs and Traditions* (London: Phillip Allan 1930): 71.

30 Ibid., 72.

31 Ibid.

32 Philip Longworth, *The Unending Vigil* (London: Leo Cooper, 1985): 51.

33 Ibid., 43.

34 Brig. Justin Maciejewski DSO MBE. Niblett Lecture (Salisbury, UK), 2010: 11.

35 In notes from the Archives of the RAChD museum on El Alamein.

36 Ibid.

37 Neil Edward Allison, "Baptist Military Chaplaincy during the Great War 1914–1918", MPhil thesis, University of Wales, 2006: 141.

38 From "Experiences and Reflections in Battle," RAChD Museum, 3/4.

39 Reverend Father Daren Brown, "Herrick IV – A Wilderness Experience," *RAChD Volume* 46 (2007): 66.

40 Sir John Smyth, *In This Sign Conquer* (London: Mowbray, 1968): 175.

41 Notes from a chaplain in Malaya, RAChD archives.

42 Brig. I. D. T. McGill, *An Investigation into the Need for Spiritual Values in the Army* (British Army Internal Report, 1999).

43 Preface, *Chaplains' Handbook*, Character Training Series 22, January 1989–December 1989.

44 The core values for the navy are commitment, courage, discipline, respect for others, integrity, and loyalty; for the army, they are selfless service, courage, loyalty, integrity, discipline, and respect for others; and for the air force, they are respect, integrity, service, and excellence.

45 Kenneth Hendrickson, "Winning the Troops for Vital Religion: Female Evangelical Missionaries to the British Army, 1857–1880," *Armed Forces and Society*, vol. 23, no. 4 (Summer 1997): 623.

46 The authors have heard Lt. Col. Keeble tell his story. See also Chris Keeble, "Forgiveness out of War," online at http://www.forachange.net/features/3266.html, 4 April, 2007.

47 Notes from RAChD Archives (Amport House, UK). These are two verses from a longer poem consisting of nine verses. The poem is included in Stephen Garnett, *Salute the Soldier Poets* (London: Allen and Unwin, 1966).

48 Jonathan Sacks, *The Politics of Hope* (London: Jonathan Cape, 1997): 122.

49 Jonathan Sacks, *Faith in the Future* (London: Darton, Longman and Todd, 1995): 14.

50 Iain Torrance, "Ethics and the Military Community," Strategic and Combat Studies Institute Occasional Paper No. 34 (Camberley, 1998): 10.

51 Martin Beckford, "Churchgoing Stabilises after Years of Decline, Research Shows," *Daily Telegraph*, 10 September 2010, online at http://www.telegraph.co.uk/news/religion/7992616/Churchgoing-stabilises-after-years-of-decline-research-shows.html (accessed, 1 May 2012).

52 McGill, *An Investigation into the Need for Spiritual Values in the Army*, 21.

53 Ibid.

54 Dan McDougall, "To Helmand and Back," *Observer*, 26 April 2009, http://www.guardian.co.uk/uk/2009/apr/26/fijians-british-army-iraq.

55 "Values and Standards of the British Army: Commander's Edition," British Army, Army Code No. 63813, 2000. For an analysis, see Stephen Deakin, "Ethics and the British Army's Values and Standards," *British Army Review* (Winter 2006): 39–46.

56 "Values and Standards," paragraph 13.

57 Reverend David Cooper, "The Falklands – Twenty-five Years On," *RAChD* 46 (2007): 53.

PART II

RELIGIOUS DEMOGRAPHICS IN THE
ARMED FORCES

4

Pakistan

C. Christine Fair

Policy makers and analysts continue to be concerned about the purported Islamization of Pakistan, particularly in the Pakistan Army.[1] This concern, which is often seen as concurrent with deepening anti-Americanism in the country and the armed forces,[2] is undergirded by the army's six-decade-long reliance on Islamist militants to prosecute its interests in India and Afghanistan. These militants can be found in the Afghan Taliban, the Lashkar-e-Taiba, Jaish-e-Mohammed, and dozens of other groups terrorizing the region.[3] The United States has long worried about these groups operating in India, because a terrorist attack in that country remains the most likely precipitant of an Indo-Pakistan war, with possible nuclear escalation – either advertently or inadvertently. Some analysts and policy makers worry (with less justification) that Islamist militants will acquire nuclear technology or related assets either by stealth or through active or passive facilitation of the Pakistan Army. Recent U.S. legislation aims to reverse many of these ostensibly worrying trends.[4]

Some analysts of Pakistan contend that the lineaments of Pakistan's future Islamization can be traced to the arguments of early proponents of an independent Pakistan who believed there was a need for an independent Muslim state. Thus, even before independence, Pakistan was already conceived as a homeland for South Asia's Muslims. Other analysts claim that Islamization began in the first decade after independence as Islamists began vying for greater influence over Pakistan's developing state apparatuses. Still others argue that Islamization did not occur to a significant degree until much later.[5]

Despite these differences of opinion, most scholars of Pakistan agree that the impact of Islamization was clearly evident in the policies of Prime Minister Zulfikar Ali Bhutto. Bhutto was an authoritarian autocrat who used lethal force to put down opposition. When his regime became increasingly compromised, he sought to cultivate Islamists by pursuing policies that would appease them, such as outlawing gambling and drinking and declaring the Ahmediya to be non-Muslim. The process of Islamizing Pakistan intensified under Bhutto's successor, Gen. Muhammad Zia-ul-Haq, and his military government. Perhaps contrary to popular expectations, however, Pakistan's urban areas, not its rural areas, have been the site of Islamization and Islamic revivalism.[6]

Several policy concerns emerge from the ways in which Pakistan in general and the army in particular are presumed to have Islamized. First, as previous collaborative work by the author has shown, the Pakistan Army is becoming increasingly representative of Pakistani society writ large and increasingly likely to draw officers from urban areas, where Islamist revivalism may be most apparent.[7] It is difficult to predict what this diversification may mean for the officer corps, much less soldiers in the ranks and the noncommissioned officers, about whom virtually nothing is known in policy analytic or academic circles. Indeed, U.S. analysts and commentators often speculate with alarm that the Pakistan Army has Islamized without consideration of what this label may actually mean.[8] There is a widespread tendency within U.S. policy circles to assume that deepening commitments to political Islam (Islamism) or increasing personal piety or conservatism is coincident with expanding support for Islamist militancy in Pakistan.[9] U.S. policy toward Pakistan aims to support "moderate" Pakistanis in an effort to marginalize those who are increasingly Islamist or conservative – or both – presumably because Islamists and conservatives will be more receptive to militant groups. This policy aim, which animates U.S. interests in expanding engagement with Pakistani military personnel, applies to Pakistan in general and to the army in particular. U.S. policy makers also tend to assume that any success in attenuating anti-U.S. sentiments will mitigate popular support for the Islamists and reduce support for terrorism. These common perceptions persist despite recent evidence that neither increased piety nor anti-Americanism explains support for militant groups once other factors are taken into consideration.[10]

Given the Pakistani state's long cultivation of Islamist militant groups as tools of foreign policy, many U.S. analysts firmly believe that some of Pakistan's army officers may be deeply sympathetic to these groups, their organizations, and their ethos.[11] This concern has produced a related fear that an increasingly Islamized or radicalized faction of the Pakistan Army may pose a security threat to the region or to the international community. There are also those who worry that a cadre of deeply Islamized, if not radicalized, army officers remains sympathetic to jihadist militants and will continue to advance their cause even if the army leadership were to strategically abandon militancy as a tool of foreign and domestic policy. Others continue to conjure the specter of an Islamist vanguard within the army that is sympathetic to global terrorists such as Osama bin Laden and may even provide terrorists access to Pakistan's growing nuclear arsenal with devastating consequences.

Despite the importance of these issues, the body of empirically sound literature that has analyzed the Islamization of Pakistan and its polity is thin.[12] Extant analyses focus on case studies of the influence of particular devotional, traditional, or revivalist movements; the rise and development of Islamist political parties (most notably, the Jamaat-e-Islami, which has ties to the Muslim Brotherhood); the electoral outcomes of Islamist parties; qualitative assessments of pietic, political, or militant groups in specific geographical areas; or localized case studies of (usually sectarian) violence.[13] Unfortunately, there are few sources of empirical data that shed light on the various processes of Pakistan's Islamization, their manifestations, and their effects.

This chapter employs the existing body of literature and data to weigh in on the complex issue of religion and the Pakistan Army. It begins with a summary of the secondary literature on Islamization in Pakistan in general and then turns to the specifics of Islam, Islamism, and piety within the army – subject to numerous caveats described herein. Following this, the chapter employs district-level data on Pakistan Army officers from 1970 through 2005 that were obtained from the Pakistan Army General Headquarters. In addition, it uses several years of district-level household data to demonstrate that, contrary to popular views that the Pakistan Army is dominated by rural Punjabis, officers are more likely to come from urban areas and areas that are socially more liberal. They are also drawn increasingly from areas such as Balochistan.[14] The chapter concludes with a call for a research agenda on religion in the Pakistani military.

The Islamization of Pakistan?

The movement for an independent Pakistan was motivated by the "two-nation" theory, which held that Muslims represented a nation apart from either Sikhs or Hindus and therefore required a separate state to ensure their protection and rights. Muslim proponents of the two-nation theory feared that if Muslims remained in a united India, the country's Hindu majority would not protect their interests. While many of South Asia's Muslims imagined Pakistan to be their homeland, Pakistan's founding father, Mohammad Ali Jinnah, believed that it should also accommodate minorities that chose to remain in the country.

Since Jinnah's death in September 1948, the role of Islam within the Pakistani state has remained a divisive issue, with successive Pakistani leaders moving away from his notion of Pakistan as a state for Muslims toward one that is in some measure an Islamic state. Shortly after independence, the Islamists demanded an Islamic constitution. Their efforts, spearheaded by Maulana Shabbir Ahmed Usmani, culminated in the Objectives Resolution of 1949 by the first Constituent Assembly. The resolution declared Pakistan to be a sacred trust of Allah, sovereign of the universe. Although the actual meaning of the resolution was unclear in practice, it was an important symbolic recognition of the role of Islam in the new state.[15]

After Pakistan's loss of Bangladesh in the 1971 war, Zulfikar Ali Bhutto sought to promote Islam as a unifying factor to mitigate fissiparous tendencies among the country's remaining ethnic groups. The government and Islamists alike viewed the embrace of Islamic ideals of governance and society as the most likely means of maintaining state cohesion. Zulfikar Ali Bhutto expanded the state's connections to the Arab Gulf states; broadened the role of Arabic in the school curriculum, creating new jobs for specialists in Islamic studies; declared Ahmediyas to be non-Muslims; outlawed drinking and gambling, among other efforts to promote his notion of Islamic socialism; and laid the foundations for an official Islamization policy by enshrining Islamization within the framework of the 1973 constitution, clearly stating that Pakistan was an Islamic state.[16]

After the 1977 coup against Bhutto, Gen. Zia worked to strengthen the place of Islam within the Pakistani state and polity. As Hassan Rizvi writes, Zia's Islamization efforts were "regulative, punitive, and extractive."[17] Zia reconstituted the Council of Islamic Ideology to allow for greater representation of conservative and orthodox ulema in advising the government of the polity's Islamization, including efforts to review extant laws and bring them into greater conformity with the Quran and Sunna. Zia amended the constitution to establish a Sharia bench within the four provincial high courts and an appellate bench in the Supreme Court in 1979. In 1980, he established a Federal Sharia Court to replace those benches.[18]

Under Zia, the government passed four laws in early 1979 to enforce Islamic punishments for various crimes. Known as the Hudood Ordinances, the laws prescribed physical punishments (e.g., whipping, stoning, and amputation) for a variety of sex-related crimes, theft of property, possession of drugs and alcohol, and other transgressions.[19] Zia also introduced interest-free banking based on an alternative system of profit and loss sharing as well as a system of compulsory Islamic tax, the Zakat, which was highly controversial.[20]

Under Zia, a Sharia faculty was established at the Qaid-e-Azam University in Islamabad in late 1979, and later a separate Islamic University was established in Islamabad with the financial assistance of Arab Gulf states. In addition, schools and colleges revised their syllabi to provide greater emphasis on Islamic principles and teachings as well as on the "Ideology of Pakistan." This concept, sometimes called Pakistaniyat, refers to the belief that Pakistan was created as a homeland for South Asia's Muslims because Muslims and Hindus could not live in one unified state after 1947. The ideology of Pakistan thus enshrines Islam as a fundamental tenet of Pakistani identity. The Zia government informed leadership of print and electronic media that their content should reflect orthodox Islamic values. The government exerted greater film censorship and issued dress codes for women, and government servants were instructed to wear national dress (*salwar kameez*). In addition, the government imposed obligatory prayer breaks during its working hours and encouraged private-sector employers to do the same.[21]

During his time in office, Zia began to posit Islamization as justification for his martial law regime. This effort only intensified as his legitimacy began to falter after he failed to hold promised elections and as the goals of his regime expanded.[22] Nonetheless, Zia's attempts to Islamize Pakistani society were hindered by the military government's failure to appreciate the diversity of Islamic schools of thought in Pakistan, most of which disputed fundamental lineaments of Sharia.

Despite the assumptions of many Western analysts that Islamic revivalism would be more popular among illiterate rural Pakistanis, the trend has been a decidedly urban phenomenon. Cities are the loci for Islamist discourse, and it is there that Islamist policies and actions are formulated by its proponents, including Islamist political parties, their student wings, and ulema. As Mohammad Qadeer has noted, "Urban Islam tends to be relatively puritanical and textual compared to the ritual/folk thrust of beliefs and practices in rural/tribal areas."[23] In Pakistan, Islamic revivalism is often rooted in the newly educated and prospering groups, which tend to have an urban outlook and lifestyle despite their personal piety. Upwardly mobile village families whose members are educated and choose service and industrial occupations are frequently drawn to this exegetical Islamic discourse. After enrolling in college in Pakistan's cities, boys and girls – including those from villages – often become involved in student wings of Islamist political organizations. Whereas in the village they may have voted for one of Pakistan's mainstream parties, once ensconced in an urban, university setting, they are more inclined to vote for Islamist parties.[24]

Currently there is no way to demonstrate empirically the impacts of the trends discussed earlier on Pakistanis' views toward Islamism, militancy, or pietism, much less the views of the army. Simply put, although the historical accounts posit a slow but steady process of Islamization of Pakistani institutions – including the army and civil society – Pakistani public opinion polls provide few consistent measures of this finding.[25] Indeed, even if they had included means of identifying members of the armed forces, none of these polls have the sample power to enable any specific assessments of the army.[26]

Islamization and the Pakistani Army

The role of Islam in the Pakistani state remains a highly volatile area of inquiry, with vocal opponents and proponents divided on the notion that the Pakistan Army has become Islamized. It is unsurprising, then, that analysts have sought their own assessments of the role of religion in the Pakistani armed forces. For example, in his 1984 groundbreaking study of the Pakistan Army, Stephen Cohen noted that on achieving independence, the army "moved immediately to emphasize Islam as a unifying force."[27] During both the 1965 and 1971 wars, the government repeatedly invoked Islam to mobilize soldiers and civilians alike.[28] This was apparent in the civil war of 1971, which pitted Bengalis in East Pakistan, aided by India, against West Pakistan. The commander in chief and president of Pakistan, Yahya Khan, motivated his soldiers by declaring the Bengali guerrillas a "kaffir" (non-Muslim) army against which the Pakistan Army was waging a legitimate jihad. Cohen cites one senior officer who told him that "expressions like the 'ideology of Pakistan' and the 'glory of Islam,' normally outside a professional fighter's lexicon, were becoming stock phrases. ... The Service Chiefs sounded more like high priests than soldiers."[29] The value of Cohen's work derives from his extensive access to the Pakistan Army, which included numerous interviews. The disadvantage, as he readily concedes, is that it preceded some of the most important changes brought about by the anti-Soviet jihad in Afghanistan.

As mentioned earlier, Zia-ul-Haq vigorously sought to Islamize the institution of the army, first as chief of army staff and later as president. Deeply sympathetic to Jamaat-e-Islami, Zia began using his post of army chief to distribute the party's literature among the soldiers and rank and file.[30] In March 1976, he gave the army a new motto: "Imam, Taqwa, wa-Jihad-fi-sibilillah" (Faith, Piety, and Holy War [or also "striving"] in the name of God). Rizvi has written that although the adoption of this motto reflected Zia's personal religious inclinations, it was not a major departure from the army's culture, because military education in Pakistan has always emphasized Islamic principles, teachings, and history as well as Muslim war heroes and their battles.[31] Reportedly dismayed with Zia's activities, Bhutto summoned him before the cabinet to explain himself. During his trial before the Supreme Court, Bhutto remarked: "I appointed a Chief of Staff belonging to the Jamaat-e-Islami and the result is before all of us."[32]

After the 1977 coup, Zia began his efforts to Islamize the army specifically and Pakistan generally. As the army chief, he set the tone of the army. His highly visible and vocal advocacy of Islamism likely encouraged similarly inclined individuals to join the army while discouraging those who did not share his views.

Rizvi has identified several developments in Zia's army that had a far-reaching impacts on the role of Islam in that institution. First, Zia mobilized conservative Islamic groups to legitimize his increasingly problematic rule, and he encouraged Islamic orthodoxy within the army. These actions dovetailed with subtle changes in army recruitment patterns, which saw officers coming increasingly from the middle to lower socioeconomic strata and from urban areas and small towns, where conservative Islamic ideology is more prevalent than in rural Pakistan. Thus the values that Zia promulgated in the army aligned with those of the new Pakistani soldier. Officers (and soldiers) were also assigned to militaries in the Arab Gulf, exposing them to ultraconservative Wahhabist teachings. The degree to which officers embraced Islamic conservatism influenced their path to promotion. Although officers' private lives were always under scrutiny, under Zia an officer's piety and religious practices became a part of assessment for promotion. This bias may have encouraged some officers to begin growing beards and eschew the consumption of alcohol. In the past, officers had been known to relax with an alcoholic beverage.[33]

Second, Zia promoted Islam as "an important part of the public profile of the in-service personnel."[34] He permitted key Islamic groups, such as the

Tablighi Jamaat (a revivalist group dedicated to proselytization that avoids political activities), to expand their presence in the army. This decision would have been anathema to past army chiefs. Zia was the first head of state to attend its annual meeting in Raiwind (in the Punjab, near Lahore) – a step that encouraged several officers to openly associate with the group in a demonstration of their piety. In addition, other conservative Islamic groups, such as Jamaat-e-Islami, made inroads into the army and other services. Many officers also began overtly affiliating with Jamaat Islami and its founder, Maulana Maududi.

Third, the 1979 Islamic Revolution had an effect on Pakistan's military and civilian institutions and civil society. In response to Iran's efforts to export its Shi'a revolutionary ideal, Pakistan's Shi'a mobilized against Zia's efforts to render Pakistan a Sunni Muslim state (as evidenced by the way he imposed the Quranic taxes of Ushr and Zakat).[35] Iran backed Shi'a militants, and Iraq supported Sunni militants. Pakistan was soon joined by Arab Gulf states that supported these groups' efforts to confront Iran's proxies. In short order, Pakistan became the site of a sectarian proxy war fought by Iran and those aligned against Tehran. Although the sectarian identity of the revolution was Shi'a, some retired and serving officers in the army were moved by the principle of an Islamic revolution and began talking openly about the possibility of a similar revolution in Pakistan. None, however, could identify the methods for fomenting a successful revolution or for preparing for a postrevolution Pakistan.[36]

Fourth, the 1979 Soviet invasion of Afghanistan mobilized Pakistani and international resources to fund and field a force of mujahideen to repel the Soviets. These mujahideen were Afghans, Pakistanis, Arabs, and other Muslims from around the world who flocked to Afghanistan to defend the Afghans against the Communists. Although Pakistan had promoted Afghan Islamist proxy groups ousted by Afghan president Mohammed Daoud in the early 1970s, it was the 1979 invasion that brought massive resources into Pakistan, allowing it to expand and deepen these efforts. Pakistan funneled the international resources through a number of explicitly Islamist militant groups to ensure that ethnic Pashtun nationalist groups would not have the resources to mobilize coethnics on Pakistani territory. Pakistan relied on a network of refugee camps, madrassahs (religious seminaries), mosques, and Islamist political parties in the Pashtun belt and beyond to provide foot soldiers and other resources for the effort. These same institutions became the breeding ground for the Taliban, which emerged in the early 1990s. Pakistan-based militant groups such as Lashkar-e-Taiba, Harkat-ul-Jihad-Islami, and Lashkar-e-Jhangvi/Sipah-e-Sahaba-e-Pakistan have their origins in the Afghan War. Some of these groups later deployed to Kashmir following the Soviet withdrawal (with support from the Pakistan's Inter-Service Intelligence directorate and the Pakistan Army).[37]

Another important development was the use of Pakistani military personnel in Arab Gulf state militaries – Saudi Arabia in particular. For example, the Pakistan Army maintained division- and brigade-strength presences in several Arab Gulf states during the Arab-Israeli wars, with Pakistani air force pilots flying on the side of the Arabs in the 1967 Six-Day War and the 1973 Ramadan/Yom Kippur War. Pakistan also established an independent armored brigade group in Saudi Arabia. While little is known about this force, it is known that Jahangir Karamat, who later became Pakistan's army chief under Nawaz Sharif, served as the first commander of this unit from 1985 to 1988. At one point, Pakistani air force pilots could enhance their chances of promotion by flying with the Abu Dhabi air force. Pakistan continues to provide technical and training assistance to Bahrain, Kuwait, Qatar, Saudi Arabia, and the United Arab Emirates.[38] The Pakistan Army chose to curtail a larger Pakistani presence in order to comply with the requests of the Gulf States to limit its deployment of Shi'a troops and because of the 1990–1991 Gulf War. Cohen notes that Pakistani and Saudi intelligence agencies have historically enjoyed strong ties as well.[39]

The long association between Pakistan's armed forces and Arab Gulf states raises an important – if unanswerable – question: Did exposure to these states and to Wahhabism encourage Islamism among Pakistanis who served in these states and those who interacted with them, including their families? Alternatively, those same individuals could have been off put by the decadence and maltreatment of South Asians living in the Arab Gulf states.

Under Zia, Islamic training was introduced into the curriculum of the Command and Staff College. In lectures by Col. Abdul Qayyum at the Staff College throughout the 1970s, officers were encouraged to respect – rather than mock and deride – mullahs and maulvis (i.e., scholars who had undergone rigorous training at a madrassah). Before Zia, the maulvis' lack of genuine religious knowledge and financially dependent social status had led many Pakistanis to see them as charlatans more worthy of derision than reverence. Zia required maulvis to go into battle with the troops. Qayyum thought of these "clerical" figures as bridges that officers could use to span their Westernized profession and their faith.[40] Qayyum also urged students to base their education on the Quran.

In his discussion of army officer training at the Pakistan Military Academy and other training institutions such as the National University of Science and Technology, Pervaiz Iqbal Cheema notes that underlying these educational programs "is a strong grounding in general Islamic teaching including the concept of Jihad. This is inevitable in a Muslim country: the concept of Jihad is an important pillar of Islam."[41] Cheema also writes that the officers and soldiers of the Pakistan Army have a solid understanding of the "concept of Jihad, as Islamic ideas have become an integral part of training in the armed forces."[42] Cheema believes that this is necessary because Pakistan confronts a larger, better-equipped Indian Army. The Pakistan Army therefore must rely heavily on a "great measure of moral superiority which encompasses a high degree of professional competence, in-depth study of modern concepts and doctrines of war, better leadership and inspired ideological orientations."[43]

Cohen has written that the Pakistan Army's professional journals contain numerous essays that study the question of the Islamization of the military and the degree to which the Pakistan Army should part ways with the traditional practices of the old Indian Army to achieve greater adherence to Islamic principles. For example, Pakistani regiments adopted distinct Islamic battle cries. The Pakistan Frontier Force began voicing the expression "Nadar Hazar Ali!" ("I am present before the Almighty!"). Signboards remind recruits that "life and death are the same thing: and when the experiment of life is completed, then the eternal life – which we call death – begins." Other boards declare that "fighting in the name of Allah, fighting in the name of truth, is the supreme sort of worship, and anybody who does service in the armed force with the intention of doing this job in worship, his life is a worship" (Photo 5).[44]

One retired officer wrote that the cumulative result of Zia's army policies was the "rise of religious orthodoxy among a cross-section of the armed forces. For this small group, ideology can be stretched to radicalism and takes precedence over professionalism. Their attitude needs to be countervailed otherwise it will erode the very foundation of a cohesive, professionally competent, and technologically adept armed forces."[45]

Despite these efforts to Islamize the army and the state, Cohen found that the changes in the officer corps were in fact modest. (Cohen's fieldwork for his book was completed before the culmination of Zia's efforts.) He also found that while there is an "Islamic presence" in the regimental training centers, it "derives from the Indian Army tradition and is moderate in tone." Further, there was considerable divergence within the officer corps over the role of Islam, which mirrored the divergence of views about the origins of the state and Islam's place in it.[46] Cohen did find other officers who were dissatisfied with the ostensibly sluggish pace of Islamization in the military. For example, he came across a number of officers who criticized the Staff College and army rules as having a "distinct aroma of subjugation suited to a colonial power" rather than "reflecting a true Islamic equalitarianism."[47]

The Pakistan Army, similar to all other armies, has long had the responsibility for territorial defense. During Zia's tenure, however, the army began assuming a new role: defending Pakistan's "ideological frontiers." Zia argued that "Pakistan's armed forces were responsible for not only safeguarding the country's territorial integrity but also its ideological basis."[48] Elaborating on this point, Zia contended that the "preservation of that Ideology and the Islamic character of the country was ... as important as the security of the country's geographic boundaries."[49] Although Zia's view was perhaps paramount given that he was both the president and chief of army staff, he was not alone in having this perspective. Rizvi contends that the army's proclaimed commitment to protecting the ideology of Pakistan has allowed the army to interfere in domestic politics when it deems necessary, presumably on the pretext of protecting this ideology.

Some in the senior army leadership who succeeded Zia appreciated the impact of Zia's policies on the army and feared that some members had come

Photo 5 Soldiers from the 57 Punjab Regiment (Cheeta Battalion), 326 Brigade, in the Makeen Valley, South Waziristan, August 2010. Their vehicle, a Hilux outfitted with a machine gun, is used for counterinsurgency operations in mountainous areas but is also vulnerable to insurgent attacks. It is inscribed "God is Great" (top) and the Islamic creed "There is no god but Allah and Muhammad is His Prophet" (bottom, partially obscured). Photo by C. Christine Fair.

to substitute "professionalism and discipline with Islam-oriented activism."[50] Gen. Asif Nawaz Janjua, who was the army chief between August 1991 and January 1993, and his successors tried to push back the politicized Islamic elements within the force and reinstate the tradition of "keeping Islam and professionalism together but treating the former as a component of the latter."[51] Nevertheless, Zia's successors continued to acknowledge the role and importance of Islam within military ideology.

Rizvi, anticipating contemporary concerns about Pakistan's military, argued that it would face major challenges in the twenty-first century. First, it would have to ensure the professional and cohesive disposition of the new breed of officers who came up during the Zia years and had begun taking command. Second, it would need to maintain the delicate balance between Islam and service discipline as Islamic and Islamist groups continued to develop inroads within the army. No doubt Pakistan's utilization of Islamist militant groups as a tool of foreign policy has fostered deeply sympathetic elements within the army for whom abandoning jihad would be very difficult. Third, the military would have to contend with ethnic imbalances resulting from the overrepresentation of Pashtuns and Punjabis and the underrepresentation of Sindhis relative to their population distribution in the country. Arguably, the army's deep involvement in running Pakistan intensified the need for a representative army. The skewing of the ethnic balance is complicated by privileges that the army has reserved for itself, such as higher-quality schools, hospitals, and other social services that are denied to nonmilitary personnel and their families.[52] The interplay between ethnicity and religiosity has undoubtedly been deeply affected by the ongoing Islamist insurgency, in which largely Punjabi and Pashtun militants terrorize Pakistan's largely Pashtun tribal belt.[53]

Army Recruitment: A District-Level Assessment

The preceding summary of the secondary literature on the Pakistan Army and the role of Islam in that organization is truncated to the early 1990s. The sanctions placed on Pakistan as a result of its nuclear program made it extremely difficult for the U.S. government to garner insights into the Pakistan Army after it excluded Pakistan from its International Military Education Training program and cut off almost all defense ties in 1990.[54] Unlike the Indian Ministry of Defense, which publishes an annual report that resembles a national security strategy document, Pakistan puts out no such documents. Moreover, Pakistan came to view the United States as an adversary keen on shutting down its nuclear weapons program and was not very interested in permitting Americans access to its military.

With the terrorist attacks of September 11, 2001, Pakistan again became (a not unproblematic) ally in the U.S. war on terror in general and the U.S.-led military operations in Afghanistan in particular. Before the launch of military offensives in Afghanistan on October 7, 2001, the United States lifted or waived its sanctions against Pakistan.[55] Concerns about the Pakistan Army and the posited "Islamists within," however, have only intensified over the past decade. U.S. analysts talk about "beard counts" at the graduation ceremonies at the National Defense University and keep track of officers presumed to have Islamist credentials, fearing they may be the masterminds of the next terror attack against India or a purveyor of nuclear technology to terrorists, among other nightmare scenarios.

Although questions about the Pakistan Army are extremely important, data do not exist to permit analysts either in or out of government to address them to any serious degree. U.S. officials – civilian and military – are extremely constrained in who they can meet from the Pakistan military. They rarely meet officers below the rank of lieutenant colonel, with the exception of those U.S. Army majors who attend the Command and Staff College for one year at Quetta. U.S. defense analysts have told the author that U.S. officials inter- act with about 100 Pakistani officers at most. They meet no junior noncom- missioned officers and no enlisted soldiers from an active army composed of approximately 550,000 personnel and an officer corps estimated to number in the tens of thousands.[56] Cooperation with the Pakistan government, and the army in particular, is fundamental to collecting data needed to understand the role of Islam and Islamism within the Pakistan armed forces, the degree of support for militant groups, and the connections – if any – among support for militancy, personal piety, Islam, and Islamism.[57]

Such support is unlikely to be forthcoming, however. While the Pakistan Army bristles at aspersions cast upon it and takes great care to put forward a modernized face of scotch-drinking generals with a fondness for women, it has not – and perhaps cannot – provide data to analysts to address this issue. The army has not been amenable to actual studies of attitudes among its armed forces personnel and guards information about its officers and enlisted person- nel with the utmost secrecy. Some Pakistan military and intelligence officials see no need for studies about the attitudes and beliefs of the officer corps, tell- ing the author that all services screen officers rigorously, particularly when the officers are promoted from major to lieutenant colonel. According to U.S. mili- tary attachés, this process involves intelligence agencies scrutinizing officers on the basis of, among other things, their personal beliefs and private lives. U.S. defense officials have told the author that Pakistani intelligence officials will even compare their "beard counts" with those of American defense officials.

Given the importance of these issues, the author assembled a research team to mine a unique – but imperfect – dataset on district-level Pakistan Army recruitment and retirement figures. These data provide aggregates of district- level officer recruitment and retirement information from 1970 to 2005. Recruitment data pertain to the number of candidate acceptances into the Pakistan Military Academy at Kakul, which is the principle means of becoming a commissioned officer in Pakistan. Data are aggregated by the officer's district of origin, including the Federally Administered Tribal Areas, Kashmir, and the Northern Areas – in other words, areas not typically included in federal sur- veys. The team also had access to district-level aggregates of the numbers of officers who retired from these districts. These data are organized according to the district from which the officer was recruited, not the district to which he retired.[58]

The optimal empirical approach to understanding changes in the officer corps requires analysis of the social and economic characteristics of officer candidates. Unfortunately, our team could obtain only district-level aggregated data, not officer-level data. The data, provided in spreadsheet form, yielded no additional information apart from aggregate counts of yearly recruits and retirements. Per force, we adopted a "second best" approach that focused on the characteristics of officers' home districts and how these have changed over time. This approach, although limited, does provide insights into the larger social and economic environment of districts that produce officers, including proxies for social conservatism. Equally important, these data do not directly weigh in on the issue of Islamization, even though they do cast light on the relative social conservatism or liberality of the persons inhabiting the districts. Although social conservatism or liberalism is not a direct proxy for Islamism and although these results may ultimately prove unsatisfying, these data offer the only available insights into this important officer corps.

Despite the suboptimal nature of the data, they did permit a unique opportunity to evaluate claims that the Pakistan Army has increasingly recruited from socially conservative areas over the years, even while they shed no light on the characteristics of individual officer candidates.[59] The data, methods, and results are briefly discussed below.

Data and Methods: A Brief Overview

Our team employed several kinds of data.[60] First, we used annual data on the home districts of officer recruits and retirees, as noted earlier, for 1970 and 2005; although again for reasons noted earlier, we could use data only from 1991 to 2005.[61] Second, we used district-level estimates of economic, demographic, and social characteristics. These data were derived from respondent-level data from the 1991, 1998, 2001, and 2005 waves of household surveys conducted by the Pakistan Federal Bureau of Statistics (FBS), such as the Household Integrated Economic Survey, Pakistan Integrated Household Survey, and Pakistan Social and Living Standards Measurement Survey. These include data on education and the kinds of schools used to educate children, economic and employment data, social factors such as rates of contraceptive usage, and demographic factors such as the age distribution. Unfortunately, the data come only from the four provinces of the Punjab, Sindh, Balochistan, and Khyber-Pakhtunkhwa (KPK, formerly known as the Northwest Frontier Province). The team constructed weights with which we collapsed the data to annual, district-level observations to match the army recruiting and retirement data. We also included other variables that could affect military recruitment outcomes, such as density of military installations, variables on economic performance nationally, assistance to Pakistan that could be used to build up its military, and so forth.[62]

For purposes of analysis, we used only those districts and years for which three conditions obtained. First, we examined only those years for which we were able to acquire and process survey data and only those districts that were covered in all waves of the survey data. Second, we examined only years for which we could create "lag" variables; that is, years in which data for the following year were also available. For example, we excluded 2005 survey data because no army data were available for 2006, as required for lag effects. Third, we examined only those districts/years for which we have full set of individual and community characteristics collected by the FBS. These restrictions left us with a dataset of 294 observations (three years for each of the ninety-eight districts).[63]

Given these limitations, we view our initial results as a call for more careful analysis, not as a definitive analysis of factors driving recruitment to the Pakistan Army. Such analytical refinement is only likely to be achieved, however, with officer-level recruitment and retirement data along with other key information about these officers, which is unlikely ever to be forthcoming. With these important caveats, this analysis is the first and most rigorous attempt to analyze extremely difficult to obtain (legally) Pakistan Army recruitment data using econometric tools. As such, this effort should have important if limited relevance to ongoing speculation about the Pakistan Army.

Because this chapter is not meant to offer a quantitative analysis, I recount only the relevant – if preliminary – findings most germane to the inquiry at hand. First, the team found that the officer corps is drawn primarily from more urban areas, a fact that has not changed much over the period in question.[64] This finding suggests that the Pakistan Army has not sought to recruit officers from more rural areas in any consistent way. Second, even after accounting for the concentration of officer recruits in urban areas, we found that the army recruits substantially more officers from places with above-average literacy rates. (This is also true of the U.S. Army.)

The Pakistan Army has also expanded the geographical distribution of officer recruitment. Although recruits from Punjab and KPK are somewhat overrepresented in annual cohorts, Balochistan appears to be producing recruits roughly in proportion to that province's population distribution. In contrast, Sindh is massively underrepresented in new officer intake per its share of Pakistan's population.[65] These changing geographical patterns may have important implications for the role of Islam, piety, and support in the army. For example, Pashtuns are often characterized as being "more pious" than other Muslims, although this claim is impossible to verify with current data and may reflect such pervasive stereotypes about Pashtuns held among Pakistanis. Moreover, Fair and Nawaz found that the southern Punjab is increasingly producing officers.[66] As this region has long been the epicenter of Deobandi-inspired anti-Shi'a sentiment and militancy, officers who embrace these stereotypes may decide in increasing numbers to enter service. Although it is impossible to evaluate these propositions with the available data, researchers should design future studies that permit assessment of these issues.[67]

When we controlled for other factors, the "urban" effect diminishes. While officers generally come from more urban parts of the country, this is an artifact of the army's tendency to recruit from wealthier areas.[68] Once economic conditions and other characteristics of the districts are controlled for, the association with urban areas disappears. Moreover, we found that army officers are likelier to come from more socially liberal districts than conservative ones. We used two variables from our survey data to evaluate this claim. First, we used the ratio of female to male literacy. The greater literacy advantage of men to women was used as a proxy for increasing social conservatism. Second, we examined household education utilization. We used the district-level aggregate of madrassahs utilization as a proxy for conservatism and private-school use a proxy for social liberality.[69]

Finally, as with other armed forces, military recruitment in Pakistan is strongly regionally and socially influenced. Although some changes are the result of growth in certain districts, the continued influence of social factors suggests that the Pakistan Army remains conservative and will change only slowly.

These findings may suggest important shifts that are germane to this study. Given disproportionately high Pashtun representation and the ongoing confrontation with Islamist militants across the Pashtun belt, it is entirely possible that this confrontation has influenced how officers who have served in these areas understand the role of Islam and Islamist militancy. For example, the ways in which some Pakistani militants justify their war on Pakistanis and the state may repulse some officers and motivate them to reconsider how the army has instrumentalized both Islam and Islamist political and militant groups. Other officers may instead understand the problem to be "Pashtun," focusing their vexation with internal affairs on an ethnic group that already suffers racist stereotypes. Still other officers may see an Indian hand behind the groups targeting the Pakistani state and embrace Islamism ever tightly as the best means to ensure Pakistan's coherence as a nation and as a state. Unfortunately, these recruitment data do not permit insight into these questions.

Similarly, given that many officers are now coming from urban areas and given the propensity in recent years of the Pakistan Taliban to target important urban areas such as Islamabad, Rawalpindi, and Lahore (in and around the Punjab) as well as important cities in KPS such as Peshawar and Mingora, the recruitment bases from which officers draw may be reconsidering the threats posed by militants. Such officers may see them as menaces who have turned on their erstwhile proxies and who must be eliminated. Others may see them as Indian agents and embrace more intently the utility of these groups to operate in India.[70]

During fieldwork in Pakistan in June and July of 2010, the author met extensively with military and intelligence personnel. The author noticed an important shift in thinking between those officers who served in the tribal areas combating militants and those who had not yet deployed. Meeting with officers in North and South Waziristan, the author observed that they referred to their domestic foes as "terrorists," whereas those who had not deployed and were training at Pakistan's new Anti-Terrorism Training Center near Mangla Dam still referred to them by the term "miscreants."

The author also observed, however, the debates about whether these militants should be properly characterized as "terrorists" or "miscreants." As suggested earlier, some officers insisted that India was behind this domestic menace. They point to noncircumcised captured militants, with obvious reference to "Hindus."[71] It is impossible to discern whether the Pakistani military high command believed these individuals to be Hindu (i.e., Indian) operatives or whether this was a ploy to mobilize both the troops and polity to support internal military operations because the actual foe is "Hindu India."[72] Given the high-profile media attention these uncircumcised militants received and given the well-known role of the intelligence agencies and the Inter-Services Public Relations arm of the military to use the domestic media to manage perceptions, both are likely true in varying measures. In October 2009, Pakistan's interior minister Rehman Malik even claimed that India was funding the Taliban, a claim India obviously dismissed.[73]

Conclusion

Historians have examined the Islamization of the Pakistan Army through the Zia period. Yet there is little if any support for conventional fears about the army becoming increasingly Islamist and thus prone to supporting militancy today. Equally important, there is no evidence that this is not the case given the data available to scholars. Even if the army as an institution is becoming more "pious" as a result of the ways in which it both uses Islam within the institution and defines the external threat from "Hindu India," this cannot be used to suggest that increasingly pious persons are more inclined to support militancy. In fact, work by the author and Jacob Shapiro employed here undermines this hypothesis. But because they are based on recent but still preliminary studies or are derived from negative evidence, all of these findings are tentative.

These data limitations should not motivate the policy community to become insouciant about developments within the Pakistan Army. The consequences of radicalization of the Pakistan Army – however unlikely – have enormous import for U.S. national security interests. This study is the first effort to empirically characterize the different environments that produce officers and to illuminate a sustained, important area of empirical inquiry.

The preliminary findings of this study suggest an urgent research agenda. The analytical community must make an effort to obtain data about army personnel (officers and enlisted) and their family backgrounds. This can be done by fielding large national-, household-, or individual-level surveys that incorporate questions about responders' military experience, veteran status, and so on. Similarly, the addition of a handful of military status questions to the census would go far in enabling clarifications of the questions that this essay has sought to address. This study provides a first glance that allows analysts to identify important districts in Pakistan that play an important role in producing officers and thus may provide important insights into how analysts can best capture information about army personnel on a local level. The sampling for such an exercise would have to be multistage to identify the distribution of military families writ large, followed up with a well-constructed and robust sample.

Such a survey effort would permit analysts to identify officer personnel as well as household characteristics and compare them to nonmilitary individuals and households, and similarly compare officer personal among themselves based on their area of residence. Repeated surveys administered regularly would make it possible to carefully assess trends and changes in army composition and under certain conditions permit more definitive inference of causal effects. Such exercises would yield important insights into how the values, worldviews, and socioeconomic and demographic background of military families differ from those of nonmilitary families, how they differ across regions, and in which directions changes are occurring. In particular, such an effort would cast enormous light on the role of Islam, attitudes toward Islamism, pietistic trends, and beliefs about Islamist militancy in the single most important institution that sets the course for Pakistan's external as well as domestic policies.

Notes

1 A version of this chapter was published as C. Christine Fair, "Increasing Social Conservatism in the Pakistan Army: What the Data Say," *Armed Forces and Society* 38, no. 3 (July 2012): 438–462.

2 See Jonathan Paris, "Prospects for Pakistan," Legatum Institute, January 2010, http://www.li.com/attachments/ProspectsForPakistan.pdf. This report derives from an earlier report by the author for Booze Allen Hamilton, under contract from the Office of the Secretary of Defense, Net Assessment.

3 Husain Haqqani, *Pakistan: Between Mosque and Military* (Washington, DC: Carnegie Endowment for International Peace, 2005).

4 One of the most recent pieces of U.S. legislation providing comprehensive assistance to Pakistan is the Enhanced Partnership with Pakistan Act of 2009, better known as Kerry-Lugar-Berman. This legislation sought to address, among other issues, a criticism lodged by the U.S. Government Accountability Office in its 2003 report (GAO-08–622). According to the report, the government had failed to develop a comprehensive plan that mobilizes all elements of U.S. national power – diplomatic, military, intelligence, development assistance, economic, and law enforcement support – to address the various forms of terrorism and extremism emerging from Pakistan. See especially "Section 3. Findings" of the legislation. http://frwebgate.access.gpo.gov/cgi-bin/getdoc.cgi?dbname=111_cong_public_laws&docid=f:publ073.111.pdf. For a more comprehensive articulation of U.S. strategy toward Pakistan, see U.S. Department of State, Pakistan Assistance Strategy Report, 14 December 2009, http://www.state.gov/documents/organization/134114.pdf.

5 Vali Nasr articulates the process of Islamization as incorporating "Islamic norms, symbols and rhetoric in the public sphere, and in the process, it has had a notable impact on politics, policy making, law and social relations." He notes that while Islamism is often seen as an ineluctable state response to social factors,

political developments, and grassroots pressure from Islamist groups (among other considerations), in many Muslim countries where Islamism has been interpolated into politics, the state has been a key agent proactively promoting Islamization. The state may do so to fortify beleaguered or increasingly illegitimate regimes, to exert social control over restless polities, and to expand control over state resources and policy among other aims. Pakistan, as Nasr notes, typifies this process. Seyyed Vali Reza Nasr, *Islamic Leviathan: Islam and the Making of State Power* (Oxford: Oxford University Press, 2001): 3.

6   See inter alia Mohammad A. Qadeer *Pakistan: Social and Cultural Transformations in a Muslim Nation* (London: Routledge, 2005); Anita Weiss, ed., *Islamic Reassertion in Pakistan* (Syracuse, NY: Syracuse University Press, 1986): 21–48; Richard Kurin "Islamization: A View from the Countryside," in Weiss, *Islamic Reassertion in Pakistan*, 115–128; Haqqani, *Pakistan: Between Mosque and Military*. For accounts of how Islamization has affected women in urban areas, in particular, see Fawzia Afzal-Khan, "What Lies Beneath: Dispatch from the Front Lines of the Burqa Brigade," Social Identities, Vol. 14, No. 1, January 2008, pp. 3–11; and Naeem Ahmed, "State, Society, and Terrorism: A Case Study of Pakistan after September 11, 2010," Ph.D. dissertation, University of Karachi, 2007, http://prr.hec.gov.pk/thesis/2511.pdf.

7   C. Christine Fair and Shuja Nawaz, "The Changing Pakistan Army Officer Corps," *Journal of Strategic Studies* 34, no. 1 (2011): 63–94.

8   Without evidence, Paris writes that "the danger for the army, and for Pakistan generally, is not Talibanisation but Islamisation from Punjab-based militants and their allies." Needless to say, not only is the claim lacking in evidence, but Paris also fails to describe what he means by "Islamisation" and why this is necessarily dangerous. This analysis suggests that Islamists are more prone to hand the country to terrorists. Paris, "Prospects for Pakistan," 7.

9   A more nuanced articulation of the Islamist-militant nexus stems from the factual argument that Deobandi ulema parties have long supported Deobandi Islamist militants, and that these militant groups and the ulema parties (factions of the Jamiat Ulema-e-Islam (JUI)) have overlapping membership. This does not mean, however, that all of the supporters of these parties (which usually pull in fewer than 10 percent of voters even during elections that are most rigged in their favor) support terrorism. Polling by the author shows that piety does not predict terrorism or support for ulema parties. Indeed, if piety did predict support for these parties, one would expect to see much higher support from them. For a nuanced discussion of these issues, see Ahmed, "State, Society, and Terrorism."

10 C. Christine, Fair, Neil Malhotra, and Jacob N. Shapiro, "Islam, Militancy, and Politics in Pakistan: Insights from a National Sample," *Terrorism and Political Violence* 22, no. 4 (2010): 495–521.

11 For an example of this analysis, see Paris, "Prospects for Pakistan." For a countervailing view, see Fair et al., "Islam, Militancy, and Politics in Pakistan"; Julian Schofield and Michael Zekulin, *Appraising the Threat of Islamist Take-Over in Pakistan*, Concordia University Research Note 34 (March 2007), http://www.ieim.uqam.ca/IMG/pdf/NOTE34.pdf.

12 A notable exception is Nasr, *Islamic Leviathan*.

13 Mumtaz Ahmad, "Islamic Fundamentalism in South Asia: The Jamaat-i-Islami and the Tablighi Jamaat of South Asia" in Martin E. Marty and R. Scott Appleby,

Fundamentalisms Observed, Chicago: University of Chicago Press, 1991, pp. 457–531; Sadaf Ahmad, "Identity Matters, Culture Wars: An Account of Al-Huda (Re)defining Identity and Reconfiguring Culture in Pakistan," *Culture and Religion*, Vol. 9, No. 1, March 2008, pp. 63–80; Magnus Marsden, "Muslim Cosmopolitans? Transnational Life in Northern Pakistan," *Journal of Asian Studies* 67 no.1 (February 2008): 213–247; Magnus Marsden, "Women, Politics, and Islamism in Northern Pakistan," *Modern Asian Studies* 42 (2008): 405–429; Masooda Bano, "Beyond Politics: The Reality of a Deobandi Madrasa in Pakistan," *Journal of Islamic Studies*, Vol. 18, No. 1, 2007, pp. 43–68. M. Zaman, "Sectarianism in Pakistan: The Radicalization of Shi'a and Sunni, *Journal of Asian Studies* 32, no. 2 (1998): 689–716; Vali R. Nasr, "International Politics, Domestic Imperatives, and Identity Mobilization: Sectarianism in Pakistan, 1979–1998," *Comparative Politics* 32, no. 2 (January 2000): 171–190; Vali R. Nasr, "The Rise of Sunni Militancy in Pakistan: The Changing Role of Islamism and the Ulama in Society and Politics," *Modern Asian Studies* 34 (2000): 139–180; Seyyed Vali Reza Nasr, *The Vanguard of the Islamic Revolution: The Jama'at-i Islami of Pakistan* (Los Angeles: University of California Press, 1994); and Yoginder Sikand, "The Tablighī Jama'āt and Politics: A Critical Re-Appraisal," *Muslim World* 96, no. 1 (2006): 175–195; Afzal-Khan, 2008.

14 This research was completed in collaboration with Claude Berrebi and Jacob Shapiro and in consultation with Shuja Nawaz, who provided these data.

15 Qadeer, *Pakistan*.

16 Christophe Jaffrelot, "Islamic Identity and Ethnic Tensions," in Christophe Jaffrelot, ed., *A History of Pakistan and Its Origins* (London: Anthem Press, 2004), pp. 9–38; and Nasr, *Islamic Leviathan*.

17 Hassan Askari Rizvi, *Military, State, and Society in Pakistan* (London: Palgrave, 2000): 170.

18 Ibid., 171.

19 Ibid., see also Nasr, *Islamic Leviathan*.

20 Rizvi, *Military, State, and Society in Pakistan*, 171–172.

21 Ibid., Nasr, *Islamic Leviathan*.

22 Stephen P. Cohen, *The Pakistan Army* (Berkeley: University of California Press, 1984): 38–43; and Rizvi, *Military, State, and Society in Pakistan*, 170–173.

23 Qadeer, *Pakistan*, 176; Kurin, "Islamization."

24 Qadeer, *Pakistan*, 176–177; see also Kurin, "Islamization."

25 *The Herald*, a prestigious monthly news magazine, has episodically polled Pakistanis on these issues, but it has relied on heavily urban samples. Pakistan is overwhelmingly rural. Sixty-four percent of Pakistanis reside in the countryside compared to 36 percent who live in urban areas (Central Intelligence Agency, World Factbook Pakistan, 2010, https://www.cia.gov/library/publications/the-world-factbook/geos/pk.html) More problematic, the magazine has used different questions across the various years in which it has conducted such surveys. The Pew Foundation Global Attitudes Survey has regularly surveyed Pakistan since 2001 – again with an overwhelmingly urban sample – using a somewhat similar core set of questions as well as new questions. The questions are poorly worded, however, and they have yielded extremely high nonresponse rates. Other surveys are done regularly, but respondent-level data are not available. Polling by the author in collaboration with various colleagues date only to 2007. For more details, see "The Sample Truth," *Herald*, January 1997,

141; "Sixty Years, Sixty Questions," *Herald*, August 2007, 87; C. Christine Fair, Clay Ramsay, and Steve Kull, "Pakistani Public Opinion on Democracy, Islamist Militancy, and Relations with the U.S." (Washington, DC: United States Institute of Peace/Program on International Policy Attitudes, 7 January 2008). The author also collaborated with Clay Ramsay, Steven Kull, Stephen Weber, and Evan Lewis on "Pakistani Public Turns against Taliban, but Still Negative on US," 1 July 2009, http://www.worldpublicopinion.org/pipa/pdf/jul09/WPO_Pakistan_Jul09_rpt.pdf. See also C. Christine Fair, Neil Malhotra, and Jacob N. Shapiro, "Islam, Militancy, and Politics in Pakistan: Insights from a National Sample," *Terrorism and Political Violence* 22, no. 4 (September 2010): 495–521.

26 See discussions in Fair, Malhotra, and Shapiro, "Islam, Militancy, and Politics in Pakistan"; and Jacob Shapiro and C. Christine Fair, "Why Support Islamist Militancy? Evidence from Pakistan," *International Security* 34, no. 3 (Winter 2009/10): 79–118.

27 Cohen, *The Pakistan Army*, 37.

28 Rizvi, *Military, State, and Society in Pakistan*, 245.

29 Cited by Cohen, *The Pakistan Army*, 87.

30 Nasr, *Islamic Leviathan*.

31 Rizvi, *Military, State, and Society in Pakistan*, 245.

32 Cited in Nasr, *Islamic Leviathan*, 97.

33 Rizvi, *Military, State, and Society in Pakistan*, 245.

34 Ibid., 246.

35 Anne Elizabeth Mayer, "Islamization and Taxation in Pakistan," in Weiss, *Islamic Reassertion in Pakistan*, 59–78; and Nasr, *Islamic Leviathan*.

36 Rizvi, *Military, State, and Society in Pakistan*, 246; and Nasr, *Islamic Leviathan*.

37 Rizvi, *Military, State, and Society in Pakistan*, 246–247.

38 Simon Henderson, "Pakistan, Proliferation, and the Middle East," Washington Institute for Near East Policy, *Policy Watch* no. 415 (14 October 1999), http://www.washingtoninstitute.org/templateC05.php?CID=1293.

39 Stephen P. Cohen, personal communication, August 2009.

40 Cohen, *The Pakistan Army*, 95.

41 Pervaiz Iqbal Cheema, *The Armed Forces of Pakistan* (Karachi: Oxford University Press, 2002): 82.

42 Ibid.

43 S. M. Rahman, "Motivation: The Ultimate Weapon," *Dawn*, 6 September 1984, cited by Cheema, *The Armed Forces of Pakistan*, 82.

44 Cohen, *The Pakistan Army*, 38–39.

45 Cited in Rizvi, *Military, State, and Society in Pakistan*, 247.

46 Cohen, *The Pakistan Army*, 37.

47 Ibid., 96.

48 Rizvi, *Military, State, and Society in Pakistan*, 256.

49 Ibid.

50 Ibid., 247.

51 Ibid.

52 Ibid., 248.

53 See discussion in Fair and Nawaz, "The Changing Pakistan Army Officer Corps."

54 For a discussion of this at length, see C. Christine Fair, *The Counterterror Coalitions: Cooperation with Pakistan and India* (Santa Monica, CA: RAND, 2004).

55 For a detailed discussion of the various nuances in the sanctions that were applied over time to Pakistan and for a nuanced discussion of the interagency process that resulted in the lifting of these sections, see Fair, *The Counterterror Coalitions.*

56 Robert G. Wirsing, "Political Islam, Pakistan, and the Geo-Politics of Religious Identity," in ed. Yoichiro Sato *Growth and Governance in Asia* (Honolulu: Asia Pacific Center for Security Studies), 2004): 173.

57 Curiously, the Russian military was amenable to survey work about attitudes of its armed forces, and some of these results were even made public. The Friedrich Ebert Foundation, using a Munich-based polling group in cooperation with sociologists at a Russian military academy, interviewed 615 officers above the rank of major, including 60 generals and admirals. For a discussion of these data, see Benjamin S. Lambeth, "Russia's Wounded Military," *Foreign Affairs* 74, no. 2 (March–April 1995): 92–93.

58 The core team for this analysis comprises this author, Jacob Shapiro, and Claude Berrebi in consultation with Shuja Nawaz. These data were obtained under highly unusual circumstances, which are unlikely to materialize again. One of the team members, Shuja Nawaz, requested and received these data from Pakistan's General Army Headquarters to support his research for his book on the Pakistan Army, *Crossed Swords: Pakistan, Its Army, and the Wars Within* (New York: Oxford University Press, 2009). The Pakistan Army gave Nawaz this extraordinary access in part because his older brother served as Pakistan's tenth army chief of staff from 1991 until his death in 1993. See Fair and Nawaz, "The Changing Pakistan Army Officer Corps." For more detail about the econometric approach, see C. Christine Fair, Claude Berrebi, Jacob N. Shapiro, and Graeme Blair, "Drivers of Change in the Pakistan Army: What the Data Say," working draft, October 2009 (available from the author).

59 For the data to shed light on the characteristics of individual officer candidates, one would need to assume that the Pakistan Army is choosing recruits who are average for their home districts. Given the selective nature of the army, this is an untenable assumption. Moreover, it is important to note that there are significant limitations to the causal inferences that can be drawn from these data. Any link between a district's characteristics and numbers or trends in officer recruitment could be the result of the district's characteristics affecting individuals' tendencies to apply for officer slots, the army targeting its recruiting efforts based on the district's characteristics, the tendency of individuals from these districts to join the army affecting the districts' characteristics, or other external factors influencing district characteristics and army recruiting regardless of whether the two affect each other (e.g., wars).

60 For a more detailed exposition of methods, see Fair and Nawaz, "The Changing Pakistan Army Officer Corps."

61 Because the internal administrative boundaries of Pakistan changed substantially over this period, we recoded these data slightly to follow 100 districts over time that correspond to the 1995 administrative boundaries. The year 1995 was the latest year for which Geographic Information Systems district boundaries coordinates were available. This approach provides comparability across time and geographical areas.

62 The team augmented the data with other variables that could influence army recruitment, consistent with military recruitment models elsewhere. National level

variables, which vary over time but not across districts, include data on gross domestic product, foreign direct investment, and foreign aid, all obtained from the World Bank's World Development Indicators database. District-level variables that do not vary across time included district size, proportion of arable land, linguistic breakdown, and the presence of major army installations.

63 These restrictions increase the reliability of our estimates but meant having to drop observations. Because the FBS did not collect data on many of the measures of social characteristics in Federally Administered Tribal Areas (FATA) and Northern Areas, these areas were dropped altogether.

64 Note that the years employed in this study are the post-Zia years and likely were after the urbanization of the army was under way. In the early years, Pakistan Army recruitment patterns followed those of the British Army, which relied heavily on rural, landed elites for its officer corps. For a discussion of the historical recruitment patterns and changes since independence, see Fair and Nawaz, "The Changing Pakistan Army Officer Corps."

65 Remember that these refer only to places of origin, not ethnicity. We cannot discern if someone from Balochistan is ethnically Baloch or Punjabi, for example.

66 Fair and Nawaz, "The Changing Pakistan Army Officer Corps."

67 Indeed, the author currently has a survey in the field with Jacob Shapiro and Neil Malhotra that will be an important first step in trying to discern differences in attitudes between military and nonmilitary families toward an array of militant groups and other issues of relevance to this query.

68 The team found that urban areas are on average wealthier.

69 We found a mixed relationship between the economy and officer production. Recruiting likely increases with long-term economic performance because this provides resources for increased recruitment. Overall, recruits are more likely to originate from wealthier areas, but at the same time, they are more likely to come at periods when the districts' economic and labor market conditions are tight. This does not mean that the army is recruiting the unemployed. Rather, when the local labor market worsens, persons of all skill levels become available and more of them pass the recruiting criteria.

70 The author found that residents in the KPK were less likely than those in the other three provinces to support Islamist militants. This may be because the KPK has borne the brunt of the violence. C. Christine Fair, "Islamist Militancy in Pakistan: A View from the Provinces," *WorldPublicOpinion.org*, 24 July 2009, http://www.worldpublicopinion.org/pipa/articles/brasiapacificra/629.php?lb=bras&pnt=629&nid=&id=. Recent work found similar results that were more robust. They employed the 6,000- person survey conducted by Fair, Malhotra, and Shapiro in 2009, which relied on an endorsement experiment to determine levels of militant support. Controlling for the level of violence using WITS data, they found that "for each group, there exists a negative correlation between the total violence in the area and the average level of support." See Will Bullock, Kosuke Imai, and Jacob Shapiro, "Measuring Political Support and Issue Ownership Using Endorsement Experiments, with Application to Militant Groups in Pakistan," working paper, 16 June 2010, http://www.princeton.edu/~jns/papers/BIS_2010_Support.pdf.

71 A pediatrician from South Waziristan explained to the author that parents in the tribal areas do not circumcise their boys for fear that something could go wrong.

The lack of hospitals could mean that medical treatment would not be available. Additionally, the Mehsud tribe does not circumcise boys at all. Thus these men will typically be circumcised as adults and only if they enter government service. Author interview with a South Waziristan pediatrician in Peshawar in July 2010.

72 For an extensive discussion of the change of public opinion toward the war, see C. Christine Fair, "Pakistan's Own War on Terror: What the Pakistani Public Thinks," *Journal of International Affairs* 63, no. 1 (Fall/Winter 2009): 39–55.

73 Kamal Siddiqi, "India Funding Taliban Fighters, Says Pakistan Minister," *Hindustan Times*, 26 October 2009, http://www.hindustantimes.com/India-funding-Taliban-fighters-Pak/Article1-469345.aspx.

5

Israel

Stuart A. Cohen

The defining characteristic of the modern state of Israel is that it is the only country in the world in which the majority of citizens are Jews. Indeed, the Law of Return passed by the Knesset (Israel's parliament) in July 1950 – just two years after the establishment of the state – explicitly granted all Jews, as well as persons of Jewish ancestry, permission to immigrate to Israel and apply for Israeli citizenship. Over the years, more than two million persons have availed themselves of this opportunity. As a consequence, notwithstanding a far higher birthrate among the country's Arab minority, Jews in 2010 still constituted more than 75 percent of Israel's total population (as opposed to almost 90 percent in 1950).[1] Because all Muslim Arabs are automatically granted exemptions from conscription, the discrepancy in the composition of the Israel Defense Forces (IDF) is even greater. Jews make up more than 97 percent of the men and women who perform military service in Israel. Recruitment among other population segments (Bedouin, Druze, and Christians of varying denominations), although sociologically interesting, is statistically irrelevant. To all intents and purposes, the IDF is an army of Jews.

The IDF is also a "Jewish" army, in the sense that traditional Jewish themes and motifs form integral parts of its texture. Only in part is that characteristic demonstrated by the fact that all IDF kitchens conform to traditional Jewish dietary requirements, that the Sabbath and Jewish holy days shape military sched-ules with respect to training and vacations, and that all Jewish military burials are performed in accordance with traditional religious practice. Equally indic-ative is the extent to which each other major rite of passage in the Israeli military experience is also deliberately suffused with ceremonies and pageants designed to arouse profound Jewish connotations. For instance, at his or her induction, each new recruit receives a copy of the Old Testament, which reli-gious conscripts necessarily consider to contain sacred scriptures, and which nonbelievers have been taught at school to regard as the formative text of the

Jewish and Hebrew literary corpus. Similarly evocative are the venues selected for the staging of parades at the conclusion of courses of instruction passing-out parades. On completion of basic training, for instance, each new cohort of paratroops has by tradition been formally enrolled during the course of a torchlight ceremony held at the Western Wall in Jerusalem. Since 2010, the same venue has also been used by the Golani infantry brigade. The location is well chosen. Apart from being located at the heart of the Old City, where IDF troops covered themselves in glory during the 1967 Six-Day War, the wall is also the sole remaining relic of the second temple destroyed in the year 70 CE, and hence a site of religious pilgrimage.

It is impossible to exaggerate the uniqueness of such phenomena, or indeed to ignore the revolution in Jewish history that they signify. True, the earliest traditions of the Jewish people were reportedly forged against a background of almost incessant military violence. As depicted in the Bible, the children of Israel (and their God, the Lord of Hosts) seem almost incessantly to have lived by the sword. So, too, did the inhabitants of the "second" Jewish commonwealth, established by the exiles the Persian emperor Cyrus permitted to return to Zion in 516 BCE. Martial values and themes pervade such postbiblical and eschatological texts as the books of Maccabees, Jubilees, and Judith as well as the Dead Sea Scrolls. Prominent among the latter is a text menacingly entitled "The War of the Sons of Light against the Sons of Darkness." Consisting of what amounts to a plan of campaign for the armies of the Messiah, this scroll graphically demonstrates the extent to which, by the time of the birth of Jesus, an aura of militarism had come to pervade Jewish religious perceptions, even among sectarians who inhabited the wastes bordering the Dead Sea.

Then, suddenly, the entire tenor of Jewish political behavior and writings underwent a shift of seismic proportions. Always fragile, the Jewish polity was pummelled into defeat by Rome in 70 CE. Survivors of that disaster were treated even more savagely during and after the Bar Kochba rebellion that broke out some six decades later. With the vestiges of the Jewish people now exiled and shorn of sovereignty, their links with their military past seemed to have been irrevocably broken. Henceforth, Jewry's default response to persecution was to be flight and martyrdom, not resistance or revolt. To all intents and purposes, the Jews became a noncombative people, exhibiting what has been termed "an aversion to bloodshed."[2]

Deviations from this norm were sporadic. One can identify a handful of Jews who fought under either the Cross or the Crescent in the great confrontations between Christians and Moors in medieval Spain, as well as one individual, Ismail ibn Nagrela (993–1055/6), vizier to the rulers of Grenada (and hence named in Jewish sources Shemuel ha-Nagid, or Samuel the Prince), who quite apart from being a remarkably talented Hebrew poet and scholar also had the unique distinction of commanding a Muslim army. In the second quarter of the nineteenth century, many more Jews of much humbler status, termed "cantonists," were forcibly conscripted into the ranks of the Imperial Russian Army while still young children, and were condemned to perform military service on behalf of the czar for periods lasting as long as twenty-five years. In yet a third category, Jews eager to become fully accepted citizens in their countries of residence voluntarily enlisted in the emerging national armies of the Netherlands (as early as the seventeenth century); of the United States (in the eighteenth century); in ever-increasing numbers, of the Austro-Hungarian Empire, Britain, France, Germany, and Italy prior to and during World War I; and in those of the Western Allies and of the Soviet Union during World War II. Nevertheless, all such instances, although significant, remained exceptional. For the vast majority of both European and Oriental Jewries, soldiering remained off limits throughout the medieval and premodern periods, and even after Emancipation, continued to be a marginal occupation. The proportion of Jews who earned their livelihood by serving in the armed forces persistently lagged far behind that of the Gentile average, and never made up more than a fraction of the total Jewish population.[3]

Overwhelmingly, traditional Jewish thought underscored the nonbelligerency thus prevalent in traditional Jewish practice. By the third century CE, at the latest, Jewish thinkers had begun to expunge virtually all memory of warfare from the national consciousness. Most notably, the Bible itself was subjected to a process of reinterpretation, whereby its tales of martial valor and heroism were deliberately divested of their plain meanings. Thanks to the alchemy of rabbinic exegesis, King David, for instance, was transformed from a warrior into a scholar. Likewise, military themes were airbrushed out of the traditions that celebrated the victorious rebellion against Seleucian rule in the Second Temple period. Chanukah, the "festival of lights" that commemorates the triumph, was instead regarded as a quintessential expression of the non-combative theme adumbrated in Zechariah 4:6: "Not by might nor by power, but by My spirit says the Lord of hosts." Making a virtue out of necessity, rabbis developed an approach to the historical process that regarded a Jewish resort to arms as sinful, especially if designed to regain the Holy Land. After all, exile had been a divine punishment for Israel's sins. Redemption, therefore, had to await God's pleasure, which would be signified by the advent of an otherworldly Messiah. Any attempt to "hasten the end" under the aegis of armies composed of mere mortals was ipso facto sinful and doomed to failure.[4]

There are indications that the handful of Jewish scholars who somehow rose to positions of influence in Diaspora lands could not avoid devoting some thought to what would today be termed "grand strategy." As Efraim Inbar discovered, scattered references indicate that those with personal experience of high politics in fact readily acknowledged warfare's utility as a tool of statesmanship in an inherently anarchical world.[5] Maimonides (1135–1204), the most authoritative of all Jewish codifiers, even devoted several chapters of his magisterial corpus of Jewish laws to summarizing whatever rulings he could glean from the biblical and Talmudic rulings relevant to the initiation and conduct of armed conflict (*Mishneh Torah*, or "Laws of Kings and Their Wars," chapters 5–8). Significantly, however, not even such titanic instances set a precedent. Not one of the numerous commentaries on Maimonides's code developed his martial themes. They were likewise almost entirely ignored in the "responsa literature," the vast storehouse of transcontinental correspondence between rabbis that ever since the early Middle Ages has constituted a principal medium of instruction on every imaginable aspect of Jewish law. The only departures from that convention – almost all of which begin to appear only in late eighteenth-century Europe – merely prove two rules. First, that enlistment was generally regarded as an anathema, and second, that where issues relating to Jewish military activity were concerned, political discretion seemed to preclude even speculative analysis. As one particularly influential rabbi put it, "Regarding this matter, silence is better than our speech."[6]

Adherents of political Zionism had begun to deviate from these attitudes as early as the 1920s.[7] Indeed, physical defense organizations were essential ingredients of their enterprise, with paramilitary "underground" units soon becoming no less characteristic of the Yishuv – the prestate Jewish society under construction in mandatory Palestine – than were such other innovations as the collective agricultural settlements (kibbutz and moshav) and labor unions (*histadrut*). Even so, the establishment of the IDF in 1948 marked a hiatus of momentous proportions. All of the prestate militias had been voluntary organizations in which Jews could, if they wished, not serve (and in fact most of the Yishuv chose not to do so, even when tensions between Jews and Arabs and between Jews and the British mandatory authorities were at their highest).[8] By contrast, enlistment in the IDF was, from the first, compulsory. The Service Defense Law passed in 1949 (which remains on the statute books today) imposes conscription on all citizens, male and female, at the age of eighteen, and requires them to be available for summonses to reserve duty once their conscript terms have ended.

Religiously based responses to that situation fall into four broad camps. One consists of avowedly "secular" Jewish citizens, who are estimated to constitute between 10 and 15 percent of the Israeli Jewish population.[9] As far as they are concerned, conscription is a nothing more than a civic obligation. It possesses no religious connotation, positive or negative, and hence generates no religious sentiments, positive or negative. For the most part, avowed secularists regard soldiering as just one more attribute of the "new Jew" whom Zionism has fashioned by deliberately rebelling against traditional stereotypes.

A second camp is made up of ultra-Orthodox (Haredi) Israeli citizens, a mélange of varying approaches to the state and its institutions that together constitute 8 to 10 percent of the population. In this sector, attitudes are far more ambivalent. Even among Haredim who do not entirely affirm traditional Judaism's antimilitarism (a minority do), most emphatically adhere to the priority that tradition has accorded to the study of the sacred texts. Conscription, because it necessarily intrudes on the observance of the latter obligation, is therefore to be avoided. This is especially true of women, whose modesty would be irrevocably sullied by military service of any sort.

A third attitude is expressed by religious Zionists (12 to 15 percent). Although claiming to follow the precepts of traditional Judaism, they nevertheless reject the secondary status accorded to military service in Haredi thought. As far as they are concerned, the establishment of the State of Israel constitutes a definitive sign of the Almighty's grace. Hence, service in a framework designed to defend God's handiwork is ipso facto a religious obligation second to none. All that has to be ensured is that the IDF will create the conditions that will enable Orthodox Jews to perform their service without compromising their adherence to the everyday practices and rituals (e.g., dietary laws and prayer) that are integral to traditional Jewish identity.

Traditionalists, those 50 to 55 percent of Israeli Jews who in varying degrees retain an attachment to traditional customs and rituals, even though they do not observe them with traditional rigidity, are also concerned about the retention of an ambience that allows for the observance of dietary laws and prayer obligations. They, too, expect the IDF to display characteristics that are identifiably "Jewish" and, even more, to operate in accordance with the mores that owe their origin to religious instruction.

How these four approaches to military service might be reconciled (indeed, whether it is at all possible for them to be reconciled) has always been a matter of acute concern, as much to Israel's political and military leadership as to the country's Jewish religious establishment. David Ben-Gurion, Israel's first prime minister and defense minister (he held both offices with only minor intermissions from 1948 until 1962), and the man who did more than any other to create the IDF and determine its ethos, considered that there was only one way to harmonize the various approaches outlined earlier. Israel's military had to be constituted as a "people's army," in which military service would be not just compulsory for all citizens but also an arena in which they could all be integrated into a unified citizenry.[10]

As far as the relationship between Judaism and military service was concerned, this credo carried three practical connotations. The first was essentially negative. Religious and secular Jewish citizens could not claim to possess different sets of national obligations. In a country that defined itself as "the state of the Jews," the duty of military service was to be equally incumbent on both communities. Second, the aspiration that conscription would serve an integrative purpose also precluded religious Jewish troops from serving in segregated military formations. Hence, Ben-Gurion brusquely rejected early suggestions that the IDF allow religious personnel to serve in homogeneous fighting formations.[11] Third, however, and on similar grounds of equity, Ben-Gurion appreciated that the military framework also had to accommodate itself to particular religious needs. Specifically, it had to be structured in ways that would alienate neither religiously observant Jews nor traditionalists – still less require them to contravene unnecessarily the dictates of traditional Jewish law.

To a large extent, the internal history of the IDF during the past six decades can be read as an attempt to accommodate that tripartite cluster of considerations. Necessarily, the story is not one of uninterrupted continuity. Probably the only factor that has remained almost static is the Israeli public's persistent commitment to the maintenance of the IDF as a people's army, in which salaried professionals are vastly outnumbered by conscripts and reservists. Even so, the composition, structure, and mores of the force have over time undergone radical changes, all of which are also reflected in its interactions with religious personnel and with religious behavior. The purpose of the discussion that follows is to trace those changes and to analyze their possible implications.

The chapter begins with a brief sketch of the shifts that have taken place in the participation and nonparticipation of religiously observant citizens in the IDF. Thereafter, it analyzes, in turn, the institutional adaptations made by the military organization in order to accommodate religiously observant troops and the various channels of communication between soldiers and rabbis that facilitate the integration of Orthodox personnel into the ranks. Finally, the chapter addresses the possible consequences of those developments, and the tensions (some real, others imagined) to which they are thought to give rise.

The Changing Demographics of Religion in the IDF

Although the IDF Manpower Branch does occasionally release random reports on the size and composition of the force, it has persistently refused to comment on the proportions of Jewish conscript servicepeople who can be categorized as religious and secular. Necessarily, therefore, assessments in this area are tentative and largely derived from other sources. Some figures are provided by the Ministry of Education, which publicizes the annual numbers of young men and women who graduate from "national religious" and "national" high schools. More morbid and less comprehensive is the information that can be gleaned from the memorial biographies published in the national media whenever a soldier falls in battle or is otherwise killed. And then, of course, there is the simpler tool of personal observation, which, although necessarily impressionistic, is especially useful in this case thanks to the distinctiveness and conspicuity of the dress codes habitually observed by religious men (especially the skullcap) and women (skirts rather than slacks).

Superficially, these sources tell a tale of remarkable continuity. They indicate that, notwithstanding the fluctuations in Israeli demographics, as far as males are concerned, the proportion of religious to nonreligious conscripts in the overall IDF complement has remained more or less constant since the 1950s, hovering between 14 and 18 percent. In other words, the contradictory effects produced by changing birthrates (on average, religious couples have more children than do secular couples) and by the influx into the IDF of successive waves of immigrants (most of whom, since the 1960s, have been secular) have tended to cancel each other out. At the end of 2011, and in keeping with overall population trends, "secular" troops were still estimated to outnumber religious troops by roughly four to one.[12]

Closer inspection, however, reveals that the impression of consistency is deceptive. First, this is because the focus on the religious/secular ratio among young males who do enlist masks the truly massive changes in the percentages of those who do not. In the secular segment, the changes have been marginal. Certainly, "draft avoidance" – a portmanteaux term that covers phenomena as different as conscientious objection, pleas of "psychological unsuitability," and claims of "physical incapacity" – became more common among secular high school graduates during and after the 1990s than had been the case in earlier decades. Even so, it remained a decidedly minority phenomenon. Whereas in the 1980s and 1990s all such categories combined amounted to 4 percent of the total number of nondraftees (i.e., roughly 1 percent of the total of young males summonsed to duty), in 2009 – the last year for which official statistics are available – the figures were still no more than 4 percent and 1.5 percent, respectively.[13]

By contrast, the same period had witnessed nothing less than an explosion in the numbers of ultra-Orthodox/Haredi males, to whom the minister of defense grants deferments from military service (which, because they are indeterminate, effectively amounted to discharges) on the grounds that the study of the Torah is their profession. When originally sanctioned by Ben-Gurion in 1948, this concession to Haredi priorities was considered to be only a minor infringement of the rule of universal conscription.[14] After all, it was limited to just 400 male students. But, in a curve that parallels the growing power and cohesion of political parties representing Haredi interests – a phenomenon that Ben-Gurion never once envisaged – the numbers have grown exponentially. The sum total of Haredi deferments rose to 8,257 in 1977, the year that Haredi parties first joined a government coalition, and jumped to 16,000 in 1985, to 30,000 in 1999, and to more than 50,000 by 2010. At the end of the first decade of the millennium, persons in this category accounted for more than half the total number of Jewish nondraftees, equivalent to some 14 percent of the overall potential recruitment pool.[15] Extrapolations from junior high and high school registration statistics show that the figure could reach 25 percent by 2020.[16]

Several attempts have been made to reverse this trend. For instance, in 1999, the IDF agreed that Haredi males who wished to retain their traditional lifestyles and yet not apply for draft exemptions (principally because they lacked the intellectual and psychological prerequisites for devotion to a life of uninterrupted scholarship) would be allowed to enlist in their own segregated unit. In practice, this means that soldiers in Battalion 97, otherwise designated Netzach Yehudah (Eternal Judah) or, more popularly, the Nachal Haredi, serve under conditions that clearly contradict the integrative guidelines laid down by Ben-Gurion and that are indeed unknown anywhere else in the IDF. These soldiers are sequestered from females, allowed regular contact with Haredi religious mentors, supplied with food that meets the most stringent standards of conformity with Orthodox Jewish dietary laws, and permitted to retain elements of their own dress code.[17] A second initiative has been the establishment of a service track known as Shachar (an acronym for *sherut charedim*, or Haredi service, which also translates as "dawn"). This service track assures more mature Haredi men (generally aged twenty-four to twenty-seven) that they will be given military assignments that also provide them with a technical training, which, on discharge, they can put to use in the civilian market. Yet a third option, contained in legislation passed by the Knesset in 2002 (the Tal Law) and renewed in a slightly revised form in 2011, is for Haredim to enlist as individuals in regular units at the age of twenty-four for drastically abbreviated terms of service.

Optimists take considerable heart from reports indicating a growing willingness among Haredi young men to take advantage of the offers thus presented. According to figures compiled on the basis of reports submitted in 2010 to the Knesset by the commanding officer of the IDF Personnel Branch, the number of persons enlisting in the Nachal Haredi, for instance, climbed from 90 per annum in the period 2000–2006 to 200 in 2007, 300 in 2008, and 360 in 2009. The popularity of Shachar has risen even more sharply. This service model, which began as the personal brainchild of the commander of the Israel Air Force in 2007, when it catered to just thirty conscripts who enlisted as technicians, has since been adopted by several other branches, including intelligence, computer services, and the navy. As a result, enlistment in Shachar jumped to 300 in 2008 and to 700 in 2009.[18]

Enthusiasts in the IDF are confident that these figures can double during the next decade. But even if that projection proves true, and even if all the current statistics are correct (a matter very much complicated by difficulties in determining who is a "true" Haredi and who is a fellow traveler), birthrates will ensure that the overall demographics of the IDF will become yet more lopsided than they already are. Even as matters stand, the rate of Haredi nonenlistment makes a mockery of the entire notion of equitable burden sharing inherent in conscription – so much so that in February 2012 Israel's Supreme Court declared that it would no longer tolerate the inequalities embedded in the Tal Law. By a majority of nine to six, the judges gave the government less than a year to come up with alternative provisions designed to cause Haredi service to be both mandatory and more widespread, either in the IDF or in some other form of public service. At time of writing (December 2012), this requirement had still not been met.

A gender breakdown of the enlistment figures likewise undermines the impression of continuity in service patters over the past sixty years. Overall, it is true that today – as in the past – by far the majority of females drafted into the IDF come from secular backgrounds. Nevertheless, the proportions are changing. Until the late 1990s, 90 to 95 percent of the annual total of Jewish female graduates from national-religious high schools, similar to their Haredi counterparts, performed no military service whatsoever. Instead, and often under instruction from their rabbinic mentors (who on this point very much agreed with Haredi religious authorities), women from this sector claimed – and were granted – exemption from the draft on the grounds that military duty would conflict with their religious lifestyles. As an alternative, a high percentage performed a year or two of voluntary civic service, an example that few Haredi women followed.

In recent years, however, two new trends have become apparent. For one thing, increasing numbers of female graduates of national (i.e., secular) high schools are claiming, and receiving, exemptions from service on "incompatibility" grounds (IDF sources report that the figure is as high as 40 percent). On the other hand, and far more remarkably, despite the persistence of mainstream Orthodox rabbinic objections to female conscription, by 2010 between a quarter and a third of female graduates of national-religious high schools were enlisting in the IDF in some capacity.[19]

In the male segment, too, the figures require closer scrutiny. What the bare statistics report is that an impressively high proportion – 85 percent – of graduates of national as well as national-religious high schools continue to answer the call to duty.[20] In other words, both segments have proved remarkably immune to the mood of postmodernism/postmaterialism/post-Zionism thought to be sweeping the country when, in April 1997, the IDF released a panic-stricken warning on a dip in "motivation to service."

What the reports on the recovery of the conscription rates do not tell us, however, is in which capacities religious and secular troops tend to serve. The answer to that question can only be obtained through observation but nevertheless seems to be unequivocal. Over the past quarter of a century, a shift of truly massive proportions has taken place in the sociological architecture of the IDF. Prior to the 1980s, its elite combat units were for the most part operated – and, even more so, commanded – by graduates of the secular (principally Ashkenazi) school system. Moreover, sons of (secular) kibbutzim figured especially prominently – and in vastly disproportionate numbers – in the ranks of junior officers in the ground forces; in training courses for fighter pilots, parachutists, and commando units; and in the rosters of persons killed in action while "commanding from the front" during battle.[21] This is no longer the case. "Secular" troops from Ashkenazi backgrounds now seem to be underrepresented in IDF combat units. Instead, and in increasing numbers, they have gravitated toward high-technology and white-collar logistical and combat support units, which have of late enormously expanded in size and prominence thanks to the IDF's growing (over?)-reliance on state-of-the-art C4I systems.

The gaps thus created in frontline ranks have been filled by groups that were once considered peripheral components of the IDF's complement – population segments whose contribution to Israel's battlefield victories had long been considered subsidiary: Oriental (Mizrachi) Jews, Druze soldiers, new immigrants (both from the former Soviet Union and from Ethiopia), and – above all – graduates (Ashkenazi and Mizrachi alike) of the national-religious educational system.[22] The knitted skullcap (*kippah serugah*), which has become the latter group's most recognizable hallmark, is especially conspicuous at graduation parades of junior officers in infantry brigades where a rough head count indicates that they may now constitute as much as half of the total (i.e., three times their demographic proportion). Their presence in the most senior echelons of the IDF, although not as dominant, is nevertheless obtrusive. The promotion of religiously observant officers to the General Staff, unheard of before 1998, now raises few eyebrows. One (Maj. Gen. Yair Naveh) was appointed deputy chief of staff in 2010.

Institutional Innovations

Adopting various tools of analysis, observers – some less charitably than others – have attributed the phenomena described above to a wide selection of causes: ideological motivations, political ambitions, and socioeconomic interests.[23] Whichever the purpose identified, the role played by institutions in facilitating its attainment seems to have been vital. The exponential growth in the numbers of Haredi draft deferments, for instance, cannot be understood without reference to the establishment and expansion of the massive Talmudic seminaries that have facilitated the emergence of "a society of scholars" in that community.[24] Likewise, the virtual disappearance of the kibbutznik from the ranks of combat units must be analyzed within the context of the way in which most of the other frameworks traditionally associated with the ethos of the kibbutz have similarly been dismantled in recent years. By the same token, institutions – and the way in which they have acted as agencies for the transmission of new attitudes toward military duty – also provide keys for an understanding of the shifts that have taken place in the service patterns of national religious youth.

I begin my survey of the relevant institutions with the military chaplaincy (i.e., the IDF rabbinate), a sequence principally justified by virtue of the seniority and size of this framework. Indeed, the chaplaincy is almost as old as the IDF (it was established in 1949) and has over the course of time grown from being just a skeleton body, whose tasks were limited to advising the chief of staff on religious affairs, to becoming a full-blown military formation. It now possesses a distinctive unit crest (the two stone tablets of the Ten Commandments upheld by a sword); a tradition of battlefield valor (supplied by the exemplary service performed under fire by those of its troops whose task it is to identify fatal casualties and bring them to burial); and an extended hierarchy, which begins with rabbis and extends down to rabbis, religious affairs officers (one of whom has since 2005 always been a female), and religious affairs coordinators. Moreover, even though it does not grant rabbinic ordination, which is the exclusive prerogative of the civilian chief rabbinate, the IDF chaplaincy does require all candidates for office within its framework to undertake distinctive programs in this field before assuming their duties.[25]

From its inception, the IDF chaplaincy was expected to perform two different roles. One was to communicate the rudiments of Jewish values and teachings to the complement as a whole – secular as well as religious – and thereby serve as a mechanism for troop cohesion and integration. At the same time, however, the IDF chaplaincy was expected to serve the specific interests of the minority of troops who desire to be religiously observant. These did not require "outreach" programs that focused on basic courses of instruction in Jewish values and customs. Rather, what Orthodox soldiers needed was proof that enlistment would not prevent them from maintaining basic standards of observance. Hence, the chaplaincy had to ensure that kitchens on every military installation would observe Jewish dietary laws, and that every military base would contain the facilities (synagogues, prayer books, etc.) that observant soldiers require on a regular basis. Absent assurances to that effect, there was always the danger that they might resist the entire notion of a people's army – either by downing arms (as did two military cooks as early as September 1948, when ordered to cook a meal on the Sabbath)[26] or by renewing demands for the establishment of segregated religious units.

During its formative period, the IDF chaplaincy focused most of its attention on the second of those priorities. Primarily, that choice was made by Rabbi Shlomo Goren, the first and most influential of all IDF chief rabbis, who held the office from 1949 until 1971. Although certainly not insensitive to the needs of the nonobservant majority, Goren considered it his duty to devote most of the limited resources at his disposal to satisfying the interests of the observant minority and ensuring that religious troops could serve, as equals, in as wide a range of IDF units as possible. Two of Goren's most recent successors, Rabbi Yisrael Weiss (IDF chief rabbi from 2003 to 2006) and Rabbi Avichai Rontzki (IDF chief rabbi from 2007 to 2010), by contrast, sought to pursue a more evenhanded approach. Goren's battles, they maintained, had in fact been won. What was now required was a program of instruction and leadership that would ensure that the rabbinate also addressed the needs of traditionalists, that large bloc of the complement who required the provision not just of physical facilities for religious observance but, more insistently, spiritual guidance and comfort before, during, and after battle. Weiss's response was to establish in 2004 a Combat Values Branch (Anaf Erkhei Torat Ha-Lekhimah), largely staffed by charismatic lecturers (in 2006 it was more modestly redesignated the Jewish Awareness Department or Ha-Makhlakah le-Toda'ah Yehudit). With even greater success, Rontzki recruited a new breed of military chaplains, searching for rabbis who were also graduates of combat units, and hence capable of empathizing directly with the troops in the field – an attribute emphasized by the fact that IDF rabbis do not observe the Geneva Convention's rules that prohibit military chaplains from bearing arms. The current IDF chief rabbi (Gen. Rafi Peretz, a qualified combat pilot), although vigorously denying charges of "missionary" activity, has nevertheless made it clear that he, too, intends to maintain "a dialogue" with all shades of religious opinion in the ranks.[27]

One of the circumstances that has allowed the IDF rabbinate in recent years to shift so much of its attention to traditionalists and even secularists within the complement is that soldiers who come from religiously observant backgrounds can now have recourse to alternative frameworks. Especially influential in this respect are two sets of educational institutions: "arrangement" academies of Jewish study (Yeshivot Hesder) and "preconscription Torah colleges" (mekhinot ha-kedam tzeva'iyot ha-toraniyot), both of which benefit from IDF sanction and cooperation. Although sharing some characteristics, they deserve to be discussed separately.

When originally muted in 1964, the Hesder system was depicted as a way of satisfying the need felt by male graduates of national-religious high schools to fulfill two apparently irreconcilable commandments: to study the Torah and to perform military duty.[28] Convinced that the circle could not possibly be squared, Haredim, as noted earlier, had overwhelmingly chosen to focus entirely on Torah study and to apply for deferments from military duty. Hesder promised to offer a happy medium. Under this arrangement, recruits from Orthodox backgrounds are allowed to perform conscript duty for abbreviated terms (amounting to eighteen to twenty months rather than the statutory three years), spread over a five-year span during which short bursts of military training are interspersed with longer periods of study in the academy.

What began as an experiment, limited to just one academy with a total enrollment of twenty students, over time mushroomed into a much larger program. Nine such establishments were founded between 1967 and 1979, three more in the 1980s, and an additional twenty-two since 1990. Official government Web sites now list forty Yeshivot Hesder, located across the length and breadth of the land, with an annual intake of some 1,300 students (about 20 percent of the total number of national-religious high school graduates).[29] During the past decade, a similar program has been instituted for women, who are now able to choose between three academies (termed Midrashot) of their own.[30]

Even more precipitous has been the growth of the preconscription (Mekhinah) program. The program requires graduates of national-religious high schools to serve full three-year conscript terms as regular soldiers but permits them to postpone their enlistment for a calendar year – during which time they undergo an intensive course of training in both physical fitness and Jewish values in the Mekhinah of their choice. Although the Mekhinah was a much later initiative than the Hesder (the first Mekhinah did not open its doors until 1988, with just a dozen students), the two programs soon became evenly matched. By the year 2000, there already existed fifteen Mekhinot. Since then, another dozen have been added (as have twelve more that cater to secular or mixed religious-secular youth).[31] Annual enrollment in the religious Mekhinot now tops 1,800 males per year, which amounts to almost a third of the annual sum total of male graduates of the national-religious high school system. What is more, here, too, changes in the service preferences of women graduates of national-religious high schools are beginning to have an effect. The year 2006 saw the foundation of the first Mekhinah for religious women who planned to enlist in the IDF.

Even though most male graduates of national-religious high schools still enlist individually, and hence not through either the Hesder or Mekhinah tracks, it would be difficult to exaggerate the impact the latter have exerted on service patterns in this segment of the population. Hesder conscripts, who were originally assigned to units in largely homogeneous groups, have traditionally been conspicuous components of the IDF armored corps and of its four principal infantry brigades. In each case, their presence has acted as a magnet for other religious soldiers, whose willingness to volunteer for those formations has been augmented by the knowledge that they will be serving in the company of a large number of persons who come from a similar background and who share similar interests and lifestyles.

Mekhinah graduates, whose timetable does not require them to enlist in groups, fulfill a different function. They act as individual role models, whose record of excellence as new recruits, noncommissioned officers, and junior officers sets standards that their brothers-in-arms – especially those who likewise come from religious backgrounds – strive to emulate. The bar is very high indeed. Religious Mekhinot claim that almost 70 percent of their graduates volunteer for service in combat units (twice the national average) and that 45 percent (nine times the national average) agree to attend the IDF junior officers' course – a commitment that requires them to reenlist for an extra year of (salaried) duty. The record of Bnei David, the first Mekhinah and still the flagship institution of this framework, is especially remarkable. On its twentieth anniversary (celebrated in 2008), its secretariat reported that of its first 1,000 graduates, 41 had served as pilots, 70 in reconnaissance squads, 400 in other elite field units, and 200 in the armor or artillery corps. Fully 50 percent of all graduates had become IDF junior officers.

Cultural Adaptations

In addition to necessitating an expansion of the wide range of physical facilities to which reference has already been made, the rise in the proportion of religiously observant soldiers and officers has also created a demand for the provision of more personal forms of religious instruction and advice. Men and women in uniform who are committed to the maintenance of the intricate web of rituals and ordinances that are embedded in Orthodox Jewish behavior are required to know whether they are expected to continue to observe traditional precepts even in a military context – and if so, how. To take just a simple example: undoubtedly, the imperative of self-defense overrides the prohibitions otherwise incumbent on Orthodox Jews against undertaking any sort of labor on the Sabbath (injunctions that extend even to such seemingly nonlaborious tasks as writing and activating electrically operated machinery). But does the same general dispensation apply when there exists no immediate danger to life, and they are simply required to stand guard or ensure that essential services are kept working efficiently? An affirmative answer (which is invariably the response) does not put the matter to rest. Does it mean that Orthodox Jewish soldiers on duty are to behave as though the Sabbath has simply been suspended? Most authorities require them to acknowledge the Sabbath by ensuring that they make some changes to their normal work habits when performing their duties. But if so, what form should they take?

Orthodox Jews drafted into the armies of the central European powers had begun to ask questions of that nature as early as the late nineteenth century. With the imposition of the draft and its extension to the United States during World Wars I and II, the inquiries became even more numerous. (In 1944, for instance, the Committee on Jewish Law appointed by the Rabbinical Assembly of the Conservative Jewish movement in the United States reported, "By far the most important questions we had to deal with pertained to the religious dilemma of the large numbers of recruits in the training camps of the United States Army.")[32] But once the IDF was established, new heights were bound to be scaled. Military service was no longer an occasional intrusion into the normal Jewish agenda. In Israel, it had become a regular and pervasive feature of national life. How Orthodox Jews were to harmonize their national and religious obligations thus required urgent and detailed attention.

Quick to appreciate the magnitude of that challenge, Rabbi Shlomo Goren here, too, exhibited pioneering initiative. Indeed, he devoted much of his time as IDF chief chaplain to crafting an integrated and comprehensive accommodation between traditional behavior and army life. To that end, he produced a torrent of learned articles, rabbinic decrees, and erudite written replies to individual inquiries addressed to him by individual service members. Many of these he later collated in his magnum opus, entitled *Meishiv Milchamah* (literally, "responding to war"), three plump volumes of "*responsa* relating to the army, war and security" that summarize a lifetime of deep personal involvement in military matters both large and small. Thus quite apart from extended discussions on Sabbath observance and dietary restrictions, his work also contains lengthy analyses on such matters as forms of prayer when on service, relationships with comrades in arms, and – not least – the basics of combat morality. In each of these areas, and virtually single-handedly, Goren created a literary corpus on topics of Jewish religious law that for more than 2,000 years had remained almost entirely untouched.[33]

As Goren would have been the first to admit, considerable though his contribution thus was to establishing Jewish law in a military context, it fell far short of being definitive. The dynamics of change in Israeli military practices, together with incessant technological innovations, ensured that virtually each new cohort of religious men and women in service would seek guidance in areas that even Goren had left untouched. Hence, although his writings continue to constitute a base for all discussions of the interface between religion and military service in Israel, in many respects they have been overtaken by more recent publications written by authors who have blazed their own paths.

For one thing, later authors have widened the span of subjects in which they seek to reconcile the practicalities of modern military life with the stringent dictates of traditional Jewish practice. In addition to continuing to address topics that were central to Goren's enterprise (e.g., Sabbath observance, dietary restrictions, forms of prayer), they discuss newer topics that changing circumstances have thrust to the forefront of troop attention. Among the most significant are gender relationships (a subject made increasingly prominent by the IDF's efforts to integrate women into a wider spectrum of military professions), the sanction required for the use of military force, and – increasingly since the outbreak of the second Palestinian intifada (uprising) in the year 2000 – the morality of military action in urban areas containing dense concentrations of civilian inhabitants.[34]

Equally noteworthy are the differences in background and affiliation that distinguish Goren's successors from their acknowledged mentor. Goren originally composed most of his writings on the religion-military interface while he was still in uniform and in command of the IDF rabbinate, a large military bureaucracy with institution-wide responsibilities. Many of the younger and more recent contributors to the field have followed very different career paths. Few are graduates of the IDF rabbinate; most have served in combat formations, sometimes at fairly senior rank, and then gone on to become communal rabbis or, more commonly, principals or senior teachers, or both, at one of the several dozen Yeshivot Hesder and *mechinot kedam tzeva'iyot toraniyot* that, as already noted, have become so popular. They participate in the contemporary rabbinic discourse on military-related matters, therefore not as members of the military framework but rather as educationalists intimately acquainted with the spiritual needs and concerns of what has become a significant proportion of Israel's combat complement.

Finally, and inevitably, there are differences in the means of communication used by the younger generation of rabbinic authors.[35] Goren had lived by his pen, writing out his papers in longhand and then sending them off for publication in either the journal published by the IDF chaplaincy, *Machanayim* (literally, "camps"; see Genesis 32:3), or in other collections of articles. Necessarily, there had therefore existed a lengthy time lag between authorship and publication. The advent of the Internet has revolutionized this situation. Most of the Yeshivot Hesder and Mekhinot now maintain Web sites that regularly publish rabbinic answers to students' questions. There also exists a range of other addresses that specialize in such matters. These venues not only provide opportunities for almost instantaneous responses to whatever dilemmas may trouble soldiers on service, they also facilitate dialogues characterized by the frequency and intensity of exchanges between participants. Together, these phenomena have ensured that there exists a vast and growing library of Orthodox Jewish texts relating to religious observance in a military setting, an area that only two centuries ago was barren of any rabbinic pronouncement.

Reactions to Cultural Adaptations

Just as interesting as the developments traced above are the reactions they have generated. These have been varied and cut across several of the boundaries that conventionally distinguish religiously observant Jews (of various sorts) in Israel from secularists, and both of those segments of the population from "traditionalists." In the main, discourse has focused on three clusters of issues: the possible political implications of the growing numbers of national-religious soldiers in the ranks, their possible impact on IDF operational behavior, and most broadly of all, the influence that religious practices and themes have exerted on the integrative ethos that Ben-Gurion considered so essential to the IDF's institutional identity. Although in many respects overlapping, each cluster warrants individual treatment.

The Political Implications

Observers began to ponder the possible political implications of the growing prominence of religion as a factor in the IDF's comportment almost from the moment the phenomenon became apparent. Indeed, they were compelled to do so largely by national religious reactions to the realignment in Israel's security thinking. This realignment was a response to the recognition of the Palestine Liberation Organization by Yitzhak Rabin's government in 1993 and the government's subsequent agreement to grant the Palestinian Authority autonomous control over sections of the West Bank and Gaza Strip. No sooner had the ink dried on the Oslo Agreements than a large group of prominent rabbis – the most illustrious of whom was Goren, by then in retirement – published a manifesto that categorically prohibited the surrender of Jewish dominion over any part of the Land of Israel. More threatening, the document also called on religious troops to refuse orders to participate in operations designed to dismantle a settlement or an IDF base prior to its transfer to Palestinian jurisdiction.[36] There followed two other milestones. First, in November 1995, Prime Minister Rabin was assassinated by an IDF reservist who had graduated from a Hesder academy and who claimed to have acted under the inspiration of rabbinic instruction. Ten years later, Prime Minister Ariel Sharon announced Israel's decision to "disengage" unilaterally from the Gaza Strip and to dismantle the Jewish settlements located there and in northern Samaria. Once again, there followed a flurry of rabbinic denunciations and exhortations to disobey orders, which this time were accompanied by efforts to get national religious reservists to sign proclamations warning that, in the last resort, they would obey their rabbis rather than their commanding officers.

In the event, this mountain of activity produced a tiny molehill.[37] Testifying to the Knesset's Foreign Affairs and Defense Committee in September 2005, a month after completing the disengagement operation, then-chief of the IDF General Staff, Gen. Dan Chalutz, stated that just sixty-three soldiers had been placed on trial for refusing orders during the operation (fifty conscripts, twenty-four of whom served in the framework of the Yeshivot Hesder; five petty officers; three other ranks in professional service; and five reservists). Tens of thousands of others, including numerous national-religious service men and women, had carried out their duties without flinching. Prophecies of doom, in other words, were proven mistaken. Although undoubtedly tormented by disengagement, the vast majority of national-religious rabbis had ultimately preached the priority of maintaining national unity. And although many of their students had clearly experienced serious misgivings, in the last analysis they, too, prioritized the national interest (i.e., subordination to the civil authority) over religious inclination.

Common sense cautions against placing too much reliance on a repetition of that precedent. There exists no guarantee that national-religious troops would display a similar rate of compliance should an Israeli government ever decide to implement a withdrawal from all or part of the West Bank. The latter, after all, encompasses Judea and Samaria, regions that lie in the very heart of the Holy Land and that therefore exercise a hold on Jewish attachments far greater than Gaza ever did. Not incidentally, they are also home to a significant number of middle-rank national-religious officers,[38] whose growing numbers will in any case make it increasingly difficult for the IDF to juggle the units involved in settlement evacuation (as it did in 2005) and thereby minimize the number of potentially disaffected soldiers involved in the "inner circle" of dismantlement operations. Even so, as matters stand, warnings that national-religious soldiers might en masse refuse to take part in future territorial withdrawals remain entirely speculative. Absent concrete evidence to the contrary, there is still no reason to consider national-religious soldiers more prone to political disaffection than other segments of the IDF's complement. Senior echelons in the IDF certainly do not seem to think so, which is why the religious identity of soldiers and officers has in no way influenced decisions concerning their promotions.

Operational Behavior

In conformity with military chaplaincies throughout history, the IDF rabbinate has always considered one of its principal tasks to be the maintenance of troop morale at moments of mortal danger. From the very beginning of his tenure as chief military chaplain, Rabbi Goren consequently sought to provide spiritual encouragement to soldiers in the field and instill them with faith in eventual victory. For the most part, his efforts were confined to inserting a message of encouragement in the flyleaf of the copies of the Bible that every new recruit received on induction and to giving occasional pep talks at individual bases. Far more dramatic, however, was the address he delivered on national radio during the tense first hours of the Six-Day War, which resonated with citations from Deuteronomy, chapter 20; Judges, chapter 7; and Psalms:

Hear O Israel. Today you approach battle against your enemies. This is the great day for the people of Israel, as you march out towards the massive and decisive engagement for the deliverance of the people of Israel from its enemies, who have come to destroy and uproot us. The eyes of all Israel are on you. Dear soldiers! Let not your hearts be faint. Do not be afraid, do not tremble before them. For the Lord your God goes with you to fight on your behalf against your enemies and to save you. Today He will give us courage! Today He will make us great! Today our enemies shall be crushed beneath us! ... Be strong and of good courage for the sake of our people and the cities of our Lord. And with the help of the God of Israel's battles, you shall win a great victory over all of Israel's enemies. ... O Lord, save us! O Lord, send us success![39]

In this sphere, too, Goren's successors have taken matters several institutional steps further. Hence, instead of being a sporadic phenomenon, rabbinic exhortations to show courage have become persistent features of the military timetable. In part, that message is conveyed during the course of informal talks that teachers in the Yeshivot and Mekhinot are invited to give when they visit their students on service, itself a common occurrence. More widely, the same message is conveyed through the activities arranged by the military rabbinate's Combat Values Branch and its successor, the Jewish Awareness Department.

At one level, these developments have generated nothing more serious than intra-IDF turf wars, prompting complaints by senior officers in the Education Corps that the military rabbinate is infringing on areas of activity that lie foursquare within their domain.[40] Far more fundamental, however, have been the concerns expressed, among others by the outgoing commanding officer of the IDF's Personnel Branch, to the effect that the force might soon have to confront a religious "takeover."[41] Some secularists in Israel's general public have added a further dimension to that warning. Protesting that the military rabbinate is using its influence to inject a religious dimension into Israel's strategic outlook and behavior, they have accused recent incumbents of the post of chief IDF chaplain of exacerbating Israeli-Arab relations (especially tensions between Israelis and Palestinians) by depicting them as a confrontation between rival faiths. Such charges became especially rife during and immediately after Operation Cast Lead in 2009 – so much so that they became items of international media interest. Thus, on March 22 of that year, a lead story in the weekend section of the *New York Times* (entitled "A Religious War in Israel's Army") quoted one soldier as saying that, in Gaza,

the rabbinate brought in a lot of booklets and articles and their message was very clear: We are the Jewish people, we came to this land by a miracle, God brought us back to this land and now we need to fight to expel the non-Jews who are interfering with our conquest of this holy land. This was the main message, and the whole sense many soldiers had in this operation was of a religious war.

Testimony such as this has created an atmosphere in which it has been possible to infer that heightened rabbinical influences over troop behavior, together with the new sociology of the IDF, might have unleashed the trigger-happy "proclivities" of some soldiers in their confrontations with Palestinians.[42] As far as national-religious troops are concerned, however, this argument carries little conviction. There exists no empirical evidence proving that units with an exceptionally high proportion of national-religious soldiers and officers (e.g., the infantry brigades) are responsible for more Palestinian casualties than others (e.g., the air force and artillery). Moreover, studies of the content of current rabbinical teachings on warfare indicate that – contrary to much caricature – the messages imparted by the second generation of national-religious spiritual leaders are no more bellicose than those of their predecessors and significantly less so in some cases.[43] All that has changed, perhaps, is that the discourse now attracts more publicity than was the case in the past.

Troop Cohesion

For many years, analyses of the role of religion in Israeli military service depicted religion's social effects in terms that conveyed an overall impression of harmony. Common service was said to mitigate the stresses otherwise generated by intra-Jewish dissension in Israel, enabling both observant and non-observant segments of society to sublimate their separate interests within a military setting that tightened their communal bonds.[44] An updated review requires significant qualifications. One obvious reason is that recent years have witnessed the steady demise of the old consociational spirit, a process itself brought about by the different ways in which traditional and nontraditional Israelis have responded to the cultural climates of recent decades. To this must be added the more specific influence exerted by Israel's territorial conquests of 1967. By the 1980s, it was already apparent that the drive to settle the new areas had injected an element of messianic purposefulness into the consciousness of many national-religious Israelis, which growing proportions of their secular fellow citizens found discomfiting.[45]

In a far more specific sense, however, the current level of secular-religious dissonance in the IDF reflects growing differences in the educational frameworks attended by the two segments of the complement prior to their enlistment.[46] Thus, whereas in the nonreligious community the mixed-gender day school still predominates, the national-religious world has witnessed the proliferation of single-sex schools, many of the most highly regarded of which (*yeshivot tichoniyot* [for boys] and *ulpanot* [for girls]) are also residential. Furthermore, national-religious schoolchildren participate in a thriving network of their own youth movements (e.g., B'nei Akivah, Ezra, and the Religious Scouts), most of which also maintain gender segregation.

Attendance at this multilayered system of educational frameworks that cater exclusively to religiously observant youth produces a cocoon-like effect. This, however, may not be the best preparation for coping with the societal challenges posed by military service, given that it accustoms national-religious teenagers of both sexes to patterns of behavior (e.g., gender relationships, language, dress, and entertainment) that are peculiarly their own. Not until enlistment will they have any meaningful contact with secular contemporaries raised in a vastly different milieu.

Reactions vary. Almost a quarter of the graduates of national-religious high schools welcome the opportunity to break out of the mold and become non-observant during the course of their military service. Many more, however, undergo a process of retrenchment. A study of the communications that pass back and forth between religious conscripts and their spiritual mentors (many of which are posted on Web sites) reveals an almost obsessive concern with the preservation of a way of life to which military service seems to present a threat. This explains why most of the communications focus on questions of personal conduct, among the most popular of which are the conditions required for prayer services, the preservation of the traditional code of inter-gender relationships in the cramped conditions of military vehicles, and even forms of everyday speech. In each of these areas, what principally worries the troops (and, it must be added, their parents) is the corrosive threat that contact with the secular world might have on their traditional mores. One of the mechanisms they develop to avoid this danger is to articulate their distinctiveness and to insist on it being acknowledged. Within this context, size certainly matters: the higher the numbers of national-religious personnel in a unit, the more likely they are to be recognized as constituting a segmented section of the complement.

This combination of pressures results in a situation in which national-religious and secular troops now frequently find themselves proclaiming their differences. Thus, at their induction, they respond in different ways to the oath of allegiance to the IDF. Whereas the standard response is "I swear" (*ani nishba*), religious troops declaim "I pledge" (*ani matzhir*); they attend different classes in the IDF's Sunday morning cultural programs; thanks to the introduction in 2007 of General Staff regulations that grant religiously observant troops the right to be provided with single-sex training exercises (termed, not altogether euphemistically, *ha-shiluv ha-ra'ui* [literally, "appropriate integration"]), they are entitled to undertake courses of instruction parallel to – but separate from – those conducted in mixed-gender settings;[47] and even when that is not the case, they invariably celebrate graduation from the program at different places of entertainment. Especially highlighted in recent years has been the increasing numbers of national-religious soldiers who have demonstrably excused themselves from attending official IDF events in which female singers provide part of the musical repertoire. Although all such instances have been harshly criticized by the IDF chief rabbi,[48] they have often been encouraged by

Photo 6 An Israeli soldier prays while another works on a mobile artillery unit near the northern Israeli border with Lebanon, July 18, 2006. Photo copyright Pedro Ugarte/ AFP/Getty Images.

some of his subordinates, thus providing a cameo portrait of the ways in which religious observance in the IDF, originally intended to serve as a force binder, now also constitutes a force divider.

True, the IDF has always sought to mitigate the most blatant of such schismatic influences by fostering frameworks that might accommodate troops with different levels of religiosity. Most regularly, even the most non-observant of IDF servicepeople are exposed to Orthodox Jewish rituals and practices, such as attendance at a festive meal welcoming the advent of the Sabbath on Friday nights. The overall impact of such measures, however, seems to be only marginal. Whatever feelings of affinity might be attained through the sharing of rituals seem to be transitory and limited almost entirely to the time spent in uniform. In terms coined by Robert MacCoun, the distinction between "task cohesion" and "social cohesion" thus becomes especially stark.[49] Religious and secular troops in a single unit certainly share what he calls a commitment "to achieving a goal that requires the collective efforts of the group," and they are motivated "to coordinate their efforts as a team to achieve that goal [task cohesion]." But they do not necessarily "like each other, prefer to spend their social time together, enjoy each other's company, and feel emotionally close to one another [social cohesion]." On the contrary, observation indicates that once religious and nonreligious personnel leave the military framework, they revert to their separate lifestyles. As one conscript remarked in conversation, "The fact that I serve in a tank driven by a non-observant fellow soldier doesn't mean that I have to spend my leave with him, still less that I need invite him to my home so that he can meet my sister" (Photo 6).

One further fissiparous circumstance warrants attention. Since the early 1990s, more than one million immigrants from the former Soviet Union (FSU) have arrived in Israel. Contrary to most previous waves of immigrants, newcomers from the FSU have resisted the "melting pot" ethos. Instead, and by means of Russian-language theaters, newspapers, and social clubs, they seek to retain and perpetuate their cultural traditions. And although the majority seeks to be classified as ethnically "Jewish," a significant minority does not. Indeed, several thousand members of the FSU community in Israel proudly proclaim themselves to be Christians.[50]

Thanks to conscription, the preferences have affected the sociological composition of the IDF. Since the late 1990s, FSU immigrants and their offspring have made up at least 10 percent of every annual cohort of new recruits (sometimes more), thus adding yet another distinctive hue to the mosaic of which the IDF is composed.[51] Indeed, every year about 200 new inductees of FSU origin declare themselves to be adherents of the Russian Orthodox Church, and hence insist on swearing the oath of allegiance to the IDF on the New Testament (copies of which it is the duty of the military rabbinate to supply). Even though their dispersal among various units prevents members of this segment from becoming a distinctive element in the IDF, it is surely only a matter of time before they, too, will require that the IDF provide them with their own religious facilities.

A more opaque "religious" boundary results from the fact that roughly one-third of the 5,000 to 6,000 FSU immigrants who enlist in the IDF every year are known to be sons and daughters of Gentile mothers. As such, even if they do not declare themselves to be Christian, they are not recognized as Jews by traditional Jewish law (*halakhah*). Instead, they seem condemned to go through their military lives in a state of uncomfortable liminality. By virtue of their performance of military duty, they can claim to have undertaken what they and many members of the general Israeli public regard as the most significant rite of passage to identification with the Jewish state and all it represents in terms of Jewish identity and survival. Yet, because they are still officially "non-Jewish," they are not recognized as fully integrated members of the Jewish-Israeli collectivity. One consequence is that the official rabbinate, which by law possesses an exclusive right to register and conduct Jewish marriages, will refuse to do so for these persons as long as their status remains unchanged. Another consequence, which affects considerably fewer individuals but possesses symbolic overtones that are even more pertinent to the subject of this chapter, is that regardless of whether these individuals are killed in action, their right to be buried in cemeteries reserved for Jewish IDF soldiers will be questioned.[52]

Recognizing the abnormality of this situation – and indeed its immorality – Gen. Elazar Stern, then-commanding officer of the IDF Personnel Branch and himself an Orthodox Jew, in the late 1990s established a framework (named Nativ ["path"]) that would enable men and women in service to undertake, during the course of their conscript terms, a program of instruction that would culminate in their conversion to Judaism by an Orthodox rabbinic tribunal.[53] But notwithstanding the considerable efforts and funds invested in putting together the program and negotiating its approval by the military hierarchy, the results have not (yet) reached expectations, and only a fraction of the potential target audience has in fact followed the course to its conclusion.[54] In part, the dropout rate can be attributed to the severity of the demands that the Nativ program imposes on participants, who are expected to display an exceptional degree of perseverance and commitment. Equally influential, however, is the deterrent effect exerted by periodic announcements issued by prominent civilian Israeli rabbis to the effect that they will not recognize the conversion certificates issued to persons who do complete the IDF course. Leaders of the Yisrael Beteinu Party, which claims to represent FSU immigrant interests, have put forward a bill that, if passed, would enshrine IDF conversions in law. But until such time as this legislation is improved (and coalition arithmetic casts doubts on the matter), the military service of FSU immigrants born to non-Jewish mothers, instead of diluting religiously based differences in Israel, will continue to demonstrate just how wide these differences are.

Conclusion

It is, of course, important to retain a sense of proportions. The IDF still provides the largest framework in Israel within which Jews (and non-Jews) who come from different backgrounds and who follow different lifestyles can meet on common ground and on equal terms. It also remains one of the few national institutions within which traditional Jewish rituals are transmitted in a form with which non-observant citizens can identify and empathize. Nevertheless, the integrative ties that for many years harmonized religion and military service are coming under increasing strain. Significant shifts have taken place in the overall environment of the military-religious equation in Israel. The IDF has now entered a phase that in 1948 neither Prime Minister Ben-Gurion nor Rabbi Goren could have envisioned.

Notes

1   Israel Central Bureau of Statistics, *Statistical Abstract of Israel*, no. 61 (Jerusalem 2010), table 2:4, http://www1.cbs.gov.il/reader/.
2   Ehud Luz, "The Moral Price of Sovereignty: The Dispute about the Use of Military Power within Zionism," *Modern Judaism* 7/1 (January 1987): 53.

3 Salo W. Baron, "Review of History," in *Violence and Defense in the Jewish Experience*, ed. Salo W. Baron and George S. Wise (Philadelphia: Jewish Publication Society, 1977): 3–14.

4 Aviezer Ravitzky, *Messianism, Zionism, and Jewish Religious Radicalism* (Chicago: University of Chicago Press, 1996): 227–228.

5 Efraim Inbar, "War in Jewish Tradition," *Jerusalem Journal of International Relations* 9 (1987): 83–89.

6 Rabbi Moses Sofer, Hungary mid-nineteenth century, cited in Judith Bleich, "Military Service: Ambivalence and Contradiction," in *War and Peace in the Jewish Tradition*, ed. Lawrence Schiffman and Joel B. Wolowelsky (New York: Yeshiva University Press, 2007): 421.

7 Anita Shapira, *Land and Power: The Zionist Resort to Force, 1881–1948* (New York: Oxford University Press, 1992).

8 Yigal Eilam, *Ha-Haganah* [The Haganah] (Tel Aviv: Zmora, Bitan, Modan, 1979): 132–133, 265–266; Pinchas Guvrin, *Tzav Keriyah Tashach* (Tel Aviv: Ma'arachot, 1976).

9 Estimates of religious affiliation in this and the following paragraphs are based on Yaacov Yadgar and Charles Liebman, "Beyond the Religious-Secular Dichotomy: Masortim in Israel," in *Religion or Ethnicity? Jewish Identities in Evolution*, ed. Zvi Gitelman (New Brunswick, NJ: Rutgers University Press, 2009): 171–192, and a survey published by the Israel Central Bureau of Statistics in the summer of 2011, reported in http://www.ynetnews.com/articles/0,7340,L-3890330,00. html.

10 Address to newly commissioned officers, 1949, reprinted in D. Ben-Gurion, *Yihud ve-Yi'ud* [Collected speeches] (Tel Aviv: Am Oved, 1971): 81.

11 Record of meeting with representatives of the Mizrachi (religious) political party, 23 September 1949, cited in Mordechai Friedman, *Ha-Yechidot ha-Datiyot Ba-Haganah u-va-Palmach* [The religious units in the Haganah and Palmach] (Ramat Gan: Bar-Ilan University Press, 2005): 109–112.

12 Interview with senior officer in IDF Personnel Branch, December 2011.

13 Stuart A. Cohen, *Israel and Its Army: From Cohesion to Confusion* (Routledge: London, 2009): 65–66.

14 Ben-Gurion's motives are analyzed in Menachem Friedman, "The Structural Foundation for Religio-Political Accommodation in Israel: Fallacy and Reality," in *Israel: The First Decade of Independence*, ed. I. Troen (Albany: State University of New York Press, 1995): 51–82.

15 Figures supplied by Hiddush, an Israeli movement for religious freedom and equality, http://hiddush.org/Categories.aspx?id=612.

16 Overall, between 2000 and 2014, the proportion of pupils registered in Haredi schools is projected to rise from 12 percent to 18 percent, while those in national (secular) schools is expected to drop from 52 percent to 40 percent. The national-religious sector will decline from 15 percent to 14 percent. D. Ben-David, ed., *Report on the State of the Nation, 2009* (Hebrew) (Jerusalem: Taub Center for the Study of Social Policy in Israel, 2010): 141.

17 The history and structure of this battalion are analyzed in Zeev Drori, *Between Faith and Military Service: The Nahal Haredi Battalion* (Jerusalem: Floersheimer Institute for Policy Studies, 2005).

18 See http://www.hiddush.com/Categories.aspx?id=462&aid=1003.

19 Interview with Yifat Selah, chairperson of Alumah, a nonprofit organization established to counsel prospective national religious female draftees, May 2010. Roughly half of the women concerned serve in the IDF's Education Corps. Others are assigned to a broad spectrum of units (intelligence, logistics, and in a few cases, combat branches).

20 Dan Soen, "All Able-Bodies, to Arms! – Attitudes of Israeli High School Students toward Conscription and Combat Service," *European Journal of Social Sciences* 6/4 (Winter 2008): 72–82.

21 Reuven Gal, *A Portrait of the Israeli Soldier* (New York: Greenwood Press, 1986): 83.

22 The differences in service patterns of the two systems have now become a topic of Israeli press discourse. See, for example, Alex Fishman, "After Me! – Please God" (Hebrew), *Yedi'ot Aharonot*, 20 October 2008. The previous November, the same newspaper had published a wide-ranging survey that highlighted the discrepancies between religious and secular high school graduates. Y. Yehoshua and T. Trebelsi, "Which Schools Do the Shirkers Attend?" (Hebrew) *Yedi'ot*, 23 November 2007.

23 Asher Cohen, "The Kipa and the Helmet – Image and Reality in the Public Discourse on Religious Zionism and Military Service" (Hebrew), in *Amadot*, vol. 1, ed. Moshe Rachimi (Elakana: Orot Israel College Press, 2009): 95–114.

24 The standard account remains Menachem Friedman, *Haredi Society: Sources, Trends, and Processes* (Hebrew), (Jerusalem: Israel Center for Israel Studies, 1991).

25 Aaron Kampinsky, "Religion, Army, and Society in Israel: Changes in the Military Rabbinate, 1948–2006" (Hebrew), Ph.D. dissertation, Bar-Ilan University, 2008.

26 In the personal diary that he kept in this period (the height of the War of Independence), Ben-Gurion referred to this incident on no less than three separate occasions. See Zahava Ostfeld, *Tzava Nolad* [An army is born] (Tel Aviv: Ministry of Defense, 1994): 748.

27 Interview with staff from the IDF journal *Ba-Mahaneh* (Hebrew), 20 May 2011, 28–32.

28 Stuart A. Cohen, *The Scroll or the Sword? Dilemmas of Religion and Military Service in Israel* (London: Harwood, 1997): 106–109.

29 See   http://cms.education.gov.il/EducationCMS/Units/Hemed/Odot/Alfon/ysivot_ hasder.htm.

30 Elisheva Rossman-Stollman, "Religion and the Military as Greedy Frameworks: Religious Zionism and the IDF" (Hebrew), Ph.D. dissertation, Bar-Ilan University, 2005.

31 See http://cms.education.gov.il/EducationCMS/Units/Mechinot_Kdam/Odot.

32 *Rabbinical Assembly of America: Proceedings*, vol. 8 (New York, 1941–1944): 34–35.

33 Aryeh Edrei, "War, Halakhah and Redemption: Army and War in the Halakhic. Thought of R. Shlomo Goren" (Hebrew), *Kathedra* 125 (September 2007): 119–148.

34 Stuart A. Cohen, "The Quest for a Corpus of Military Ethics in Modern Israel," *Journal of Israeli History* 26/1 (Spring 2007): 35–66.

35 Stuart A. Cohen, "The Re-Discovery of Orthodox Jewish Laws Relating to the Military and War in Contemporary Israel: Trends and Implications," *Israel Studies* 12/2 (Summer): 1–28.

36 For the text and its background, see Cohen, *The Scroll or the Sword?*, 65, 129–131.

37 The following paragraph draws on Stuart A. Cohen, "Tensions between Military Service and Religion: Real and Imagined," *Israel Studies* 12/1 (Spring 2007): 103–126. See also Etta Bick, "Rabbis and Rulings: Insubordination in the Military and Israeli Democracy," *Journal of Church & State* 49/2 (Spring 2007): 305–327.

38 For one portrait of the community of national-religious officers residing in the West Bank settlement of Eli, see Nava Horowitz, "Neighbor Practice," (Hebrew) *Ba-Mahaneh*, 4 October 2010, no. 37: 51–54.

39 Cited in Menachem Michaelson, "The Military Rabbinate " (Hebrew), in *Tzahal be-Cheilov* [The IDF and its arms], vol. 16, ed. Ilan Kfir and Ya'akov Erez (Tel Aviv: Revivim, 1982): 83–132.

40 IDF chaplains rebut this charge with the observation that they are simply fulfilling their responsibility for maintaining Jewish identity in the ranks. In March 2009, the commanding officer of the IDF's Personnel Branch, Gen. Avi Zamir, defined – in writing – the boundaries of the activities of the contesting parties. It is generally agreed, however, that the document has been honored more in the breach than in the observance. See Uri Blau, "A Jewish Army for Israel" (Hebrew), *Ha'aretz* weekend supplement, 2 May 2012.

41 Zamir's valedictory report to the chief of staff was the main headline in *Ha'aretz* on 20 July 2011.

42 Yagil Levy, "The Linkage between Israel's Military Policies and the Military's Social Composition: The Case of the Al Aqsa Intifada," *American Behavioral Scientist* 51/11 (July 2008): 1575–1589.

43 Ronen Lubitch, "Army and War in Religious Zionist Thought" (Hebrew), in *Amadot* (Hebrew), vol. 1, ed. Moshe Rachimi (Elakana: Orot Israel College Press, 2009): 115–138.

44 See, for example, Samuel Rolbant, *The Israeli Soldier: Profile of an Army* (New York: Yoseloff, 1970): 154.

45 Asher Cohen and Bernard Susser, *Israel and the Politics of Jewish Identity: The Secular-Religious Impasse* (Baltimore: Johns Hopkins University Press, 2000).

46 Ido Lieberman, "Religious Zionism: Towards Segregationalism" (Hebrew), Ph.D. dissertation, Bar-Ilan University, 2004.

47 General Staff Order 33.0207, cited in Orna Sasson-Levy, "Gender and the Decline of Israel's Citizen Army," in *The New Citizen Armies*, ed. Stuart A. Cohen (London: Routledge, 2010): 191–192.

48 Interview with Rabbi Rafi Peretz in *Mekor Rishon* (Hebrew weekly), 27 January 2012, 20–22.

49 Robert J. MacCoun, "What Is Known about Unit Cohesion and Military Performance," in *Sexual Orientation and U.S. Military Personnel Policy: Options and Assessment* (Santa Monica, CA: RAND, 1993): 283–331.

50 Asher Cohen, "Non-Jewish Jews: Non-Halakhic Approaches to the Question of Joining the Jewish Collective," in *Ambivalent Jew: Charles Liebman in Memoriam*, ed. Stuart A. Cohen and Bernard Susser (New York: JTS Press, 2007): 157–172.

51 Rivka Eiskovits, "Intercultural Learning among Russian Immigrant Recruits in the Israeli Army," *Armed Forces & Society* 32/2 (January 2006): 292–306.

52   For a critical review of the intra-rabbinic discussion generated by one such incident in 1993, see Rabbi Yehudah Shaviv, "Loved in Life [II Sam. 1:23] – and in Death?" (Hebrew), *Techumin* 14 (1993–1994): 319–330.

53   Stern provides a personal account of his efforts in this regard in his autobiography: *Masa Kippah* [The weight of the skullcap] (Tel Aviv: Yediot, 2009).

54   As late as the autumn of 2008, and notwithstanding almost a decade of generously funded activity, the total number of conversions to Judaism resulting from the Nativ program had barely reached 3,000, which is only a fraction of the potential during that period. Of the 3,000 troops who registered for initial Nativ courses in 2008 (out of an estimated cohort of roughly 7,000 possible candidates), only 800 (most of whom were women) completed the entire seven-month cycle and went on to convert. Interview with the director of the Nativ program, Amichai Eitam, 15 February 2009.

PART III

RELIGION AND MILITARY OPERATIONS

6

Iran

Mahsa Rouhi

The 1979 Islamic Revolution drastically changed the structure of Iran's military forces. The Iranian Imperial Army (IIA), one of the most powerful armies in the region, underwent a comprehensive restructuring process to become the Islamic Republic of Iran Army (IRIA). New institutions were established to provide religious and ideological education to members of the army. Supreme Leader Ayatollah Ruhollah Khomeini ordered the establishment of two new forces based on the Islamic Revolutionary ideology: the Islamic Revolution Guards Corps (IRGC) and the Basij. Their main responsibility was to defend the revolution and protect its religious values and ideals. Thus, from the very beginning, Iran's religious leadership sought to expand its influence in the military, and religion came to play an even more dominant role in the military establishment after the Iraqi invasion in 1980. Iran's religious leaders perceived the Iran-Iraq War as a threat to the Islamic Revolution and its ultimate religious ideal, the "Return to the True Islam." Khomeini named the war a "War of Islam against Blasphemy" and closely tied its symbolic significance to religion.

In this chapter, I argue that the Iranian military intertwined nationalism, revolutionary ideals, and religious and cultural norms after the 1979 revolution. I focus on the role of religion and how religious passion drove masses of young revolutionaries into battle to defend the Islamic Revolution. These volunteers inspired a new strategy of self-sacrifice, or "martyrdom seeking." As the demographics of war casualties testify, these martyrdom operations came to play a major role in the Iran-Iraq War. Religiously motivated volunteers also expanded and strengthened the IRGC until it became the primary organization responsible for waging the war. By relying on strategies shaped by religion and ideology, the IRGC was able to marginalize the IRIA, which insisted on pursuing classical war strategies.

In particular, I explore the role of religion in the Iranian military after the Islamic Revolution. I argue that the revolution introduced religion as a significant factor into the Iranian military, and this role was consolidated during the course of the Iran-Iraq War. The first section expands on the process of reconstruction of the military after the revolution and the transition from a secular, professional military to an ideologically trained one. It then looks at the establishment of the IRGC as an ideological military and its evolution into a parallel military force. In the second section, I discuss the various roles religion played in the Iran-Iraq War. I examine the demographics, organization, and leadership of the military during the war based on statistics, memoirs, and interviews. I conclude with observations on the role of religion in the Iranian military today.

This chapter focuses on the Iran-Iraq War for two reasons. First, there is little reliable data available on current religious practices in the Iranian military. Second, and more important, this phase was an extremely important transition period for the Iranian military because two different military forces, one a professional military and the other a purely ideologically driven force, participated in the war. Therefore, it is a unique historical case that allows a comparative examination of how and to what extent religious values and practices played out within Iranian military establishments.

The Islamic Revolution and the Structure of the Military

Following the Islamic Revolution, the Iranian military underwent a thorough restructuring. Although the equipment and training of the military were sound, the new government emphasized a program of integrating its religious-ideological principles into its organizational structure. It then built on this by forming the Basij, a populist militia to augment the army and "guard the revolution."

The Army

Prior to the Islamic Revolution, the Iranian military was "the most powerful for its size in Asia."[1] It was a major player in the Middle East and came to be known as the "Gendarme of the Region." The Iranian Imperial Army had more than 500,000 employees in 1979.[2] The shah sought to develop a professionalized army that would serve the goals and values of a "modern Iran." He founded the IIA on three ideological principles: laicism, nationalism, and authoritarianism.[3] These premises were intended to secularize the military forces and preserve the shah's authority.

Although the IIA had declared neutrality during the revolution, both religious and secular hard-liners pushed for its dismantlement after the fall of the shah, arguing that the IIA could not be trusted to support revolutionary and religious ideals. Others, including Khomeini, opposed the idea of a comprehensive military purge, arguing that the process of replacing the IIA with religious and revolutionary militias had to take place gradually. He believed that most IIA members, many of whom were conscripts, were trustworthy and that a purge of the high-ranking officers and supporters of the shah would be sufficient to avoid a coup d'état. "Religious officers," meaning those who had strong religious beliefs and close ties to moderate clerics, became key contact points in the subsequent reconstruction of the military.[4]

Within five days of the revolution, Ayatollah Khomeini appointed a group of revolutionaries to conduct a series of army reforms. According to Sepahbod Mohammed Vali Gharani, the first postrevolutionary commander of the army, the reforms were primarily ideological: "We have inherited a crumbled army which was claimed to be one of the most equipped armies in the world. ... What our army did lack was faith. ... There will be essential purges undoubtedly, and the old ideology will be replaced with a new one."[5] The first secretary of defense, Mostafa Chamran, revealed the comprehensive nature of this ideological reform: "First of all, we need to redefine the ideology and philosophical foundation of our armed forces. In the past, it was based on the shah. Today we will base the ideology on God. ... Second, the vision of our army will be to defend the regime and Islamic monotheistic ideology."[6]

The transition from the IIA to the IRIA created great difficulties. The commanders of all three branches of the IRIA were replaced more than three times over a period of fifteen months, and more than 12,000 members of the IIA were dismissed from duty. These purges not only damaged the spirit of solidarity in the armed forces but also produced a crisis in the military's leadership.[7] As a result, the capability of the IRIA had been considerably weakened by September 1980, when Iraq invaded Iran.

The IRGC and the Basij

Immediately after the revolution, Iran faced insurgencies, external threats, and the risk of a coup d'état – all of which the army was in no position to confront. The need for security led to the formation of a trusted group of revolutionary armed forces that would later form the Islamic Revolutionary Guard Corps. The IRGC was closely allied with the religious leadership and saw its goal as protecting the revolution against imperialism, primarily with regard the United States.[8] In April 1979, the Revolutionary Council, composed primarily of clerics close to Khomeini, appointed the first commander in chief of the IRGC and published its first statute.[9]

The IRGC's broad goals were to guard the revolution and spread it throughout the world by disseminating Islamic ideology. Its missions were a mix of sustaining internal security in different cities, facing armed struggles against the revolution, and supporting liberation movements – particularly Palestinian movements. Members of the IRGC were required to believe in Islamic ideology, the Islamic origins of the revolution, and anti-imperialist ideas. Senior members provided ideological and religious training to new members. More important, the IRGC operated under the supervision of the Revolutionary Council and was therefore completely independent of the government. Thus, from its founding moment, the IRGC has been a genuinely religious and ideological armed force within which Iran's religious leaders had the greatest influence.

The Revolutionary Council deemed the IRGC to be necessary, but not sufficient for countering the so-called imperialist threat. This perception was bolstered by documents, found in the U.S. embassy in November 1979, that mentioned possible plans for restoring the shah to the throne. In response, Khomeini suggested a new organization for public mobilization that would recruit volunteers from across society and provide basic military training in case of war. Khomeini argued: "We must gather all our resources to protect the country. ... All the people in an Islamic country should be soldiers and be militarily trained. ... Our youth have to be prepared, ideologically and militarily trained. ... This country that would have 20 million youth population in the future must have 20 million soldiers. ... In that way we will be invulnerable."[10]

Khomeini's speech led to the founding of the Basij militia. According to its statute, the Basij was designed to guard the revolution, accomplish jihad as the will of God, and reinforce the defense capacity of Iran's military forces.[11] This militia was placed under government control and was based in mosques and governmental offices. Although members of the Basij had religious and military training, it began as a social, nonmilitary organization, independent of the IRIA and IRGC.[12]

In July 1980, Iran's Parliament approved a revised statute for the IRGC that would broaden the influence of religious leaders in the corps.[13] This revision resulted in the establishment of two new institutions within the IRGC: the Supreme Leader Representative (SLR) and the Ideological-Political Directorate (IPD). The SLR's responsibilities included supervising all of the activities and decisions of the IRGC, including the performance of its commander in chief, to guarantee conformity with religious law. The IPD was responsible for providing essential ideological and religious education to members of the army.[14] This was the first major step in the ideological transformation of the IRIA into an Islamic organization. IPD members had to be clerics appointed and approved by the supreme leader or his representative. The revised IRGC statute also attached the Basij to the IRGC and thus placed its organizational structure, training, and activities under the authority of the IRGC. This revised statute thus provided the foundation for placing the military under the full supervision of Iran's religious authorities. During the war with Iraq, these small organizations would develop significantly and assume a leading role in Iran's armed forces.[15]

The Iran-Iraq War and the Armed Forces

Iraq's 1980 invasion of Iran led to one of the longest and deadliest wars of the twentieth century. Ninety-five-plus months of war resulted in more than one million casualties. These eight years were a trial for the newly restructured Iranian military, as strategists struggled to balance military power with sharp rates of attrition. In keeping with the ideals of the Islamic Revolution, they capitalized on Shi'a ideals and traditions, invoking the story of Hussein and glorifying martyrdom to facilitate "human wave" tactics. This brutal form of warfare met with limited success and wore down public morale, but the legacy of service has figured prominently in building the credibility of postwar politicians and clerics.

Demography

The restructuring of the Iranian military undermined its effectiveness, as the purge had broken command chains and replaced high-ranking officers with commanders lacking professional training. Moreover, the Iranian military relied on Western military equipment for which it was unable to obtain ammunition or spare parts after the deterioration of relations between Iran and the West. In contrast to Iraq, which could rely on ongoing weapon acquisitions and the use of chemical weapons, Iran's military equipment suffered significantly from international sanctions.[16]

What enabled the Iranian military to endure the eight-year struggle was its human wave strategy, in which masses of volunteers charged into enemy positions and across battlefields.[17] Religious narratives played an important role in sustaining these human waves. According to official records, 75 percent of Iranian troops during the war were volunteers who participated in 95 percent of the war's 182 operations.[18] Of the 200,000 estimated Iranian dead, IRGC and IRIA members are said to have accounted for 22 percent and 25 percent, respectively; Basij volunteers are estimated to have accounted for 47 percent.[19]

These figures are a testament to the crucial role that religiously motivated volunteers played in the war. According to official statistics, most of the casualties were young men: 74 percent were between the ages of sixteen and twenty-five. More specifically, 31 percent were aged fifteen to nineteen, and 41 percent were between the ages of twenty and twenty-three. Moreover, 38 percent of the casualties were either illiterate or had completed only primary school, 26 percent had passed secondary school, and only 31 percent had graduated from high school. In other words, more than 60 percent of the war casualties were undereducated.[20] This finding reveals that the majority of the war's human waves were youth who were motivated by their passion and religious values.

Elementary and high school students made up the largest group of martyrs, comprising 17 percent of the dead. The next two highest figures belonged to laborers and farmers, which accounted for 6.5 and 3.6 percent of the dead, respectively. This suggests that the majority of volunteers originated from working-class families or, as Khomeini called them, "oppressed classes."[21] The geographical distribution of the casualties indicates that the more religious regions in Iran yielded a disproportionate number of martyrs.[22] For instance, provinces such as Esfahan, Qom, and Yazd, which are known as the most pious provinces, suffered the largest proportions of casualties given their populations.

The number of casualties over the course of the war reveals that Iran's strategy became increasingly dependent on religiously motivated volunteers. These individuals were considered to be Iran's only advantage over Iraq's growing military capabilities. Iran incurred 40 percent of its total war casualties in the last two and a half years of the war. Twenty percent of the casualties occurred in the final year. It was during this time that Iraq expanded its military in terms of personnel, even as international sanctions took their toll on Iran's military equipment. It appears that Iran's volunteer surge during the war was the main basis for its enduring resistance.[23] The following section sheds light on the different motivations of these human waves.

Religion, Ideology, and Culture

Iran's use of human waves during its war with Iraq was inspired by cultural norms rooted in Shi'a religious values.[24] Historically, religious values have always formed an integral part of Iran's culture and have played a significant role in social life. Religious values that had played a minor role in Iran's military in the past grew to play a vital role after the revolution and the war.[25] It was the redefinition of these cultural norms before and during the revolution and the war that empowered religion and ideology to become such vital elements in the military establishment. This long-established relationship between Shi'a values and Persian culture makes it difficult to separate nationalist motivations for the human waves from cultural and religious motivations. In this section, I focus on the role of religious values while acknowledging that nationalistic motives also played an important role.

Although the revolution cannot be considered a thoroughly religious movement, Khomeini's religious leadership and his religious philosophy had an indisputable influence on intertwining revolutionary ideals with religious ideals. Thus, concepts such as jihad and martyrdom, which grew out of Islamic culture, were redefined in association with revolutionary ideas. This redefinition did not merely apply to Islamic cultural concepts. Even Marxist concepts such as the proletariat were applied to Iranian society. Iranian revolutionaries conceived of Islam as an ideology that could eliminate injustice and inequality and save them from oppression.

The Iran-Iraq War was similarly reinterpreted as a war between "Islam and blasphemy." In a speech given two days after the Iraqi invasion, Khomeini mentioned neither the motherland nor the danger of losing territorial integrity. Rather, he stated: "You all know that this war is not between Iran and Iraq. It is a war between Islam and blasphemy, between the Holy Quran and atheism. And thus it behoves all of us to defend the treasured Islam and Holy Quran and send these criminals to hell."[26]

The war was thus grounded in religion from the very beginning.[27] Khomeini's interpretation of the war as directed against the Islamic Revolution mobilized volunteers who believed in "true Islam" as the only path to salvation. The combination of Marxism and ideological Islam redefined the notions of defense and war, which in turn provided an optimal opportunity to merge nationalism and religion.[28] Many participants perceived the war as an opportunity to revive the ideals of "true Islam." As one volunteer wrote in his will, "This war is one of God's mercies. ... It gives us the chance to accomplish jihad in the will of Allah. ... What a rewarding war between the Islam and blasphemy!"[29] This sacred view of war acted to unite Iranian society.

Moreover, the attempt to replace nationalism with Islam led to a rereading of history, designed to highlight similarities between the early days of Islam and current events.[30] For example, religious leaders compared the oppressive confrontation between the revolution and its opponents around the world to the loneliness of early Muslim pioneers. The concept of oppression was tightly tied to Shi'a culture and is associated with the Ashura ceremony marking the martyrdom of Imam Hussein. Hussein, a grandson of the Prophet Mohammed, had rebelled against the Caliph Yazid to defend his grandfather's mores. He was brutally killed in Karbala, in today's Iraq, along with seventy-two of his followers. Shi'a Muslims perceive these events as symbols of martyrdom and oppression and commemorate them annually at the Ashura ceremony.

In their war against Iraq, Iranians were fighting the country in which Karbala is located. Iranian soldiers employed Karbala as a metaphor for a struggle in which they held positions similar to those of Imam Hussein: they were isolated and outnumbered by the numerous enemies supporting Iraq. This metaphor transcended time and space, allowing participants to see Iraq's leader, Saddam Hussein, as a modern Yazid and Khomeini as a contemporary Imam Hussein. Because fellow Muslims who were intimidated by Yazid's power had abandoned the imam, Iranians felt obliged to prevent the same fate befalling Khomeini. One martyr's will is representative of this thinking: "Today we declare from our strongholds that we heard the appeal of our Hussein and passionately hurried to martyrdom."[31]

This rereading of Shi'a history generated a new military ideology that was as powerful as nationalism.[32] The redefinition of the religious, cultural, and historical metaphors not only motivated society to fight but also created the new strategy of "martyrdom seeking."[33] The concept of seeking martyrdom established a mystical relationship between the leader and his followers, who sought to accomplish his will without questioning it. The main emphasis was on self-sacrifice; the results were of secondary concern. A former high-ranking officer in the war describes the following scene:

We were informed that the battalion of the Lovers of Hussein (Asheghane Hosein) was coming to clean the minefields. ... Just after their arrival they started firmly embracing each other. It was a weird scene. All the troops were crying watching those young Basijis. We did not know yet what they were going to do. ... They lined up behind the minefield and stared at it, their faces covered with tears. The silence was everywhere and we were watching them anxiously. Suddenly, a young man who was about 20 said: "All of us should die for Hussein. The Master is waiting, don't upset him." "Ya Hussein," he screamed and ran into the minefield and the others followed him. The successive bursts created a hell in front of us.[34]

The young soldiers apparently felt that they had to complete a religious duty, one that could be accomplished only through martyrdom.[35] Both failure and death were meaningless in this context. As Khomeini suggested, "We are responsible to fulfill our duty, the result does not matter." Victory would result regardless of whether one's own forces or the enemy's forces were defeated. Elsewhere Khomeini stated, "You are the conquerors. ... You people who embrace death and run toward martyrdom, you will win. ... Whether you defeat the enemies ... or fail. You greet death because it is martyrdom, it is the defending of Islam."[36] Thus, Shi'a mysticism refers to martyrdom as the reunion with the Master (God), an idea that encouraged massive numbers of young Iranian volunteers to sacrifice their lives in the defense of Iran and Islam. Those who failed to meet this objective viewed their failure with genuine regret.

Religious Practices

The Ashura metaphor also inspired Iranian war propaganda in an effort to strengthen the troops' religious passion and to intensify the spirit of martyrdom.[37] Members of the army participated in daily readings from the Ashura Prayer – a prayer unique to Shi'a Muslims that glorifies the Shi'a cause and emphasizes hatred toward Imam Hussein's enemies.[38] Prior to military operations, soldiers and volunteers often gathered to participate in Noha-khani, recitations of elegies expressing sorrow and mourning at Imam Hussein's martyrdom. These elegies had always played a role in Iranian funerals and religious memorials. During the war, they took on an epic-like character designed to mobilize soldiers and prepare them to face death.[39] The influence of these gatherings was so profound that they were banned along the front on some occasions to avoid unauthorized and spontaneous suicide attempts.[40]

Symbols related to Ashura pervaded the battlefield.[41] Signs at the front showed the distance to Karbala rather than Baghdad. One popular chant favored by the troops was "Karbala is waiting for us, we shall go." In January 1987, the largest battle in the war began with an Iranian offensive named "Karbala 5." Using such names as metaphors and engaging practices that emphasized Ashura culture consolidated the new ideology of martyrdom in the minds of the troops. Iranian propaganda created an atmosphere in which volunteers became more obsessed with martyrdom than with winning the war.

According to Iran's leaders, faith in their holy cause, divine aid, and the promise of the next world would suffice to motivate the volunteers.[42] They did not acknowledge that at some point reality would overtake their idealism. In the last year of the war, the large numbers of Iranian casualties along with Iran's failure to achieve a decisive victory decreased the number of volunteers. For instance, in one of the last deployment caravans, only 200 volunteers registered from Qom, the religious capital of Iran.[43] Citizens began facing the reality of the war and realized they needed more than just faith to survive.

Organization and Leadership

At the outset of the Iran-Iraq War, Iranian domestic politics were in turmoil. The Islamic Republican Party, including Khomeini's followers, fought the Liberals, led by President Abulhassan Banisadr, for supremacy in the newly established government.[44] As the commander in chief, Banisadr refused to permit the IRGC and the Basij militia to interfere in the war.[45] He argued that public and revolutionary resistance in the form of martyrdom operations did not constitute a professional military strategy. Concerned with the religious leadership's growing authority over the IRGC, Banisadr rejected the idea of supplying IRGC members with weapons, even though many of them hurried to the battlefields to defend the revolution.[46] At the same time, the religious leadership was concerned about Banisadr's intentions and tried to limit his influence. Suspicious of any army that was not directly under its supervision, the Revolutionary Council purged IRGC members who allied with Banisadr and accused several high-ranking IRIA officers of treason.[47]

The weakened IRIA failed in most of its major operations against the Iraqi military.[48] Although Banisadr succeeded in reconquering half of the territory captured by Iraq, his hostility toward the IRGC led to increased pressure from religious leaders who claimed that he was trying to eliminate Islam from the military and society.[49] Nine months into the war, the Iranian Parliament dismissed Banisadr from the presidency, a decision approved by Khomeini. This event proved to be a turning point in both the conduct of the war and the role of religion in it.

It was at this moment that the IRGC and the Basij militia joined the war effort and that IRGC commanders joined the Supreme War Council. Because they lacked a professional military organization and structure, the IRGC and the Basij relied on the IRIA model to organize their military forces. The IRGC grew into an irregular military force that could employ volunteers and train them on the basis of religious narratives. The Basij militia was transformed into a social force with a military identity.[50]

IRGC commanders argued that a conventional military strategy could not ensure victory. Given the significant deficiencies in Iran's armed forces, they suggested using surprise and the quick deployment of troops.[51] It was obvious that this approach would result in high casualties and thus require self-sacrifice, yet the new strategy proved successful in several minor operations. The IRIA and IRGC then cooperated in designing and performing a series of major operations and retrieved most of the territories that had been occupied by Iraq.[52] One year after Banisadr's dismissal, the religiously dominated military succeeded in liberating the port city of Khoramshahr in one of the early major battles of the war.

As the war continued, conflict escalated between the IRIA and IRGC over how to lead the war.[53] The IRIA was a traditional military force. In contrast, the rapidly growing IRGC insisted on pursuing the martyrdom strategy, resulting in high casualties. As long as the IRIA remained the leading force in the war, it could moderate the IRGC's use of human waves. As the IRGC expanded in size, power, and influence, conflict between the two organizations became more frequent. The inability to coordinate their plans led to successive failures in Iran's first operations inside Iraq, the most important of which was Operation Valfajr in February 1983.[54] IRGC commanders sought to control the war because they believed their volunteers were the real power behind Iran's military force. However, IRIA commanders were unwilling to operate under IRGC supervision because they suspected the IRGC was not able to train and logistically support its volunteers on the battlefield.

In March 1984, Khomeini sought to ease this tension by appointing Hashemi Rafsanjani as commander in chief of the war, superior to the commander of both the IRIA and the IRGC. IRIA logistics would now be used to support IRGC infantry.[55] This change meant that the IRGC would be responsible for directing offensives against Iraq while the IRIA would become more of a defense force.[56] Consequently, IRIA casualties dropped from 30,000 before March 1984 to only 18,000 subsequently, indicating the limited role that the IRIA played in the second half of the war.[57] In the last four years of the war, the IRGC directed all major operations.[58]

The IRGC grew from 10,000 members at the beginning of the war to 150,000 in 1983 and increased to 450,000 in the last year of the war.[59] In September 1985, in a symbolic attempt to strengthen the IRGC and balance against the IRIA, Khomeini ordered that the IRGC be divided into an army, an air force, and a navy to parallel the structure of the IRIA.

Iran's military failures led its political and military leaders to the realization that the probability of a rapid and decisive victory was low.[60] The war was consuming human resources at an ever-increasing pace. In a public speech, Hashemi declared: "Now we need to firmly resist. The war might take very long. I am saying this so that the nation of Iran understands the situation and does not expect the war to end today or tomorrow."[61]

The rapid erosion of manpower meant that the Basij could no longer rely on mosques as its main bases for recruiting volunteers. Starting in November 1985, nationwide caravans deployed to the battlefield in the hopes that visible recruitment would intensify public enthusiasm for the war.[62] During Friday prayers, clerics appointed by the Islamic Development Organization, which played a significant role in advancing the religious narratives during the war, invited Iranians to join the war to defend Islam.[63] According to official records, the Iranian military grew from 240,000 soldiers in 1981 to 1,250,000 by the end of the war.[64]

More than 72,000 clerics participated in the war at a casualty rate three times higher than that of nonclerics.[65] They were instrumental not only in recruiting soldiers but also in raising troop morale. Most clerics volunteered and fought alongside regular soldiers, contributing to the troops' confidence and religious enthusiasm. Missionaries from the Islamic Development Organization did not participate directly in combat but strengthened soldiers' faith and confidence by inculcating the value of martyrdom. Military clerics who were members of the IRGC performed the dual role of soldier and missionary.[66] Many clerics would later use their participation in the war to increase their influence in the political establishment. Several clerics succeeded in assuming key positions in the military and the government after the war.[67]

The Iranian Military Today

After the war, the military began to restore and develop its resources, both in manpower and institutional capacity and support. The IRIA became a professional military organization loyal to Iran's national and security interests without turning into an ideological military force.[68] The IRGC, on the other hand, focused on religious and ideological education in its military academies.

Religion also influences the structure and leadership of the armed forces. Unique to Iran, there are two leadership positions at any level of the IRIA and the IRGC. One leader comes from a military background and has professional military training. The other leader is the head of the Ideological-Political Department. He is a cleric and is not required to have military training. The two leaders enjoy the same rank, salary, benefits, and authority. The head of the IPD is directly in charge of recruitment, staff evaluations, and promotions. This individual is also consulted on all decisions and participates in all operational and strategic decision-making sessions with equal authority.[69]

Moreover, the IPD head has direct access to the supreme leader's military office. The supreme leader, who is the commander in chief of Iran's armed forces, directly appoints the commanders in chief of the IRGC and the IRIA, and they report directly to him. The supreme leader's military office appoints the head of the IPD, based primarily on religious merits. He, in turn, receives his instructions from this office and reports back directly to this important bureau (Photo 7).

Religion also shapes recruitment into the military, a topic that has generated controversy. Iran's population consists primarily of Shi'a Muslims (89 percent) and Sunni Muslims (9 percent), with a small minority of Christians, Jews, Baha'is, and Zoroastrians (2 percent). After the revolution, several officers met with members of the Parliament and the supreme leader to argue against the recruitment of religious minorities. For example, in a letter to Lotfollah Saafi Golpaygani, secretary of the Guardian Council of the Islamic Republic Parliament, Gholamreza Safayee, head of the IPD at IRIA, argued that Islam should be a prerequisite for military recruitment.[70] The reply was as follows: "In recruiting military personnel based on Article 144 of the Constitution, the recruit is required to be a believer in a religion and

Photo 7 Iranian supreme leader Ayatollah Ali Khamenei, center, confers a rank to an unidentified member of Iran's army during a ceremony in Tehran, Iran. Photo copyright STR/AP/Corbis.

loyal to revolutionary values. Thus, there is no objection to the recruitment of religious minorities. The military can determine conditions based on organizational interests."[71]

In practice, the participation of religious minorities in the military is limited. They are not recruited to the IRGC, and in the IRIA they can serve only as conscripts, medics, engineers, and low-level administrators. The greatest challenge to the participation of non-Shi'a soldiers is not the constitution but widespread religious practices at military bases. The intensity of religious activities in all parts of the military isolates non-Shi'a soldiers to such an extent that members of other religious groups rarely consider enrolling, and those who do often end up resigning.[72] For instance, a great deal of the networking and socializing among soldiers occurs at daily prayers or weekly Thursday prayers. Even Sunni Muslims find that these prayers diverge from their religious practices and refuse to participate. This alienating institutionalized religious practice has led to feelings of segregation among minorities and a search for employment outside the military.

Religious rituals and beliefs continue to affect practices in the Iranian military. The IRGC and IRIA require their members to take part in ideological and religious workshops during basic training. Conscripts are also required to attend fifty to sixty hours of religious and ideological classes during their two-year mandatory military service. Further, soldiers must attend courses on Islamic law, philosophy, history, teaching, and practice.

Daily prayers are observed at all military bases, as is fasting during Ramadan. Although these practices are not mandatory, they are seen as indicators of piety and observed by most soldiers. During Ramadan, no food or drinks can be consumed from sunrise to sundown, and more soldiers participate in daily prayers and supplications. Throughout the year, there are weekly supplications on Thursdays (Du'a al-Kumayl). Front-row seats are reserved for military commanders during Friday prayers in city centers, particularly when the prayer is conducted by the supreme leader. As mentioned earlier, the military observes daily prayers and supplications during Muharram, including the Ashura supplication.[73] Military offices and bases have religious names, as do several weapons, military operations, and exercises.

Economic and political reforms initiated by postwar governments gradually moderated the military's revolutionary idealism. The religious leadership responded by revising the IRGC's ideology to strengthen its influence over the corps. IRGC educational centers developed courses to educate IPD instructors in the new ideology. Martyr Mahallati University in Qom, founded in 1982, became the most advanced center for ideological-political training for IRGC instructors. Today, this and other centers employ roughly 4,000 "political guides."[74]

Conclusion

The Islamic Revolution changed the structure and ideology of Iran's military forces, which until then had relied on secular values. The religious leaders of the revolution formed a new military force, the IRGC, to balance the professional regular army with a religious and ideological military force. The ideological structure of the IRGC, along with the religious values that sustained the human waves of martyrs during the Iran-Iraq War, produced tactical successes during the war and drastically strengthened the power of the IRGC. Thus, with the support of the religious leadership, the IRGC was able to expand into a full military establishment parallel to the IRIA. The strengthening of the ties between the religious and the military leadership has succeeded to such an extent that the legitimacy and survival of each now depends on the other.

Notes

1   Mark J. Roberts, *Khomeini's Incorporation of the Iranian Military*, McNair Paper no. 48 (Washington, DC: National Defense University Press for the Institute for National Strategic Studies, 1996).

2   Ahmad N. Farsangi, *Artesh dar tarikh va Enghelab-e-Eslami* [The military in the history of the Islamic Revolution] (Tehran: Entesharat-e Zohd, 2006): 107.

3   Ibid.

4   Heshmatollah Azizi, *Tarikh-e shafahi-e artesh dar Enghelab-e-Eslami* [Oral history of the military in the Islamic Revolution] (Tehran: Markaz-e Asnad-e Enghelab-e-Eslami, 2007): 190.

5   Ibid.

6   Ibid.

7   Ali Gharib, *Istadeh Bar Armaan* [Standing for ideals] (Frankfurt: Entesharat-e Enghelab-e-Eslami, 2006): 56–58.

8   Mohammad Doroudian and Gholam Ali Changi Zadeh, "Negaresh-e koli bar naghsh-e jang dar zohour va shekl-giri-e nirou-ha-ye defaei dar jomhouri-e eslami" [An overview of the role of war in the formation and evolution of the defense forces in the Islamic Republic], *Mahnameh Siasat-e Defaei* [Journal of Defense Policy], no. 28 (1999): 74–78.

9   First Statute of the Islamic Revolutionary Guards Corps, 5 June 1979.

10 Ayatollah Ruhollah Khomeini, *Sahifeh-ye-Nour* [Pages of light], vol. 11 (Tehran: Vezarat Ershad Eslami, 1982): 121–122.

11 Statute of the Basij, 9 June 1982.

12 Doroudian and Zadeh, "Negaresh-e koli bar naghsh-e jang dar zohour va shekl-giri-e nirou-ha-ye defaei dar jomhouri-e eslami."

13 Statute of the Islamic Revolutionary Guards Corps, 9 June 1982.

14 Statute of the Ideological-Political Directorate, 7 July 1983.

15 Doroudian and Zadeh, "Negaresh-e koli bar naghsh-e jang dar zohour va shekl-giri-e nirou-ha-ye defaei dar jomhouri-e eslami."

16 Ehsan Khoramdareh, "Chegonegi-e shekl-giri-e sakhtar-e siasi-e Jomhouri-e-Eslami-e Iran va tasir-e an bar ravand-e aghaz va tadavom-e jang-e Iran va Iraq" [The formation of political structure in the Islamic Republic of Iran and its impact on the start and continuation of the Iran-Iraq War], *Fasl-nameh Negin* 1 (2002).

17 Mohammad Amini, "Esterategy Defai-e Iran dar jang-e hasht sale ba Iraq" [Iran's defense strategy during eight years of war with Iraq], September 2010, http://www.bbc.co.uk/persian/iran/2010/09/100927_war30th_iran_strategy.shtml.

18 Jafar Mohaghegh, "Naghsh-e velayat-e faqih dar defa-e moghadas" [The role of the Supreme Leader during the holy defense], 2009, http://www.dsrc.ir/view/article.aspx?id=1078.

19 This figure is based on official records kept by the Foundation for Martyrs and Veteran Affairs (Markaze Amare Bonyade Shahid), 2006. Unofficial estimates set a much higher figure.

20 Ibid.

21 Emad-al-din Baghi, "Jame'e shenasi-e jang" [The sociology of the war], *Shargh*, 26 August 2005, http://www.emadbaghi.com/archives/000617.php.

22 Reza Hossein Pourpoyan and Ali Vali Gholizadeh, "Tahlil-e GSI joghrafiya-ye shahidan-e jang va defa-e moghadas" [A demographic analysis of the martyrs of holy defense], 2009, http://www.dsrc.ir/view/article.aspx?id=1149.

23 Amini, "Esterategy Defai-e Iran dar jang-e hasht sale ba Iraq."

24 Ali T. Akbari et al., *Avamel-e ma'navi va farhangi dar defa-e moghadas* [Spiritual and cultural factors in the holy defense], vol. 1 (Qom: Pajohesh-kadeh Tahghighat-e Eslami, 2008): 150–152.

25 Mohammad Rahbar, "Jangi baraye Eslam: Sarmaye-i baraye Jomhouri-e-Eslami" [War for Islam: An asset for the Islamic Republic], 2010, http://www.bbc.co.uk/persian/iran/2010/09/100919_war30th_nationalism_islam_rahbar.shtml.

26 Ayatollah Ruhollah Khomeini, *Sahifeh-ye-Nour* [Pages of light], vol. 13 (Tehran: Vezarat Ershad Eslami, 1982): 221.

27 Doroudian and Zadeh, "Negaresh-e koli bar naghsh-e jang dar zohour va shekl-giri-e nirou-ha-ye defaei dar jomhouri-e eslami."

28 Mohsen Motaghi, *Goftogo ba Farhad Khosrokhavar: Negahi be ara va asar* [A conversation with Farhad Khosrokhavar: An overview of theories and publications] (Tehran: Nashr-e Nazar, 2007): 95.

29 Mohammed Ali Elahi, *Safiran-e Nour* [The ambassadors of light] (Tehran: Markaz-e Pajohesh haye farhangi-e bonyad-e shahid, 1989). Wills such as these were often composed by martyrs on the battlefield.

30 Akbari et al., *Avamel-e ma'navi va farhangi dar defa-e moghadas*, 307–311.

31 Elahi, *Safiran-e Nour*.

32 Rahbar, "Jangi baraye Eslam."

33 Akbari et al., *Avamel-e ma'navi va farhangi dar defa-e moghadas*.

34 "Interview with Eskandar Pir-Alvand," *Etelaat*, 27 September 1997, 12. Pir-Alvand was a high-ranking officer during the war.

35 Motaghi, *Goftogo ba Farhad Khosrokhavar*, 102.

36 Ayatollah Ruhollah Khomeini, *Sahifeh-ye-Nour* [Pages of light], vol. 16 (Tehran: Vezarat Ershad Eslami, 1982): 69.

37 Akbari et al., *Avamel-e ma'navi va farhangi dar defa-e moghadas*, 40–352.

38 Mohammed Fahimi, *Farhang-e Jebheh (oghat-e feraghat)* [The culture of the war front] (Tehran: Entesharat-e Soroush, 2001): 36.

39 Akbari et al., *Avamel-e ma'navi va farhangi dar defa-e moghadas*.

40 "Interview with Sadegh Ahangaran," *Soroush*, 19 July 1992, 13–15. Ahangaran was the most famous Noha-khan during the war.

41 Akbari et al., *Avamel-e ma'navi va farhangi dar defa-e moghadas*.

42 Kiomars Ashtarian, "Zaman, divan salari-e jangi va ta'amol-e arman-vagheiat" [A theoretical overview of Iran's policy making during the Iran-Iraq War], 19 October 2009.http://www.dsrc.ir/view/article.aspx?id=807.

43 Baghi, "Jame'e shenasi-e jang."

44 Khoramdareh, "Chegonegi-e shekl-giri-e sakhtar-e siasi-e Jomhouri-e- Eslami-e Iran va tasir-e an bar ravand-e aghaz va tadavom-e jang-e Iran va Iraq."

45 Ibid.

46 Abolhassan Banisadr, *Rooz-ha bar raees-e-jomhour che migozarad* [Memoirs of the president], vol. 4 (Tehran: Entesharat-e Enghelab-e-Eslami, 1980): 78.

47 Gharib, *Istadeh Bar Armaan*.

48 Doroudian and Zadeh, "Negaresh-e koli bar naghsh-e jang dar zohour va shekl-giri-e nirou-ha-ye defaei dar jomhouri-e eslami."

49 Gharib, *Istadeh Bar Armaan*; Fatemeh Hashemi and Ghader Bastani, *Pas az bohran: Hashemi Rafsanjani: Khaterat va Karnameh* [After the crisis: Memoirs of Hashemi Rafsanjani] (Tehran: Markaz-e Nashr-e Ma'aref-e Enghelab-e-Eslami, 2002).

50 Doroudian and Zadeh, "Negaresh-e koli bar naghsh-e jang dar zohour va shekl-giri-e nirou-ha-ye defaei dar jomhouri-e eslami."

51 Hasan Rahimi, *Az soghot-e Ganjeh ta fath-e Khoramshahr* [From Ganjeh to Khoramshahr] (Tehran: Entesharat-e Sarir, 2006): 156–158.

52 Mohammad Doroudian, *Seyri dar jang-e Iran va Iraq* [An overview of the Iran-Iraq War], vol. 1 (Tehran: Markaz-e Motaleat va Tahghighat-e Jang, 2001): 46.

53 Alireza Lotfollah Zadegan, *Rooz-shomar-e jang-e Iran va Iraq* [A chronology of the Iran-Iraq War], vol. 20 (Tehran: Markaz-e Motaleat va Tahghighat-e Jang, 2002): 93.

54 Hashemi and Bastani, *Pas az bohran.*

55 Ghodratollah Rahmani, *Bi-pardeh ba Hashemi Rasanjani* [Directly with Hashemi Rafsanjani] (Tehran: Entesharat-e Keyhan, 2003): 73–75.

56 "Interview with Gholam Ali Rashid," Fars News Agency, 26 September 2008, 2–3.

57 "Interview with Ali Shahbazi," *Etelaat*, 18 April 2000, 3.

58 Ali Akbar Raeesi, *Zang-e tarikh* [History time] (Qom: Entesharat-e Nasim-e Hayat, 2005): 125.

59 Anonymous, "Jang-e Iran-Iraq: Zohor-e Sepah va eslami shodane Artesh" [Iran-Iraq War; Formation of the IRGC and the Islamization of IRIA], 6 March 2010http://www.dsrc.ir/view/article.aspx?id=942.

60 Doroudian, *Seyri dar jang-e Iran va Iraq.*

61 Hashemi and Bastani, *Pas az bohran.*

62 Akbari et al., *Avamel-e ma'navi va farhangi dar defa-e moghadas.*

63 Ibid.

64 More than 600,000 conscripts escaped the battlefields according to unofficial reports. "Interview with Gholam Ali Rashid," 6–7; Amini, "Esterategy Defai-e Iran dar jang-e hasht sale ba Iraq."

65 Ebrahim Ali Barzi, "Naghsh-e Rohaniat dar basij-e mardomi va taghviat-e Manavi-e razmandegan" [The role of clerics in Basij and strengthening the spirituality of soldiers] (Tehran: Pajoheshkadeh Tahghigh Eslami, 2007).

66 Ibid.

67 Mahdi Khaladji, "Amameh va tofang; Rohanion-e shia-ye Iran dar jebheh haye jang" [Iranian Shi'a clerics during the Iran-Iraq War], September 2010, http://www.bbc.co.uk/persian/iran/2010/09/100912_war30th_spirituality_khalaji.shtml.

68 Azizi, *Tarikh-e shafahi-e artesh dar Enghelab-e-Eslami.*

69 Personal interview with a senior Iranian official, July 2012.

70 Correspondence between Gholamreza Safayee and Lotfollah Safi Golpaygani, 13 June, 1979. Letter No. 801–07–93 and Response No. 735 (Tehran, *Communications with the IRIA, Shoraye Negahban* [Archives of the Guardian Council of the Islamic Republic]).

71 Correspondence between Gholamreza Safayee and Lotfollah Safi Golpaygani, 11 January 1982. Letter No. 701–03–121 and Response No. 2630 in *Communications with the IRIA Recruiting Office* (Tehran: *Communications with the IRIA, Shoraye Negahban* [Archives of the Guardian Council of the Islamic Republic]).

72 Author interview with a senior Iranian official, May 2012.

73 Telephone interview with a senior Iranian official, June 2012.

74 Ali Alfoneh, "Indoctrination of the Revolutionary Guards," *Middle East Outlook*, no. 2 (February 2009).

7

India

Amit Ahuja

Religion can be a source of comfort and motivation for soldiers. It can also be a source of conflict in a diverse army. How then do religiously diverse armed forces engage religion? How do they maintain cohesion while recruiting from a religious society and conducting operations in multifaith environments? By drawing on the experience of the multifaith Indian Army, which has recruited from and operated in a conflict-ridden religious society, this chapter identifies the challenges religion poses for the military and outlines the institutional mechanisms the army relies on to cope with these challenges.

The multifaith Indian army defends a constitutionally secular state, yet it remains a force of believers.[1] This poses distinct challenges for the institution. First, the military has to accommodate religiosity – faith and culturally embedded religious practices – while establishing the primacy of institutional authority over religious authority in the minds of its soldiers. In India, religious conflict is a staple of the political environment in which the military exists. The army is regularly deployed to enforce the writ of the state during periods of Hindu-Muslim communal violence and domestic insurgencies. Second, given this backdrop, the open acknowledgment of religiosity with its accompanying practices exposes the military to the danger of faith-driven mutinies and interfaith conflict within its own ranks. These faith-related challenges have a bearing on the military's organization and operations.

The Indian military includes army, naval, and air forces. Instead of discussing religion across the Indian military, this chapter confines its focus to the army. There are three reasons for this choice. First, the army is the largest component of the Indian armed forces. Second, it has been the most widely used and consequential arm of the military during all domestic and international military operations. Third, many of the practices described are not restricted to the army but rather are common to the other branches of service.

This chapter draws on field research and interviews conducted between December 2009 and January 2011 in addition to incorporating materials from secondary sources. I do not reveal the names, regiments, and locations of officers and soldiers unless they have already appeared in public elsewhere. I conducted a total of 174 interviews with retired and serving officers and soldiers across six states in India. These individuals belonged to four infantry and two support regiments. Overall, I interviewed 45 officers and 129 soldiers from other ranks.

The chapter begins by describing how the army engages religion, then outlines two challenges it poses for the institution. The next section enumerates the institutional mechanisms put in place to cope with these challenges. The final two sections illustrate these mechanisms during an army operation in a religious shrine and evaluate their efficacy during the subsequent mutiny among soldiers triggered by the events surrounding the operation.

Religion in the Indian Military

India is one of the most religiously diverse countries in the world and is home to Hindus (80.5 percent), Muslims (13.4 percent), Christians (2.3 percent), Sikhs (1.9 percent), Buddhists (0.8 percent), and Jains (0.4 percent).[2] Moreover, Indian society is religious. In the 2009 Indian National Election Study, 74 percent of respondents reported praying weekly, and 54 percent reported attending a place of worship weekly. Among my interview subjects, 88 percent were comfortable describing themselves as "religious."[3] Today, the Indian Army has a volunteer force of more than 1.15 million active personnel recruited from this diverse and religiously observant environment.[4] It is difficult to obtain precise figures on the religious composition of the army; the army does not provide these data.[5] Still, it is well known that not all communities are represented in proportion to their total populations. Hindus make up the largest section of officers and soldiers. Sikhs are believed to be overrepresented, comprising perhaps as much as 10 percent of the army, while Muslims are thought to be underrepresented, perhaps amounting to 3 percent. The religious composition of the Indian Army has changed over time, especially after the departure of British troops in 1947 and the creation of the newly independent states of India and Pakistan. Muslim and Christian proportions were most affected by this; the large majority of Muslim officers and soldiers joined the Pakistan Army.[6] It is noteworthy that despite widespread communal violence at the time, officers and soldiers of different faiths did not turn on each other.[7] The Indian Army has recently increased the total number of Christians serving by raising new battalions from Northeast India, a region with a high concentration of Christians.

Most armies in secular states provide for the spiritual needs of their soldiers. The Indian Army, however, goes to great lengths to accommodate religion and uses it instrumentally to motivate its ranks.[8] When joining the army, all soldiers

Photo 8 A Buddhist soldier, a Christian soldier, a Sikh soldier, a Muslim soldier, and a Hindu soldier stand with their religious scriptures during a Presidential Colours Presentation ceremony in Rangreth on the outskirts of Srinagar, November 3, 2006. Photo copyright Danish Ismail/X01584/Reuters/Corbis.

take an oath on the Constitution of India and their respective religious text. The army celebrates a variety of religious holidays and regional festivals. Officers, regardless of their faith and ethnicity, are required to participate in these observances with their soldiers. The army maintains places of worship on its bases and provides a religious teacher – a pandit, granthi, maulvi, priest, or monk – for every 1,000 soldiers (a battalion). This teacher remains with the unit during regular operations and accompanies it to forward areas of battle. Army grooming and uniform regulations allow Sikhs to wear turbans, Muslims and Sikhs to keep beards, and Hindus to wear sacred threads (Photo 8).

Religion is a source of motivation in the Indian Army. Regiments predominantly made up of Hindus frequently adopt deities that reflect their regional character. Religious teachers use folktales and stories from holy texts such as the Hindu Mahabharata and Sikh Dasam Granth to inculcate their troops with the concepts of pride and valor. Battle cries are frequently religious in nature.[9] Pictures of fallen soldiers are kept inside places of worship on army bases. Religious teachers offer prayers before military exercises. Officers call on these teachers to give inspiring sermons and reassuring advice ahead of operations. Finally, weapons themselves are worshipped through certain rites.

Accommodating religion through state policies further entrenches the power of religion.[10] That said, religiosity is a defining feature of the lived experience of many soldiers. The challenge for a professional army, therefore, is to acknowledge this reality and to harness the benefits religion has to offer while still limiting its pernicious effects. The accommodation of religion and its instrumental use pose two challenges for the army: (1) subordinating religious authority to military authority, and (2) maintaining unit cohesion. These are explained in the next two sections.

Two Competing Authorities

Both religion and the military impose a set of regular practices, behavioral constraints, and a moral code on their members. These are supposed to order individuals' lives. When the military can accommodate the essential attributes of a religion, the two coexist, and religion can even reinforce the military's goals and objectives. It is when religious attributes come into conflict with the military that insubordination, interfaith conflict among the ranks, and even mutinies can arise.

Distinct hierarchies with different centers of authority define the Indian Army and the multiple faiths of its troops. Historically, one major organizational challenge for the army has been to establish the supremacy of the nation-state over religion. The Indian Army makes a concerted effort to accommodate religious tenets, but that effort is fundamentally limited. In instances when the two hierarchies are in conflict, the military's authority overrides religious authority.[11] One retired officer characterized this tension between simultaneously accommodating and subordinating religion. He said, "Since faith can often be an important part of a soldier's life, he must know that it is respected in the army. At the same time, his training must instill in him the belief that his duty and loyalty to the army, his fellow men, and his country are greater than his obligations to his faith."[12] Another former officer described his efforts to assist his brigade's religious teacher, but within clearly defined limits. He related, "Our brigade was moving during a military exercise. We had a Sikh battalion and I asked the Sikh granthi to travel with me in my helicopter, instead of moving with the rest of the battalion in vehicles." The officer extended this courtesy to the granthi because he knew that the granthi would ritually carry the heavy Sikh holy book, the Guru Granth Sahib, on his head during the move. Military regulations require passengers in military aircraft to wear their uniforms, but religious teachers do not wear uniforms. The granthi expressed reluctance to don one. The officer stated, "I told him, if you are not in uniform, you do not travel with us. He had to fall in line."[13]

Officers understand the management of religion is not as simple as establishing rules and commanding they be followed. In practice, subordinating religious authority to military authority can be difficult, especially during periods of communal violence, and is an ongoing process. A major general heading a division explained, "Suspicions of loyalty do arise, even among officers, especially when things are difficult in the country like they were around the Babri Masjid demolition and Operation Blue Star. It is not possible for the soldiers and officers to shut the world out completely in this day and age."[14] A majority of officers interviewed agreed with this view. At the same time, they felt the army had the means to reinforce its claim to the soldiers' loyalty over rival claims. Another brigade commander pointed out, "Life in the army is tough and people, irrespective of their faith, caste, or regional identity, go through these experiences together. This shared experience binds us. The honor of our regiments and our fellow men is at stake."[15]

Officers and soldiers alike adopt the distinct codes and practices of a regiment. The regimental history, traditions, mottoes, insignias, and awards are used to immerse personnel in the regimental identity. Long tenures of duty with the battalion of the regiment cement this identity over time. The adoption of the regimental identity helps establish the army's authority over the other allegiances of the soldiers. By grounding the idea of honor in regimental identity, the army undercuts the hold of faith on soldiers.

The army's operations, especially when forces are conducting counterinsurgency duties or restoring order in the aftermath of communal violence, also require it to remain sensitive to religious concerns. The army's accommodation of, and attentiveness to, faith lend it some credibility. And yet, every time the army's operational success comes at the expense of violating religious practices or codes, it endangers the trust that the army enjoys among its own ranks and society at large.[16] Historically, because religion has been one of the most potent triggers for civil disturbances, a less-than-cautionary approach while negotiating religious considerations would seriously undermine the military's legitimacy.

Internal Cohesion

Managing diversity while retaining an effective fighting force has been a long-standing challenge for Indian armies. It is important to point out that in India, identity politics – religious and ethnic – remains one of the key motifs of democratic politics. The army exists within an environment where religious and ethnic conflict is commonplace, and the state regularly turns to the army to enforce law and order during communal riots and to conduct counterinsurgency operations. The army therefore needs effective mechanisms to remain apolitical and maintain cohesion.

Religion presents the military with two possible challenges related to internal cohesion. First, religious bonding potentially provides both the issue and the resources for mutiny. After all, it is easier to politicize religion among collectives in which soldiers already share religious beliefs. A sense of group solidarity, it has long been feared, could enable group rebellion. Second, recognition of the salience of religion poses the danger of interreligious conflict within a multifaith army. For example, the religious cleavages common to the society could easily be imported into the military, causing it to rupture as has been the case in Bosnia, Lebanon, and Nigeria.

Because the army draws from and operates in a multifaith society, it must enjoy the support of the population. More important, to maintain force cohesion, it must have in place mechanisms that will allow it to manage religious diversity effectively and maintain interfaith harmony. The following section identifies four institutional mechanisms: (1) institutionalization of interfaith respect, (2) an apolitical organization, (3) selection of ethnicity as an organization principle, and (4) elite control. Together these are used to ensure the primacy of organizational authority and contain religiously motivated conflict within the army.

Four Institutional Mechanisms

The literature on ethnic and religious conflict suggests that institutional design matters for controlling violence. It points to a variety of institutional mechanisms that can variably exacerbate or reduce the prospects for conflict.[17] These range from electoral rules to power-sharing arrangements. States sometimes consciously select institutional designs that lower the probability of conflict. In other cases, conflict containment is an unintended consequence of institutional design. In either case, institutions are implicated in producing peace and preventing and containing violence. The Indian military also turns to institutional mechanisms to meet its faith-related challenges. The modern Indian Army imbibed the concern over the politicization of religion in the military from its parent institution – the British colonial army.[18] From it, the Indian Army also inherited some of the institutional mechanisms to address these concerns.[19]

Institutionalization of Interfaith Respect

In keeping with its secular approach, the army insists on interfaith respect. Criticism of faiths or religious practices is viewed as detrimental to troop discipline and is punished. More important, the large numbers of religious teachers recruited into the army are required to undergo a yearlong training program together at the Institute for National Integration, irrespective of their faith. The program is directed at making the religious teachers aware of the need for religious harmony and fostering a spirit of cooperation. These religious teachers are required to abide by army rules at all times and to adhere to the same command structure as other soldiers.

The army is very particular about presenting itself as a national institution, and respect for all faiths is a fundamental tenet of this image. The army, for example, celebrates men belonging to different faiths among its heroes, including the winners of gallantry awards. In the schools that it runs for the children of soldiers and officers – effectively catchment areas – prayers from multiple faiths are drawn on during school assemblies. Despite relying on religion to motivate soldiers during battle, the Indian Army does not define the enemy in religious terms because doing so would prove counterproductive for a mixed-faith force. In interviews with 126 soldiers belonging to different regiments that took part in operations during the Kargil conflict in 1998, 67 percent of soldiers talking about the Pakistani forces used terms such as *dushman* (enemy) or "Pakistani."[20] Pakistani opponents were almost never referred to directly as Muslims. The construction of the Indian soldier as the enemy has occurred differently within the Pakistani military, where Indian and Hindu identities are synonymous.

An Apolitical Organization

Traditionally, the army has remained apolitical. It has not demonstrated any inclination toward interfering in politics and has resented attempts by politicians to interfere in its internal affairs.[21] As a result, it takes an adverse view of serving officers who express political views or associate with political or social outfits, especially those that have religious leanings. This again is a legacy of the British colonial army which, fearing the influence of nationalist politicians and sporadic religious strife, turned distance from politics into a virtue for a soldier.

Similar fears and a desire to preserve its isolation continue to make the Indian Army into an apolitical organization. It maintains its distance from political parties, does not comment on political issues, and does not allow political parties or leaders to campaign before its personnel on military bases.[22] The appearance of these guidelines being violated draws a sharp response from inside and outside the army. The army also resists regular political demands in matters of recruitment from a particular ethnic or religious community or the creation of new ethnic regiments.

Selection of Ethnicity as an Organizational Principle

At the national level, religion, in India, makes a claim on a larger community than ethnicity. Hence, the politicization of religion potentially poses a greater threat to the army than the politicization of ethnicity. In multiethnic and multi-faith societies, the social cleavage structure can take two possible forms. It can be cumulative, where the different cleavages reinforce each other, or it can be crosscutting, where people united by one attribute could be divided by another. When cleavages cumulate, the fault lines run deeper, and a master or central cleavage can often divide societies. When cleavages crosscut, differences do not reinforce each other, and it becomes difficult for a master cleavage to emerge.

Indian society is characterized by crosscutting cleavages. As a result, where a common religious identity can potentially unite a people, their ethnic differences – understood as regional, linguistic, and caste differences – can potentially divide.[23] Through its organizational design, the army harnesses the cleavage structure to act as the first line of defense against a small, faith-based mutiny turning into a large-scale revolt. One of the lessons British commanders drew from the Sepoy Mutiny of 1857 was that religion could be a potent trigger for revolts and had to be managed carefully.[24] Similarly, ethnic, religious, and cultural sensitivies had to be accommodated. Another was that when the loyalty of a group broke down and the group rebelled, other ethnic groups could be used to subdue it.[25] There has been a long-standing predisposition in India toward organizing the army ethnically.

The colonial army followed a martial race theory for recruiting soldiers. According to this idea, some groups were especially well suited to soldiering because of their physical and cultural attributes. This system has been discontinued. Instead, each Indian state, a sizable number of which are organized along ethnic lines, has a quota for contributing soldiers to the military based on its population. Nevertheless, certain regions continue to contribute a disproportionate share of soldiers because of a tradition of military service.[26]

Today, the army is made up of mixed and ethnic regiments. The combat support and logistic support regiments have always been mixed. For example, in the engineer, artillery, and signal regiments, as well as in the service, medical, and ordinance corps, troops are drawn from different ethnic and religious groups. By contrast, a significant number of the infantry regiments remain ethnically organized. For example, the troops in the Jammu and Kashmir Light Infantry Regiment are recruited from the state of Jammu and Kashmir, and troops in the Bihar Regiment are recruited mostly from the state of Bihar. Although there are now a growing number of mixed infantry regiments, the battalions (1,000 men led by a colonel) and companies (120 men led by a major) in these regiments are often ethnically homogeneous (i.e., their troops are all drawn from the same region).[27] Despite not always sharing the same religious faith, they often share language and similar customs. As a result, regiment insignias, colors, and symbols of valor are mostly rooted in regional cultures.

Under this arrangement, the emphasis on ethnicity undermines the significance of faith. So, for example, even though the Rajputana Rifles, the Gurkhas, and the Jat regiments share the same faith – they are mostly Hindus – each one of these groups has an ethnically rooted, distinct regimental identity. The formation structures through which the soldiers of a particular regiment are deployed further limit the possibility of internal conflict. These structures disperse them into smaller groups, making containment of religiously or ethnically motivated group action easier.

Although regiments can be homogeneous or mixed, army formations are always mixed during times of both peace and conflict. A brigade formation typically brings together battalions from different regiments. Thus, even if a battalion is ethnically homogeneous, at the brigade level it may serve with other battalions composed of soldiers from other ethnic groups. This arrangement also ensures that any identity-motivated conflict within a company or a battalion can be easily isolated. Because the army draws from multiple ethnic groups, and emphasizes ethnicity in its organizational setup, any force-wide rebellion would have to overcome the significant challenge of cross-group coordination. This arrangement then allows the army to use forces belonging to different ethnic groups to quell any mutiny within a particular formation. In this way, using a largely ethnicity-centered organizational principle, the army defends itself from religiously and ethnicity-motivated internal conflict.

Elite Control

On the whole, the army relies on a professional and well-trained officer class for the success of the mechanisms it has put in place to maintain cohesion. In this sense, these mechanisms remain primarily elite-centric, with their efficacy dependent on the quality of officers. An officer is expected to adopt a paternal relationship with his men. The officers usually belong to a higher socioeconomic class and are better educated than the soldiers they command. Although among themselves officers converse in English, they converse with their men in the regional languages of their units or in Hindi. This social distance is also maintained through the segregation of dining and recreational facilities for the officers and soldiers. The considerations of ethnicity and religion followed for soldiers are overlooked in the case of officers. Whereas soldiers are often assigned regiments based on their ethnic identities, officers join regiments irrespective of their religious or ethnic identities. Thus, a Sikh officer can command Hindu troops and a Bengali officer can command a Gurkha battalion. In this way, officers become fluent in a multireligious and multiethnic discourse during their careers.

For officers, a group identity–based discourse enables them to relate to the soldiers under their command. At the same time, a nationalist-secular discourse, although acknowledging group identities, privileges national identity over group identity. For example, although officers are expected to immerse themselves in the religious and cultural practices of their troops, in areas that are designated exclusively for the use of officers (such as the officers' mess), discussions of religion are discouraged.[28] Religious teachings do not feature in the curriculum at any of the officer training academies. In addition, officers are trained and tasked to overcome coordination-related challenges arising when battalions made up of different groups must work together in a brigade. Multiple tenures with different formations enable the development of these skills; military exercises further test this ability.

In India's highly religious society, military operations in and around sacred sites are embedded with many difficulties. The symbolism and the danger of desecrating a sacred site can inflame an ongoing conflict. The army is vulnerable to appearing partisan, which can result in the loss of support among a group. If this group forms a part of the army, offending group sensibilities can provoke revolts among its own ranks. For these reasons, security forces find such sites especially challenging for carrying out counterinsurgency operations. By contrast, groups opposed to the state find such sites to be especially useful because of the protection they can provide against state action and the publicity they can bring to causes. Over the years, then, insurgent and terrorist groups in India have attacked sites of worship and have taken shelter there.[29]

The efficacy of institutions is tested in moments of crisis. Next, I draw on the Indian Army's experience in one such crisis to illustrate how the mechanisms outlined here fared during a period of stress. The crisis was triggered by the army's operation in a religious shrine and subsequent mutinies in some of its battalions. Operation Blue Star severely tested the Indian Army's engagement with religion. In setting aside sacred considerations in favor of operational requirements, it angered the Sikh community. A mutiny among its ranks then tested the mechanisms the army had in place to contain internal conflict.

Operation Blue Star and the Indian Army's Accommodation of Faith

In June 1984, the Indian Army was ordered to enter the Golden Temple to flush out armed men who had already been holed up in the complex for a few months. Located in Amritsar, the capital of the North Indian state of Punjab, the Golden Temple is the most sacred site to the Sikhs. The decision to use military force was triggered by an impasse in negotiations between a militant Sikh faction demanding a separate state and the federal government. The violence – assassinations and arsons – perpetrated by this group had paralyzed the civil administration in the state of Punjab.

The army's operation lasted seventy-two hours. Estimates on the number of casualties vary. According to the Indian government's figures, 83 army personnel were killed and 249 were wounded, and 493 people – including both militants and civilians present in the shrine – were killed, and 86 others were wounded.[30] Operation Blue Star occurred near the anniversary of the death of Guru Arjan Dev, the fifth among the lineage of Sikh gurus, and a large number of pilgrims who presumably could not leave the complex were trapped in the crossfire.

The operation conducted at the most sacred site in the Sikh faith had far-reaching effects. It deeply angered the Sikh community within India and beyond, and the army immediately confronted and quashed mutinies among Sikh soldiers in its ranks. In October 1984, Prime Minister Indira Gandhi was assassinated by two of her Sikh bodyguards. A resulting anti-Sikh pogrom claimed more than 3,000 lives and destroyed entire Sikh neighborhoods in the national capital of Delhi. Sikh militants also assassinated the chief of the Indian Army, who had retired one year after the operation.

The following discussion illustrates the conflict between the desire to accommodate religious sensitivities and the need for operational success, and how in one instance the army set aside religious considerations to meet its objectives. Prior to and during Operation Blue Star, the army took steps to demonstrate its respect for Sikh religious sentiments. As the operation progressed, however, some of these were set aside. To begin, a Sikh officer, Maj. Gen. K. S. Brar, was chosen to lead Operation Blue Star. Although no exclusively Sikh battalion participated in the operation, Sikh officers and soldiers participated as members of mixed battalions. The operation was made voluntary, and soldiers of all four of the participating battalions were given the option to opt out on religious grounds; few did, however.[31]

According to Gen. Brar's account of the operation plan, soldiers were instructed to use light weapons to avoid damage to key structures inside the temple complex, especially the Harmandir Sahib (the central sanctuary); pilgrims were to be separated from the militants and brought out safely; all troops taking part in the operation were to uphold the religious sanctity of the temple; and their personal behavior and conduct were to be unimpeachable.

The operation began at dusk on June 5, 1984. The planners were eager to accomplish their task before dawn, after which they believed soldiers would find it difficult to move in the complex without the cover of darkness. The army also feared that a protracted struggle could encourage an uprising in rural Punjab, where there was support for the separatists and their charismatic leader, Jarnail Singh Bhindranwale.[32] The separatists' group was headquartered in the Akal Takht, the second holiest structure in the complex and the seat of Sikh religious authority. This initially ruled out the use of heavy weapons during the assault. Multiple assaults on the Akal Takht by commando teams using CS gas – a stunning agent – were all repelled. The structure was well fortified, and without good intelligence, it seemed impossible to access it. As dawn approached and army casualties mounted, the army decided to use tanks to end the resistance. In the process, the Akal Takht suffered extensive damage.[33]

After the operation, when the army gained entry into the Harmandir Sahib, care was taken so that Sikh soldiers entered the shrine first. With the assistance of army granthis, the recitation of prayers was resumed in Harmandir Sahib within forty-eight hours after the operation commenced.[34] In its statements, the army insisted it had gone to great lengths to preserve the sanctity of the Golden Temple complex in keeping with its respect for the Sikh faith. Recounting his experience, Gen. Brar wrote, "In order to fight a battle righteously, there is no doubt that the army paid a heavy price in terms of casualties, and its soldiers never disobeyed the orders given to them, despite extreme provocation."[35] Speaking to journalists, the officer commanding troops in all of Punjab during the operation, Lt. Gen. Dayal, himself a Sikh, said, "As all of you know, the Indian army is a very religious army. Once the orders are given to them they follow them to the letter and once it was told to them [not to damage the Golden Temple] I was sure they will obey this and I am proud to say they did until the end."[36] Lt. Gen. Sunderji, the man who oversaw the entire mobilization as the area commander of the Western Command under which the state of Punjab falls, said, "We went inside with humility in our hearts and prayers on our lips. We in the army hold all places of religion in equal reverence."[37]

With the aim of accommodating religious sensitivities, the army chose a Sikh commander to lead Operation Blue Star, Sikh soldiers were given the option to remove themselves from the operation, instructions were given to keep the Harmandir Sahib out of the line of fire, and heavy weapons were not deployed in the early stages of the operation. Only when soldiers failed to enter the Akal Takht after repeated attempts and when casualties mounted, did the army seek permission from the prime minister's office to use tank fire in the temple complex. One retired officer who was closely connected with the operation recounted the dilemma for me. He said, "All hell had broken out. ... We had bad intelligence. ... We had taken heavy casualties on the Parikrama. ... After losing so many men, there could be no turning back. Had we done that, it would have been a disaster for the morale. So we used tanks against the Akal Takht, which was also a disaster."[38]

The operation angered many Sikhs. Although the Harmandir Sahib, a square structure at the center of the fight, remained largely untouched, the damage suffered by the Akal Takht and other buildings, in addition to heavy civilian casualties, represented the desecration and defilement of the Sikh religion's most sacred site by the army.

The tactics and implementation of Operation Blue Star point to the tightrope the army had to walk to meet its objective. To the extent possible, soldiers respected the religious sensitivities associated with the sacred site, perhaps at the expense of higher casualties. The operation was guided by military objectives, however, and when these conflicted with sacred considerations, operational success took priority. This success came at a heavy price.

Operation Blue Star: Managing the Sikh Mutiny

The reports of the assault on the Golden Temple and the accompanying rumors spread a wave of anger among Sikhs worldwide. The Indian Army did not remain untouched. Sikh soldiers stationed in different cantonments revolted. They looted armories, deserted their positions, and, in one instance, killed their commanding officer. The modern Indian Army had not faced a revolt of this nature before. A complete information blackout ordered by the government during the operation resulted in the circulation of highly inflammatory rumors. In many instances these triggered the revolts. But there was no denying the grievance of Sikh soldiers. When soldiers chose to break army rules and overrule their commanders, the claim of faith trumped the claim the army made on these soldiers. Operation Blue Star had turned religion, an ally that the army used to motivate men, into a rival. A Sikh Regiment soldier who participated in the revolt in his battalion said, "When I joined the army, I took an oath on the Guru Granth Sahib. The army tells us to be good warriors in the name of our faith. Then how could I sit quietly when the very foundation of my faith was attacked by the army?"[39]

The cantonment revolts highlighted the difficulty of isolating the military as an institution from the social and political upheavals occurring around it. It was discovered that separatists had managed to influence some army units. As a result, soldiers had provided the separatists with financial, emotional, and material support in the form of weapons. There were close to a dozen instances of revolts spread over multiple locations.

The mutinies seem to represent a failure of the army's institutional mechanisms. On the whole, however, these measures prevented a catastrophe from unfolding. Only 2,000 men, or 3 percent of the Sikh soldiers serving in the army, participated in the mutinies. In the most sensational case, in which around 1,400 soldiers deserted after killing their commanding officer and arming themselves, a significant number of the participants were found to be new recruits unschooled in regimental traditions, and who, as a result, were incited easily or, in some instances, were forced to participate at gunpoint. None of the Sikh battalions stationed close to the shrine revolted. And, perhaps most important, no serving Sikh officer joined the mutiny. For a large part of the army, the fallout remained limited. The mechanisms it had in place to deal with such a contingency, as I argue in the following section, curtailed the incidence of mutiny and its spread.

Ethnic Organization
Among Sikhs, religious identity is reinforced by a territorial identity because most Sikhs originate from the Punjab. Sikh grievances centered on both regional and religious issues, making them potent for use. And yet, the decision to participate in the mutiny reflected caste differences. Higher-caste Jat Sikhs join different regiments from lower-caste Mazhabi Sikhs. Despite a common grievance related to the desecration of their holiest site, the mutinies occurred mostly in the Jat Sikh battalions from the Sikh and Punjab regiments. Battalions from the Sikh Light Infantry – the regiment of the Mazhabi Sikhs – did not participate. Where mutinies occurred, help was often at hand because of the mixed nature of the formations. Soldiers from the adjoining non-Sikh battalions were used to disarm and round up the mutineers. New recruits at the regimental center were found to be most easily incited. They had yet to be socialized into the traditions of their units and failed to grasp the stigma their actions would impose on their regiment.

Elite Command
As noted earlier, the efficacy of the institutional mechanisms turns on the quality of leadership shown by the officers. In its official and unofficial assessments of the factors responsible for the revolts, the army assigned blame to its officers. For the army, a mutiny was symptomatic of a broken officer-soldier relationship. In some instances, assessments suggested that officers had failed to communicate with their soldiers and had not preempted their potential for incitement. They also found that officers had failed to check the influence of religious preachers who were advocating for the Sikh militants inside army cantonments. These situations marked a failure of the officer-centric elite command structure.

According to comments appearing in the Indian press, retired officers – even those who disagreed with the government's policy to send the army into the temple – concurred with this official view. Lt. Gen. Harbaksh Singh said, "They thought their villages were being attacked when they heard the announcement that the army was being deployed in the Punjab. Regiments should have sent small parties under the command of officers to the Punjab to see what was happening and to report back to their colleagues." Lt. Gen. S. K. Sinha went further. In a newspaper interview, he said, "As far as the mutiny goes, I will squarely blame the officer corps, because they apparently did not know what their men were thinking. ... I am very clear in my mind on this issue. Officers must know their men better than their mothers. In this case they obviously did not."[40] A survey of approximately 100 Sikh and non-Sikh officers echoed similar sentiments. Both groups blamed poor performance among officers for the mutinies more than any other factor.[41]

Still, no serving Sikh officer joined the mutiny. To appreciate fully how consequential the lack of participation by Sikh officers turned out to be, consider the following. One of the reasons Operation Blue Star ran into heavier resistance than expected was because of the involvement of a retired army general in fortifying the Golden Temple complex. Maj. Gen. Shahbag Singh (ret.), a decorated officer and an expert in guerrilla warfare, had joined the Sikh militants and was commanding the resistance. His early discharge in 1976 following charges of corruption had caused him to become disaffected.[42] If mutinying soldiers had been organized under the leadership of serving Sikh officers, the effects would have been catastrophic.

There are also instances in which Sikh and non-Sikh officers were able to prevent a mutiny among their Sikh soldiers. It is fair to assume that without the intervention of these men the mutiny could have spread across additional Sikh battalions. During field research for this project, I identified officers commanding Sikh battalions in June 1984 and then interviewed those who were willing to discuss their experiences. Among those identified and interviewed, five officers played a pivotal role in calming passions and reassuring troops. When asked why his troops listened to him, one officer explained, "They had respect for me. I had been there for them. That night, if my men did not trust me, they would have shot me. They were very angry. They had been hearing all types of stories about what was going on in their villages." Another officer, recounting a nightlong conversation with his troops, said, "I was like a parent, sometimes I had to shout at them, while at other times I had to be gentle with them."[43] Officers also said that, in trying to calm the passions of their soldiers, they appealed to their regimental and battalion identity and its honor, telling their soldiers that if they revolted, their units would be dishonored forever.[44]

Ethnic organization and elite control mechanisms were not sufficient to prevent a mutiny among all Sikh battalions during a politically charged period. At the same time, these measures were able to limit the damage in instances where the soldiers revolted. Caste divisions among Sikhs and the mixed-deployment model prevented the mutiny from spreading across all the Sikh battalions. The army turned to its elite command structure as the primary bulwark against the widespread breakdown of discipline. Where mutinies occurred, fault was found with the army's command structure.[45] Although some retired Sikh officers openly backed the militants, no serving officer joined them. A few senior Sikh bureaucrats resigned to protest Operation Blue Star, but no Sikh officer resigned in protest. Under remarkable stress, the army strived to remain apolitical throughout the conflict; it deferred the decision to increase force to the prime minister's office. Soldiers followed norms of interfaith respect. Sikh soldiers were not attacked by non-Sikhs, and mutinying Sikh soldiers did not turn on soldiers of other faiths stationed in their vicinity. When investigations revealed that in a few instances Sikh granthis had played a role in instigating troops to rebel after Operation Blue Star, the army acted swiftly and in 1985 set up the Institute for National Integration, a school for training all religious teachers who join the armed forces.

The two parts of the case study illustrate the religion-related challenges the Indian Army faces and the four institutional mechanisms it relies on to meet them. The army has been deployed regularly for internal security duties within India and suffered very high numbers of casualties in the process. The conflicts it is involved in have implications for its internal cohesion, organizational discipline, and the support it enjoys among the civilian population.

Conclusion

According to conventional wisdom, the organization of militaries should be driven by the objective of projecting maximum military power during battle. Militaries are not perpetually engaged in fighting wars with other states, however. They are often called on to perform duties related to internal security or to assist with state administration. Officers and soldiers alike have to live and train while still being a part of society. In multiethnic and multireligious societies, militaries are exposed to the social conflicts that surround them. Militaries can build barriers to shield themselves from these pressures, but an active role in the preservation of internal security can make them vulnerable to social conflicts. Therefore, they must strive to ensure self-preservation. As organizations, militaries also have an institutional memory informed by their experiences.

The modern Indian Army inherited from its colonial predecessor the fear of internal conflict and a concern for its own preservation while existing in a society prone to religious and ethnic volatility. Because religion could not be separated from the soldiers recruited into the force, it was accommodated and, where possible, harnessed to provide motivation and comfort. The army has continued to use and refine the institutional mechanisms it inherited to contain the danger religion poses to the organization. Even as it has repeatedly been assigned internal security responsibilities, it has accepted these reluctantly. Given the political backdrop against which it operates, and the internal security-related responsibilities it is instructed to discharge, it is faced with the constant danger of being influenced by the politicization of religion in Indian society.

Today, from Iraq to Afghanistan, constructing national armies remains a challenge for multinational states. The experience of the Indian Army offers important policy lessons for managing issues related to religious and ethnic diversity. The Indian Army recruits from a society with a history of identity conflict and political violence. As a result, it has had to develop mechanisms to manage diversity; these should be instructive for other multireligious and multiethnic militaries.

Notes

1 The army takes a "neutrality approach" to secularism, which emphasizes equal respect for all faiths by state institutions and has been preferred for centuries in India. This is different from the more austere "prohibition approach," which enforces strict separation between religion and state institutions and has found favor in Western democracies. See Amartya Sen, *The Argumentative Indian: Writings on Indian History, Culture, and Identity* (London: Penguin, Books Ltd. 2005): 16–19.

2 "Religious Composition," *Census of India*, 2001.

3 The Indian National Election Study is conducted by the Centre for the Study of Developing Societies in New Delhi.

4 James Hackett, ed., *The Military Balance, 2010* (London: Routledge, 2010).

5 For information on religious diversity in the Indian Army, see Raju G. C. Thomas and Bharat Karnad, "The Military and National Integration in India," in *Ethnicity, Integration, and the Military*, ed. Henry Dietz, Jerrold Elkin, and Maurice Roumani (Boulder, CO: Westview Press, 1991); and Omar Khalidi, "Ethnic Group Recruitment in the Indian Army: The Contrasting Cases of Sikhs, Muslims, Gurkhas, and Others Source," *Pacific Affairs* 74, no. 4 (Winter 2001–2002): 529–552. Khalidi references data from a 1997 parliamentary debate indicating that there were "religious teachers of the following categories: Hindu pundits, 1568; Sikh Granthis, 194; Muslim Maulavis, a mere 54; Christian padres, 27; and 11 Buddhist monks" (544). The Indian Army purportedly provides one religious teacher for every 1,000 soldiers of each faith. This allows for a rough extrapolation of the religious composition of the Indian Army. The army itself collects data on soldiers' religions but does not make them available, a fact lamented by the government's own Sachar Committee Report (2005) on the social, economic, and education status of the Muslim community of India.

6 Khalidi, "Ethnic Group Recruitment in the Indian Army."

7 For the role demobilized soldiers played in partition-related violence see Jha, Saumitra and Steven Wilkinson. "Does Combat Experience Foster Organizational Skill? Evidence from Ethnic Cleansing during the Partition of South Asia," American Political Science Review, vol. 106. no. 4 (November 2012), pgs. 883–907.

8 This instrumental use of religion can be traced to the British colonial army and before. After the Sepoy Mutiny in 1857, the British colonial army executed and imprisoned hundreds of Muslim religious teachers. And yet, in the following decades, the colonial military had once again begun to tolerate independent maulvis and faqirs in its cantonments. According to Nile Green, the relationship between the religious traditions of the soldier and the exigencies of the British Empire was

one of give and take. He writes, "The Islam of the Indian soldier was capable of assisting or resisting imperial agendas, lending mechanisms of loyalty no less than rebellion" (xi). The British consciously tolerated these teachers in spite of their danger – they were the brokers who promised protection, promotion, comfort, and miracles to their soldiers. The significance of these men in the lives of the sepoys required their accommodation. See Nile Green, *Islam and the Army in Colonial India: Sepoy Religion in the Service of Empire* (Cambridge: Cambridge University Press, 2009).

9 Hindu Gurkhas are known to use the battle cry *"Jai Ma Kali"* (Victory to the Goddess Kali). The cry *"Jo Bole So Nihal, Sat Sri Akal"* (Blessed is the one who proclaims the truth of God) can be heard among the Sikh Light Infantry and the Sikh Regiment. Muslim soldiers in the Jammu and Kashmir Rifles, Jammu and Kashmir Light Infantry, and the Grenadiers have used the battle cry *"Allah hu Akbar"* (God is great).

10 David Laitin, *Hegemony and Culture: The Politics of Religious Change among the Yoruba* (Chicago: University of Chicago Press, 1986).

11 In countries with officially recognized state religions, militaries may remain autonomous (as in Pakistan and Bangladesh) or subordinate their authority to religious officials to varying degrees (as in Iran and the Holy See). In the latter instances, the army's capacity to act can be heightened by religion.

12 Personal interview, June 2010.

13 Personal interview, July 2010.

14 Personal interview, March 2010. The Babri Masjid was a sixteenth-century mosque in a small town in North India purportedly built on the birthplace of the Hindu god Ram. It was destroyed on 6 December 1992 by hundreds of right-wing Hindu nationalists. The event sparked Hindu-Muslim communal violence across the country that killed more than 2,000 people. Operation Blue Star was a military exercise conducted to remove Sikh militants from the Golden Temple in Amritsar. The events surrounding the operation and its aftermath are related in further detail later in this chapter.

15 Personal interview, July 2010. Honor, or *izzat*, is a powerful norm in Indian society.

16 The army ranks among one of the most trusted national institutions. The 2005 State of Democracy in South Asia survey project by the Centre for the Study of Developing Societies found 73.5 percent of Indians expressed trust in the army. The corresponding figure for the police was 51.4 percent.

17 Donald. L. Horowitz, *Ethnic Groups in Conflict* (Berkeley: University of California Press, 1985) and *A Democratic South Africa?: Constitutional Engineering in a Divided Society* (Berkeley: University of California Press, 1991); Arend Lijphart, *Democracy in Plural Societies: A Comparative Exploration* (New Haven, CT: Yale University Press, 1977) and *Patterns of Democracy: Government Forms and Performance in Thirty-Six Countries* (New Haven, CT: Yale University Press, 1999).

18 Rajit K. Mazumdar, *The Indian Army and the Making of Punjab* (Delhi: Permanent Black, 2003).

19 The mechanisms developed by the colonial army cast a long shadow because, over the decades, the army has undergone a limited transformation. The modern Indian state inherited a variety of state institutions from the colonial state. But more than

any other institution in India, the army retains the strongest resemblance to its colonial parent. The political pressures that have transformed other institutions have affected it to a far lesser degree. Although as compared to its colonial predecessor it enjoys a vastly reduced role in the decision-making structure with the civil-military relations skewed significantly in favor of the civilian bureaucracy and the politicians, it has been able to resist political interference in its organization and its internal functioning. See Stephen P. Rosen, *Societies and Military Power: India and Its Armies* (Ithaca, NY: Cornell University Press, 1996); Stephen P. Cohen, *The Indian Army: Its Contribution to the Development of a Nation* (Berkeley: University of California Press, 1971).

20 I conducted these interviews in 2010 across three cantonments.

21 The Indian Army can be distinguished from the U.S. and Israeli armies with regard to military officers becoming political candidates. Retired Indian military officers seldom seek political office. One exception was the first chief of the Indian Army, General K. M. Cariappa, who contested elections on the ticket of the Hindu Nationalist Party and lost.

22 For details on how the Kargil conflict with Pakistan became politicized, much to the chagrin of the military, see the chapter "Leave Us Alone" in General V. P. Malik, *Kargil: From Surprise to Victory* (New Delhi: HarperCollins Publishers India, 2006): 303–319.

23 Ashutosh Varshney and Amit Ahuja, "Antecedent Nationhood, Subsequent Statehood: Explaining the Relative Success of Indian Federalism," in *Sustainable Peace: Power and Democracy after Civil War*, ed. Philip G. Roeder and Donald Rothchild, (Ithaca, NY: Cornell University Press, 2005).

24 The Vellore Mutiny of 1806 and the Sepoy Mutiny of 1857 were both triggered by the religiously rooted grievances of soldiers.

25 Charles Wood, British Secretary of State for India from 1859 to 1866 articulated the intension clearly: "I wish to have a different and rival spirit in different regiments, so that Sikh might fire into Hindoo, Goorkha into either, without any scruple in case of need." Cited in Perry Anderson, "Gandhi Center Stage," *London Review of Books*. Vol. 34. No. 23, 5 July 2012, 3–11.

26 Rosen, *Societies and Military Power*; Cohen, *The Indian Army*.

27 The Parachutes and Guards are elite regiments, which can be completely mixed even at the unit level.

28 Cohen, *The Indian Army*; Pradeep P. Barua, *Gentlemen of the Raj: The Indian Army Officer Corps, 1817–1949* (Westport, CT: Praeger, 2003).

29 For the special challenges posed by counterinsurgency operations in sacred spaces, see Ron E. Hassner, *War on Sacred Grounds* (Ithaca, NY: Cornell University Press, 2009); and C. Christine Fair and Sumit Ganguly, *Treading on Hallowed Ground* (Oxford: Oxford University Press, 2008).

30 Mark Tully and Satish Jacob, *Amritsar: Mrs. Gandhi's Last Battle* (Calcutta: Rupa and Company, 1985). The government did not break down the casualty figures into combatants and noncombatants. While few questions have been raised over military casualty figures, the veracity of the nonmilitary casualty figures has been widely questioned. The police official charged with cremation recalls counting more than 550 bodies.

31 K. S. Brar, *Operation Blue Star: The True Story* (New Delhi: South Asia Books, 1993).

32 Ibid.
33 In *Amritsar*, Tully and Jacob write that, in a statewide operation, the army also surrounded thirty-seven other Sikh temples the same night to eject separatists from them. With the exception of the temple in Patiala, where twenty-one people were killed, it did not encounter significant resistance.
34 Ibid.
35 Brar, *Operation Blue Star*, 127–128.
36 Tully and Jacob, *Amritsar*, 158.
37 Ibid.
38 Personal interview, January 2011.
39 Personal interview, December 2010.
40 Tully and Jacob, *Amritsar*, 197–198.
41 Apurba Kundu, "The Indian Armed Forces' Sikh and Non-Sikh Officers' Opinions of Operation Blue Star," *Pacific Affairs* 67, no. 1 (Spring 1994): 46–69.
42 According to Tully and Jacob, *Amritsar*, 89–90, many retired officers were sympathetic to the Sikh extremists, although few advocated an armed insurrection.
43 Interviews conducted between March and July 2010.
44 Kundu, "The Indian Armed Forces' Sikh and Non-Sikh Officers' Opinions of Operation Blue Star."
45 In the Sikh revolt, the army was facing one of its worst nightmares. Sikhs formed a substantial component of its fighting forces. A religious divide, if it had taken hold, could have split the army. Therefore, the army was quick to learn lessons from Operation Blue Star. Since then, similar situations have arisen twice in Punjab, and subsequently in Kashmir. In the two occupations of the Golden Temple precincts by Sikh militants in 1986 and 1988, and of the Hazratbal shrine by Kashmiri separatists in 1993 and 1996, the army laid siege to the complexes but did not enter. A Sufi shrine besieged by the army in Kashmir was gutted in a systematic fire started by Pakistani militants. See C. Christine Fair, "The Golden Temple: A Tale of Two Sieges," and Sumit Ganguly, "A Mosque, a Shrine, and Two Sieges," in Fair and Ganguly, *Treading on Hallowed Ground*.

PART IV

CONSTITUTIONAL CHALLENGES

8

United States I

Martin L. Cook

No religious Test shall ever be required as a Qualification to any Office or public Trust under the United States. (U.S. Constitution, Article 5)

Congress shall make no law respecting an establishment of religion, or prohibiting the free exercise thereof. (U.S. Constitution, First Amendment)

This chapter begins with a short note about the author's context and approach to the topic.[1] Unlike the social-scientific approach of many of my colleagues' chapters in this volume, I write from the perspective of a military ethicist who has had the privilege of working closely with U.S. military officers at the United States Air Force Academy, the Army War College, and now the Naval War College. The perspective I bring to bear on the role of religion in the military is more normative than descriptive. Because the foundation of professional military ethics in the United States is the oath each member takes to the Constitution of the United States, the question of the proper role of religious belief, practice, proselytizing, and so on, is necessarily framed in terms of how individuals understand constitutional guidance on such matters and, more important, how they ought to understand that guidance.

As the following discussion shows, these questions of constitutional understanding are by no means fixed and clear. Indeed, they are highly controversial topics among military members in the United States and in U.S. society and government itself. To some degree, this is inevitable, because the tension between the two guarantees of the First Amendment of the U.S. Constitution, the right to free exercise of one's own religion and the restriction on the federal government's endorsement of any particular religious belief or practice, virtually enshrines struggle about religion into the foundation of the U.S. government. This chapter explores these tensions as they have played out in the experience and practice of the U.S. military in recent years. Because the author's professional location entails leading officers to explore and understand the proper normative behavioral standard that should guide their professional behavior in these areas of religious practice, this chapter necessarily reflects that quest for normative clarity and the importance of correcting faulty understandings and behaviors in the U.S. military.

I taught at the United States Air Force Academy during three periods: 1991–1992, 1993–1994, and 2003–2009, when I was part of the "permanent" faculty and deputy department head of the Philosophy Department. I was present when issues of religious proselytizing and advocacy made national news for a period of time. This attention was precipitated by a report, written by a team from Yale Divinity School, that observed such practices during cadet basic training. As the investigation widened, many routine and accepted practices at the academy came under scrutiny for not sufficiently maintaining a religiously neutral atmosphere required under the Constitution for any institution of the federal government of the United States. Unlike Pauletta Otis (see Chapter 9), I found that particular event to be a manifestation of a deeper and fairly widespread tendency by some individuals and units to fundamentally misunderstand, either deliberately or through ignorance, their constitutional duties with respect to religion.

This misunderstanding is further complicated, I argue, by the emergence of a significant misrepresentation of U.S. history with respect to religion's role in the country's constitutional form of government. This misrepresentation is primarily propagated among the Evangelical community in the United States. Inevitably, anything widely taught among Evangelicals will find its way into the minds of Evangelical chaplains and service members. I therefore argue that the United States faces a significant educational mission, as well as an occasional requirement for disciplinary action, to stamp out this pernicious alternative history and to prevent it from influencing policy and practice in the services.

It is inevitable that religion will play a significant role in the U.S. military. As the most religiously active developed society on earth, it is certain that many American officers and enlisted personnel will have significant religious convictions and that those convictions will frame, at least partially, what they think and do. Furthermore, the understanding of patriotism for most Americans has from the very beginning of the country been cast in religious terms – if not those of specifically Christian religion, at least in terms of what sociologist Robert Bellah called American "civil religion."[2] In the tenets of that vague but widely shared civil religion, the United States is God's "chosen nation," and its founding and institutions are in some sense the example to the world. Finally, the importance of religion and spirituality in the U.S. military is reflected in the institution of the military chaplaincy, an institution that reaches back to the Revolutionary Army.

Military Chaplains

The Continental Congress established the role of military chaplain in 1775, believing that chaplains would help maintain the moral standards of the troops (and perhaps attract divine favor to the revolutionary cause). Furthermore, since Constantine, it was a bedrock assumption of Christendom that political unity required (in his slogan) "One God, one Lord, one faith, one Church, one Empire, one Emperor." In keeping with that assumption, all of the colonies except Pennsylvania and Rhode Island had established churches, financed with tax monies.

The relationship between religion and politics in the United States grew more problematic after the ratification of the Constitution with its Bill of Rights. Most obviously, the First Amendment's twin restrictions on the role of the federal government regarding religion prohibited any "establishment" of religion or any actions that might restrict the "free exercise" of religion by residents and citizens of the United States. Of perhaps even greater importance than these First Amendment restrictions on interference by the federal government in religious matters is the prohibition within the body of the Constitution itself of any religious test for the holding of political office in the United States. Constitutionally, therefore, the principle was very clear that individuals' religious convictions or lack thereof were not in any way to be considered in assessing their worthiness for holding federal office, including military rank.

The existence of a chaplain corps was and continues to be justified on the grounds that the relatively isolated locations of many military installations, and especially of deployed troops, requires chaplains to assist in facilitating the free exercise of religion by military personnel.[3] Needless to say, that rationale was easier to maintain when the range of religious opinion among military personnel was relatively narrow (i.e., when most soldiers were Protestant Christians). The steady increase in religious diversity has created tensions between the confessionally specific convictions of chaplains and their confessionally neutral role of facilitating the free exercise of religion for members of any and all religious persuasions – including, it is important to highlight, no religious convictions at all.

Changes in the demographics of the military chaplain corps pose further challenges. As in the larger society, Roman Catholic priests are in short supply. The process of accrediting chaplains has opened up, and the social forces that created what used to be called "mainline" Protestantism, which provided the vast majority of Protestant military chaplains through World War II, have shifted the theological fulcrum of the Protestant chaplaincy considerably. Changes within Protestant Christianity in the broader society have also manifested themselves in the religious convictions of service members, causing many to seek religious community outside the military chapel/chaplain system entirely. For example, one of the largest megachurches in the United States (the New Life Church, formerly and famously associated with the Reverend Ted Haggard, president of the National Association of Evangelicals) is located directly across the interstate highway from the United States Air Force Academy. Many cadets attend New Life's very popular Friday night service/social mixer.[4] Therefore, it would be a mistake to focus one's analysis of the role of religion in the military exclusively on the base chapel and military chaplain aspect of practice. Doing so would exclude the role of parachurch groups, such as the Officers' Christian Fellowship, Campus Crusade for Christ's military ministry, and others that play a significant role in the religious lives of many officers.[5]

Recent years have witnessed a number of significant demographic shifts within American Protestantism. The old establishment "mainline" churches of Protestantism (Episcopalian, Methodist, Presbyterian, etc.) have dramatically declined in membership, while nondenominational Evangelical churches and a few Evangelical and Pentecostal denominations have grown dramatically in size and organization.[6] There has also been a marked shift in the theological slant of the Protestant chaplaincy in the military services, as chronicled by Anne Loveland.[7] Broadly speaking, Loveland shows that Evangelicals rightly felt they had been excluded from the military chaplaincy during World War II. Until that point, only a relatively small number of denominations were recognized as "endorsing agents" (i.e., recognized groups that were approved to send their ordained personnel into the chaplaincy). Evangelical ministers, with the help of like-minded senior military officers, set about to broaden the range of recognized "endorsers" who could put forward chaplains.[8] In parallel with that trend, Loveland further shows how the great unpopularity of the Vietnam War among the mainline/liberal churches led them to send fewer and fewer chaplains into the service. The effect of these two trends was to dramatically shift the Protestant chaplaincy toward the Evangelical side of the spectrum. Today, according to one reliable source, 33 percent of the chaplains come from Evangelical traditions, and the Air Force reports that 87 percent of those now seeking to become chaplains are Evangelicals, even though only 3 percent of military members identify themselves as Evangelical.[9]

Jeff Sharlet brings that account up to the present time.[10] Sharlet documents, in detail and by name, activities of senior military officers endorsing specific religious organizations. These officers used their positions of authority and rank to foist their personal religious convictions on their subordinates and commands. After surveying actions of a number of very senior officers and the civilian secretary of the army, Sharlet summarizes as follows:

What such men have fomented is a quiet coup within the armed forces: not of general encroaching on civilian rule but of religious authority displacing the military's once staunchly secular code. Not a conspiracy but a cultural transformation, achieved gradually through promotions and prayer meetings, with personal faith replacing protocol according to the genuinely best intentions of commanders who conflate God with country. They see themselves not as subversives, but as spiritual warriors, "ambassadors for Christ in uniform," according to the Officers' Christian Fellowship (OCF) which, with fifteen thousand members active at more than 80 percent of U.S. military bases, is the biggest fundamentalist group in the military.[11]

In addition, since the 1970s, the Evangelical churches have become highly politically partisan, virtually a guaranteed element of the Republican base.

The Evangelical movement has made a specific set of claims about the religious nature of the Constitution and the American founding that has become widely taught and believed within that segment of American Protestantism. This poses special challenges because it affects fundamentally how the oath to the Constitution, which lies at the heart of military ethics in the U.S. military, should be understood.

Finally, much of the military conflict in which U.S. forces are engaged around the world is with predominantly Muslim forces. This requires soldiers to understand the nature of the motives and beliefs of the adversary and invites them to frame those conflicts in religious terms. Given that religious beliefs do indeed play a central role in the motivations for the conflict, some interpretation of those beliefs is not only inevitable but required. Nevertheless, a religious construal of the conflict may constrain the abilities of the U.S. military to successfully engage and understand opponents and exacerbate religious misunderstanding.

Religious Practices

For those with a clear understanding of the religious issues surrounding the writing and ratification debates of the Constitution, the fundamental issues are relatively clear: the federal government and its officers are in no way to support any particular religious denomination or set of convictions, nor are they to impermissibly (i.e., when interference is not truly necessary for mission accomplishment) interfere in the free exercise of religion by citizens generally. Because military officers and enlisted personnel are agents of the federal government and have sworn an oath to preserve, protect, and defend that Constitution, one might think the role of religion in the public and official life of the military would be pretty simple to understand and enforce: the military ought to be a religiously neutral place in its public acts and activities, and professions of faith and religious practices ought to be confined to private actions and voluntary gatherings of like-minded coreligionists in the military.

In practice, of course, matters are hardly that simple. Because the nation was overwhelmingly Protestant Christian in the first century or so of its national life, many religious practices have become customary in military organizations. Given that the military necessarily seeks to preserve tradition, many of these practices remain in place.[12] These include prayers at many public, and often mandatory, military gatherings, such as change of command ceremonies and convocations at various schools of professional military education and graduation ceremonies. They include nightly prayers broadcast throughout every ship in the U.S. Navy. Prayers are said publicly at meals at the Naval Academy.

Often these prayers and activities are generic, and sometimes their content reflects American civil religion more than confessionally specific Christian (or other) religious convictions. This is not always the case, however. There

Photo 9 A U.S. Marine chaplain baptizes a marine during a Sunday Protestant service for marines from the 1st Marine Division, February 23, 2003, in Kuwait. Photo copyright Robert Nickelsberg/Getty Images.

is a strong sentiment in some quarters of the military that chaplains and others should express robust and particularistic religious convictions at times of prayer and that generic expressions are too tepid to bother with.

There are further confusions regarding what events warrant or justify the "solemnizing" benefits of public prayer. At one end of the spectrum are events that, while publicly witnessed, are essentially private. These include promotion ceremonies and retirement ceremonies convened to commemorate and celebrate an event in the life of a single individual. Although some in the audience may not share the religious views expressed, they usually attend because of personal respect and friendship and understand that the event allows wide latitude for self-expression on the part of that individual. Furthermore, although attendance at such events may be highly "expected," it remains within the realm of personal discretion to absent oneself from them if one anticipates religious activities in which one does not wish to participate.

At the other extreme, and clearly unwarranted constitutionally, are mandatory unit formations of a relatively routine nature such as staff meetings, change of command ceremonies, dinings-in (formal dinners organized by military units), and so on. Although it is true that a great deal of customary inclusion of religious activities at such events has occurred, it is equally true that no one of good faith and a deep appreciation of the intent of the First Amendment can justify their use in such circumstances. To cite one example from the author's own experience, the annual Fall Convocation at the United States Naval War College – a mandatory gathering of all faculty and staff, including officers from more than fifty nations – begins and ends with a Christian prayer led by a Christian navy chaplain.[13] One might think that the distinction between appropriate and inappropriate occasions for prayer should be clear in the minds of chaplains and officers in general. Unfortunately, actual practice deviates from respect for pluralism in a large number of cases.[14]

Initially prompted by events at the Air Force Academy, Mikey Weinstein, a retired air force judge advocate general (i.e., lawyer) created the Military Religious Freedom Foundation (MRFF).[15] The foundation has broadened its mandate to hear complaints from across the Department of Defense from members and civilians who observe practices, teaching, and events that appear to them to be constitutionally inappropriate intrusions of confessionally specific religion into their units. A review of the foundation's Web site will give the reader a sense of how widespread such events actually are. Mikey Weinstein, the head of the MRFF, has recently published a narrative account of his foundation's activities, *No Snowflake in an Avalanche*.[16] While the rhetoric of the book is somewhat heated, the author was present for many of the events recounted in the narrative and can vouch for the factuality of the account.

For example, on September 1, 2011, Chief of Staff of the Air Force Gen. Norman Schwartz issued a memo to the entire U.S. Air Force, instructing all units to ensure that all teaching, training, and events show no favoritism to a specific religion or group.[17] The memo was prompted by a complaint from a number of officers who had received training on ethics while preparing to be missile launch officers. The training included a section of Christian just war materials that, while historically accurate, appeared to some to be suggesting that the proper framing for the ethics of their practice was Christian. The students' nickname for the course was "Jesus Loves Nukes."[18]

Naturally, most units simply forwarded the memo throughout their commands, as one would expect when one's chief issues a general directive. In the Air Force Academy, however, senior staff seem to have briefly discussed the memo but did not distribute it widely, despite the repeated urging of MRFF that they do so. The somewhat amusing response by MRFF was to purchase billboard space near the main entrance of the academy to post the entire text of the memo. Why the resistance to wide distribution of the memo? Such behavior is difficult to explain if the intent of the leaders in question is to send an unambiguous message of constitutionally mandated religious neutrality throughout their commands.

The Need for Civic Education

To the extent that understanding of and respect for the Constitution are at the root of the problem, the solution is straightforward: the U.S. military needs to do a better job educating its personnel to comprehend the remarkable achievement that the American experiment in religious pluralism and liberty represents. The

United States is, after all, the first predominantly Christian country since the time of Constantine to offer anything more than (at best) grudging tolerance to religious minorities. A proper education into the heroic stories of tolerance represented by the colonies of Pennsylvania and Rhode Island, or by the coalition between Deists such as Thomas Jefferson and conservative Baptists of the Danbury Baptist Association in Virginia, who for totally different reasons found common cause around the issues of religious liberty, ought to be a foundation of every American's understanding of the remarkable achievement of American democracy.[19]

Unfortunately, from the Evangelical side of Protestantism, the vision of this achievement has been deeply blurred if not lost entirely. Historically, the Evangelical communities were the most ardent defenders of religious liberty. Initially, they were the looked-down-on religious minorities fearing mistreatment by established churches such as the Congregationalists of Massachusetts or the Anglicans of Virginia. How, then, did the clarity of these convictions come to be muddied, and what are the implications for constitutionally legitimate understandings of military service?

One aspect of the evolution of the religious right and its move into partisan politics has been the development and propagation of a specific historical account of the American founding and Constitution according to which the United States was intended to be a Christian nation. In this version of history, the idea that the government should be neutral regarding religion is a recent invention, propagated by the liberal Supreme Court of the mid-twentieth century.[20] This belief feeds the rhetoric that the country needs to be "taken back" or "restored" from this unfortunate turn and deviation from the ideals of the founders. It has been amplified by the symbolic role of the Constitution in the recent Tea Party movement, despite the often amusing examples of ignorance of the actual content of the Constitution among many of its members. Finally, all of this is surrounded with conspiratorial language that claims the "true" story of the history of the United States has been suppressed or misrepresented by the intellectual elites who have previously written the histories of the nation.[21] The most important author, speaker, and radio talk show host spreading this counterfactual history is David Barton, through his organization, Wallbuilders.

Propagators of this claim have sought to make their materials available to chaplains and members of the armed forces.[22] Chaplains and chapel programs have explicitly endorsed such views in military installation newspapers.[23] Claims about the liberal conspiracy to distort the truth are designed to blind audiences to evidence. Indeed, one often encounters individuals under the influence of these distortions whose ignorance of the facts is not merely profound but also virtually impenetrable.[24]

Transgressions and Discipline

What are the implications of this distorted version of American history for the place of religion in the U.S. military? The foundation of professional military ethics for U.S. military personnel lies in their oath to the Constitution. What an individual believes to be appropriate or inappropriate conduct with respect to religion, in their official capacity as agents of the federal government of the United States, will necessarily depend on their understanding of the Constitution with respect to religion. Specifically, if individuals are persuaded that the Constitution never intended to place restrictions on the establishment of religion or it established an explicitly Christian nation, then they will feel it legitimate and compatible with their oath to proselytize subordinates, invoke personal religious convictions in uniform, or to encourage or even require religious practices in their commands.

Examples of senior officers doing precisely that are well documented by Sharlet and Weinstein, as mentioned earlier. The author's own direct experience includes hearing a deputy department head at the Air Force Academy weep as he described the "oppression" he had felt at being told that the "humongous cross" he had in his office, and the proselytizing cards he distributed to cadets who came to him for academic help, needed to be removed. On another occasion, when the Mel Gibson movie *The Passion of the Christ* was released, the author discovered that a group had hung posters for the movie throughout the fourth floor of the main academic building of the academy, every 20 feet along a nearly half-mile-long corridor.[25] Speakers at the National Character and Leadership Symposium, one of the year's most important events at the academy, included evangelical proselytizers who falsely claimed to be converted terrorists.[26] The lack of serious effort to alter these practices is evident in the whitewashed report of the official investigation into religious intolerance at the Air Force Academy. According to the *New York Times*, the report "strains credibility."[27]

If the problem is not simple ignorance but rather willful ignorance or invincible ignorance, individuals may be rendered impervious to persuasion short of legal disciplinary action against them. Because an individual's interpretation of the Constitution is entangled with their personal religious beliefs, critique may be perceived as an attempt to change those religious convictions. Thus conversations about the appropriate role of religion in the military risk degenerating into disputes about personal beliefs.

This is unfortunate because, to date, even the most egregious violations of law and regulation regarding religious matters by military personnel have met mild punishment if any. Further, the political clout of religious misinformation has only grown recently because it has formed one of the foundational building blocks of the Tea Party movement's rhetoric. A large segment of the population and the political leadership espouse the very mistaken views in question as a matter of deep religious conviction. Disciplining misbehavior has thus become an even more politically volatile act. As a matter of political reality, any commander or political leader who did discipline inappropriate use of military authority to promote these religious convictions could reasonably expect some pushback – or worse – from the political or senior military leadership.

As examples, one might cite a 2007 investigation by the inspector general of the Department of Defense. The investigation centered on a number of senior officers who, appearing in uniform on official duty, endorsed the activities of a private Evangelical organization, the Christian Embassy.[28] Although the investigation found the officers in question in violation of law, no serious consequences followed and all were promoted. Another egregious example is the inspector general's response to the conduct of the commandant of cadets at the United States Air Force Academy, then Brig. Gen. Johnny Weida. Weida made a practice of leading cadets in Evangelical chants in mandatory cadet formations. The inspector general ruled very narrowly on Brig. Gen. Weida's conduct and excused his behavior. Weida's promotion to a second star was delayed for a couple of promotion cycles, but he was eventually promoted and continues to serve with all back pay, as if he had been promoted as originally scheduled. As one who was present at the time, it was pretty clear to me that Weida had no intent to respect constitutional limitations on his conduct. One could recount many such examples, but the general point is the same. This was part of a large pattern of overtly Evangelical proselytizing and conduct at the Air Force Academy in that time period, well summarized by Kristen Leslie, then of Yale Divinity School, who completed a report on the status of religion at the academy at the time.[29]

What renders these challenges especially problematic is that one ordinarily gives a wide berth (as one should) to the personal religious convictions of military personnel. Military leaders are warranted in questioning or interfering with personal convictions only if these convictions lead to behaviors that are injurious to good order and discipline or if they lead to clear violations of law or policy. Examples might include the deeply held religious conviction of a male copilot who, believing that women should not serve in the military, refuses to accept orders from a female.[30] Commanders would also intervene if religiously inspired racism caused a military member to mistreat others, for example. Similarly, military personnel who believe they have the constitutional right to proselytize to their subordinates have crossed the line of acceptable behavior. If it is not possible to persuade them that their convictions are factually in error, then the only alternative involves discipline or separation from military service.

So far the military's track record does not inspire confidence in its ability to take meaningful disciplinary action in response to such unconstitutional conduct. The health of the profession and appropriate civil-military relations require that more attention be given to appropriate religious behavior in the military. Commanders and political leaders must garner the political courage to use the military justice system for investigations and disciplinary action in response to significant violations. Some religiously motivated behaviors are incompatible with military service under the Constitution, no matter how sincerely they are held.

Conclusion

Certain religious beliefs have implications for operational questions, such as the ability of U.S. forces to operate effectively in a counterinsurgency environment. One of these beliefs is the conceptualization of conflict as "spiritual warfare." Rather than think of their service as professional military service rendered to a secular state for purposes defined by political leadership, Evangelical military personnel are exhorted to see their "real" conflict in spiritual terms.

For example, at an appreciation dinner for chaplains and pastors, Brig. Gen. Donald C. Wurster (U.S Air Force, ret.) of the Officers' Christian Fellowship, gave an address entitled "Centurions in the Conflict" in which he said: "The struggle of demons and holiness is invisible to the unenlightened. The most caring of the unsaved have no realization of their unfortunate alliance with evil. All around us, though, we see the casualties of the battle. Many do not even perceive that the battle is joined or know that they are spiritual casualties in need of a Savior."[31] Wurster proceeded to exhort his audience as follows: "Your responsibility as the centurions of the modern age is to prepare those under your leadership at the tactical level. ... The battle is won ... with the proclamation of the Word of God and the application of His power to change lost souls into new recruits."[32] This is obviously somewhat heated religious rhetoric, and patient of a relatively wide range of interpretations. One of these interpretations is that anyone who fails to share the general's religious views, including any subordinates and peers in the military, is in "unfortunate alliance with evil." An officer sincerely in the grip of these convictions would have a difficult time perceiving of such lost souls as trusted, equal professionals. Such convictions threaten leadership, fairness, and religious neutrality.

It is also worth reflecting on the dangers of framing "the other," whether allies serving alongside U.S. forces or the cultures into which these forces deploy, in spiritual terms. Jeff Sharlet, for example, recounts the story of one army unit spending Easter in Iraq by painting "Jesus Killed Mohammad" on the sides of their vehicles and driving through an Iraqi town while having their interpreter shout the phrase over their loudspeakers.[33] Many media sources, including Al Jazeera, showed videos of Army Chaplain (Lt. Col.) Gary Hensley speaking to a group of soldiers at Bagram Air Force Base in Afghanistan, telling them to "hunt people for Jesus." The video further displayed stacks of Bibles intended for distribution to Afghans in direct violation of orders against proselytizing in the theater.[34] Private manufacturers have inscribed Bible verse citations on gunsights widely used in Iraq and Afghanistan.[35] Actions taken by private corporate entities do not raise constitutional questions, but they do reflect the difficulties caused by the need to profess one's religious faith in another culture. Such events clearly undermine efforts to prevent Muslims from interpreting the conflicts in Iraq, Afghanistan, and elsewhere as a crusade against Muslims generally.

More recently, an elective course offered at the Joint Forces Staff College in Norfolk, Virginia, called "Perspectives on Islam and Islamic Radicalism," taught explicitly anti-Muslim perspectives. The course argued for "total war" against Muslims as the proper response to terrorism. It advocated "taking war to a civilian population" (i.e., indiscriminate war, in violation of international law). The instructor went so far as to teach that the Geneva Conventions were "no longer relevant." The response by Gen. Martin Dempsey, the chairman of the Joint Chiefs of Staff, was to condemn the material as "totally objectionable" and "against our values."[36] Subsequently, a requirement went out to the entire Defense Department to report any and all teaching at all institutions that dealt in any way with Islam.[37] Here, the response was clear and appropriate because of the fairly obvious negative consequences of publicity about such teaching among Muslims worldwide.

The strong need felt by some Christians to proclaim the Gospel under any and all circumstances makes it difficult if not impossible to serve within the bounds of a general order banning proselytizing. Proselytizing is disobedient to direct orders, undermines mission effectiveness in cross-cultural environments, and may well heighten passions and hatreds on both sides. As with the internal religious issues discussed earlier, this behavior calls for far better training and education in cross-cultural and cross-religious matters at every force level. Individuals who cannot restrain their impulses to witness and proselytize, even when ordered not to do so and even when their actions are demonstrably dangerous or injurious to mission accomplishment, must face discipline and possibly be discharged from service. The services' track record on this important constitutional point thus far is not reassuring.

Notes

1 The views expressed in this chapter are solely those of the author and do not necessarily reflect the policy or position of the government of the United States, the United States Navy, or the United States Naval War College.

2 Robert Neelly Bellah, "Civil Religion in America," *Journal of the American Academy of Arts and Sciences* 96, no. 1 (Winter 1967): 1–21. For an anthology of historical documents that trace the idea of the United States as home for God's chosen people throughout history see also Conrad Cherry, *God's New Israel: Religious Interpretations of American Destiny* (Chapel Hill: University of North Carolina Press, 1998).

3 The most recent court case on point is *Katcoff v. Marsh*, litigated before the Second Circuit Court in 1984. For a discussion of the constitutionality of the chaplaincy, see http://repository.law.ttu.edu/bitstream/handle/10601/378/Rosen%20Toledo.pdf?sequence=1.

4 This weekly event, called "The Mill," is enormously popular and combines a lively worship service with a social mixer for college-age students. See http://themillonline.org/.

5 Examples of these groups include the Officers' Christian Fellowship (http://www.ocfusa.org/), Christian Fighter Pilot (http://www.christianfighterpilot.com/about.htm),

and the Military Ministry of Campus Crusade for Christ (http://www.militaryministry. org/about/campuscrusade/).

6 For a glimpse at the religious demographics of the United States, see the Pew Forum on Religion and Public Life, "U.S. Religious Landscape Survey" (February 2008), http://religions.pewforum.org/affiliations.

7 Anne Loveland, *American Evangelicals and the U.S. Military, 1942–1993* (Baton Rouge: Louisiana State University Press, 1996).

8 For a full list of endorsers recognized by the Armed Forces Chaplains Board, see the Web site of the Department of Defense on personnel and readiness, http://prhome. defense.gov/mpp/chaplains%20board/endorsements.aspx. For a short description of the process by which chaplains are selected, see the Web site of the National Conference on Ministry to the Armed Forces, http://www.ncmaf.org/chaplain. htm.

9 Noell Brinkerhoff, "Pentagon Chaplains Heavily Skewed towards Evangelicals," http://www.allgov.com/Controversies/ViewNews/Pentagon_Chaplains_ Heavily_Skewed_Towards_Evangelicals_110112.

10 Jeff Sharlet, "The War," in *C Street: The Fundamentalist Threat to American Democracy*, ed. Jeff Sharlet (New York: Little Brown and Company, 2010): 204–258.

11 Ibid., 209.

12 It is important to note, however, that the degree to which some of these activities are embedded in historical practice is often exaggerated by those who wish to defend them.

13 As there are navy chaplains representing other religious traditions in uniform, it is of course possible that a chaplain from a religion other than Christianity might be called on to lead those prayers. But so far, in the author's four years on the faculty, this has not happened.

14 For a definitive legal review of issues of religious practice in the military, see David E. Fitzkee and Linell A. Letendre, "Religion in the Military: Navigating the Channel between the Religion Clauses," *Air Force Law Review* 59 (2007): 1–71.

15 See http://www.militaryreligiousfreedom.org/.

16 Michael L. "Mikey" Weinstein and Davin Seay, *No Snowflake in an Avalanche: The Military Religious Freedom Foundation: Its Battle to Defend the Constitution and One Family's Courageous War against Religious Extremism in High Places* (Petaluma, CA: Vireo Books, 2012).

17 See http://www.airforcetimes.com/news/2011/09/air-force-schwartz-warns-commanders-on-religious-programs-091611/.

18 See http://www.military.com/news/article/af-pulls-jesus-loves-nukes-training-.html.

19 Thomas Jefferson, "Letter to the Danbury Baptists," 1 January 1802. This letter is the origin of the famous phrase regarding the "wall of separation" between church and state.

20 Of course, it is critical to note that there are important half-truths in much of this literature. Indeed, that is why sorting fact from fiction is so difficult in this area of American history. For example, it is true that the original meaning of the First Amendment was to restrict only actions of the federal government, leaving states free to try various ways of establishing religion in the states. It is also true that the United States in its early history could assume a broad Protestant consensus and could therefore avoid questioning many public religious practices that

would become problematic as the religious and cultural pluralism of the country increased. Many historians have argued that the Great Awakening and the Evangelical preaching of George Whitfield throughout the colonies was a significant factor in building an American identity out of the disparate colonies. It is beyond the scope of this chapter to deal in detail with the nuances of these questions, however. For a detailed discussion of these efforts, see Leonard Williams Levy, *The Establishment Clause: Religion and the First Amendment* (Chapel Hill: University of North Carolina Press, 1994).

21 See, for example, David Barton's "Wallbuilders" Web site, http://www.wallbuilders.com; Glen Skousen, *The Five Thousand Year Leap: Twenty-Eight Great Ideas That Are Changing the World* (Frankling, TN: American Documents Publishing, LLC, 1981). Both Barton and Skousen influenced Glenn Beck's views.

22 See, for example, http://shop.wallbuilders.com/Contribution-Military-Fund; http://usheritagebible.org/Default.aspx.

23 Chris Rodda has documented the impact of these efforts on military chaplains in *Liars for Jesus: The Religious Right's Alternate Version of American History* (Charleston, SC: BookSurge, 2006).

24 An excellent discussion of the reasons why factual debunking of Barton's claims have little impact within Evangelical culture can be found in Paul Harvey, "The Quixotic Task of Debunking David Barton," *Religion Dispatches*, 3 June 2012, http://www.religiondispatches.org/books/atheologies/6033/the_quixotic_task_of_debunking_david_barton/. This piece is a review of a book-length refutation of Barton by two Evangelical scholars. See Warren Throckmorton and Michael Coulter, *Getting Jefferson Right: Fact Checking Claims about Our Third President* (Grove City, PA: Salem Grove Press, 2012).

25 For a summary of issues regarding religion at the military academies, see Neela Banerjee, "Religion and Its Role Are in Dispute at the Service Academies," *New York Times*, 25 June 2008.

26 Neil MacFarquhar, "Speakers at Academy Said to Make False Claims," *New York Times*, 7 February 2008.

27 "Editorial: Obfuscating Intolerance," *New York Times*, 23 June 2005.

28 The inspector general's official report can be found on the Web site of the Department of Defense Office of Inspector General, http://www.dodig.mil/fo/foia/ERR/Xtian_Embassy_072707.pdf.

29 An excellent quick summary of Leslie's findings appears in the Yale Divinity School newsletter, http://www.yale.edu/divinity/notes/050516/notes_050516_kl.shtml.

30 A distinguished air force lawyer who dealt with this case reported it to the author. Because it was handled administratively, however, there is no official record of the case.

31 Brig. Gen. Donald C. Wurster, "Centurions in the Conflict," Officers' Christian Fellowship, http://www.ocfusa.org/articles/centurions-conflict/.

32 Ibid.

33 Jeff Sharlet, "Jesus Killed Mohammed: The Crusade for a Christian Military," *Harper's*, May 2009, 31–43.

34 Anne Szustek, "Al Jazeera Accuses U.S. Military of Proselytizing in Afghanistan," 5 May 2009, http://www.findingdulcinea.com/news/Asia-Pacific/2009/may/Al-Jazeera-Accuses-U-S–Military-of-Proselytizing-in-Afghanistan.html; "Witness for

Jesus in Afghanistan," *Al Jazeera*, 4 May 2009, http://english.aljazeera.net/news/asia/2009/05/2009532013158854832.html.

35 Michael Winter, "Pentagon: Bible-Verse Gunsights Don't Violate Rules," *USA Today*, 19 January 2010.

36 See http://usnews.msnbc.msn.com/_news/2012/05/11/11659853-outrage-calls-for-action-over-anti-muslim-materials-in-military-training?lite.

37 See http://www.guardian.co.uk/world/2012/may/11/anti-islam-teachings-us-law-enforcement. See also http://www.nytimes.com/2012/04/26/us/new-review-ordered-on-anti-islamic-themes-in-military-courses.html.

9

United States II

Pauletta Otis

The terrorist attacks of September 11, 2001, brought religious issues into the public forum. Questions about the religious composition of the U.S. military and its influence on foreign and defense policy were not new, but they reemerged with renewed vigor. Prior to that time, it was assumed that religious faith and identity, whether within the U.S. military or in the military services of allies and enemies, was a matter of personal choice and did not significantly influence international security. Because the Department of Defense (DOD) was often the most visible tool of U.S. foreign and defense policy, many questioned the role of religion in the DOD and the extent to which religious factors influenced policy and practice.

The Department of Defense was unprepared to deal with religion as a cause or contributor to warfare, as were the Department of State, the Department of Justice, and the Department of Homeland Security. Uncertainty within the DOD about how to respond to this new environment reflected an inability to understand how religion factored into modern warfare rather than an inability to understand the religiosity of military personnel. Regarding the emotive reaction of individuals, the DOD tried to ignore the "religious factor" both within its ranks and as a variable shaping the battlefield. Despite the immediacy of the problem, the U.S. government and the U.S. military continued to address the issue of religion in conflict, war, and terrorism in an ad hoc, haphazard, and superficial manner. This approach reflected long-standing and reasonably successful DOD policies toward the department's own internal religious pluralism and diversity. It did not contribute to an understanding of how religion influenced the emerging conflict and war in the Middle East.[1]

Training within the U.S. military, constrained by long-established DOD policies and doctrines, reflected historical patterns. It consisted of classes in comparative world religion for operators and analysts, training in cultural awareness that included religious factors, and a continuous stream of briefers who represented anyone and everyone who saw an opportunity to help. This echoed the training the DOD used to address religious, racial, and gender diversity within the U.S. military. It took place in a constrained environment, addressed a "captive audience," and set forth a reasonable set of rules. The result was an improvised montage of teaching that offered no consistent theoretical base to address why or how religion was associated with violence.

Adapting to this new environment proved to be even more of a challenge in the field. At the ground level, soldiers, sailors, marines, and airmen were left to deal with their own religious instincts and preferences. They were then asked to deal with the religious instincts, preferences, and behaviors of people in an entirely different historical and cultural context. With significantly less training than regular units, the Reserves and the National Guard units depended on personal preferences and codes of conduct unless otherwise instructed. Each of the services handled the teaching and training regimes differently, but all were required to stay within DOD doctrinal guidelines. These guidelines, however, focus on the principles of religious accommodation and religious pluralism within the U.S. military, not on religion as a factor in combat.

Even though command and control, good leadership, and common sense have successfully tapped down efforts by radical actors to promote religious agendas in the military, critics have used minor incidents as evidence for a crisis in the operational environment. These incidents include those of 2007–2008 at the U.S. Air Force Academy that factionalized faculty as well as students; religious explanations for the 2009 shootings at Fort Hood, Texas; a deceptive video of chaplains ostensibly distributing Bibles in Afghanistan (created by the photographer's manipulation of the photos in 2009); and a curriculum dispute at the Joint Forces Staff College in 2012. Despite these incidents, the military considers it axiomatic that its forces represent the U.S. government and should not be hijacked by one political or religious agenda at the expense of maintaining its primary role, the "defense of the U.S. Constitution against all enemies, foreign and domestic."

Three Theoretical Frameworks

The polarizing disputes noted in the previous section highlight the importance of building strong theoretical frameworks for analysis and collecting facts while reserving judgment and maintaining balance. Scholars have proposed three basic theoretical approaches that can be termed "the sacred, the secular, and the separated." In the first framework, the United States and its military are regarded as inherently Christian and are fighting a war of religion. In the second, the United States and its military are seen as strictly secular, and U.S. wars reflect the hegemonic interests of a major world power. The third approach defines the United States as a nominally Christian country. Its history and policies of religious accommodation and pluralism reflect the ideal and the reality of religious diversity within the country.

Unfortunately, the first approach is common around the world. It suggests that the U.S. military is a direct reflection of the United States as a Christian country, and therefore all DOD policies and the activities of individual service people may be interpreted in the light of adherence to Christian beliefs and behaviors. If the U.S. military is, at its very core, a Christian army, fighting in support of Christian ideals and principles, then the conflict becomes one between two religious forces – Christianity and Islam – a modern replay of the Crusades. In this view, the Christian religion plays an integral role in all areas of foreign and defense policy at all levels of the chain of command, from commander in chief (the president) to the U.S. Army private. Accordingly, the enemy is spiritual and religious, characteristics that in turn lead to the conclusion that the "war of ideas" is basically a return to "wars of religion." Many who hold this extreme version are either Christians who wish the U.S. military to embrace the Christian identity of the state or strict secularists who believe the Christian right is taking over the secular principles of the U.S. Constitution.

The second, opposing explanation holds that the United States is a secular country with military forces that are motivated solely by power and self-interest. This position is generally derived from an interpretation of the Constitution and the Federalists Papers that supports a strict "wall of separation" between church and state. Proponents of this view do not deny that the United States has religious elements and that these elements are part of the American social and political life, but they maintain that the separation of church and state precludes religious influence within the public arena. They also tend to support such separation, arguing that religious diversity has a tendency toward extremism and fundamentalism, both of which are detrimental to the workings of good government. If the U.S. military is self-defined as "secular," neither the beliefs of individual service members nor institutionalized religion is an important factor in U.S. foreign and defense policy.

The third view, held by this author, synthesizes the first two views. The United States includes religious people and institutions, but the U.S. military employs law and policy to prevent their undue influence. This perspective reflects both the Constitution and the history of religious accommodation in the United States. In this view, the "Christian-ness" of the U.S. military is not pertinent to the pursuance of foreign and defense policy objectives. Differences in religion and religious practices, until they result in conflict, should be understood, tolerated, accommodated, and even embraced.

The perception that U.S. military policies and practices reflect exclusively Christian values is seriously flawed in logic, unsubstantiated by research, and a case of hyperbolic rhetoric that is not only misleading but dangerous. The religious profile of the U.S. military does not predict the behavior of the U.S. armed forces in either policy or practice. At the same time, the U.S. military is not strictly secular. The separation of church and state cannot mean that individuals and institutions are barred from behaving in accordance with their religious beliefs and practices while employed by the government. This is especially true in a combat environment where individual beliefs and practices regarding morality and ethics are often put to the ultimate test. Military members are forced to think about the concepts of "just war" and "justice in war" as part of their profession. If there is a dearth of institutionalized handling of the topic of religion and warfare, it is not because individual soldiers are unaware of the relationship. As a matter of principle, individual service members follow their faiths insofar as they do not affect their professional duties.

In conclusion, the U.S. military accurately embodies U.S. constitutional provisions: individuals of faith are free to express and practice their religion, but the power of institutionalized religion is precluded from becoming de facto established. The U.S. military reflects the values and behaviors of a religious constituency while its policies and practices are constrained by law and tradition.

Empirical Data

The population of the United States is the most religiously diverse in the world. It stands to reason that if the U.S. military replicates the demographic profile of the civilian population, its composition would reflect the same religious diversity.[2] Statistics are difficult to find because the U.S. government is precluded by law from census or population surveys that inquire about religion. The numbers available are derived from public research institutes, universities, or religious organizations. The Department of Defense, however, collects information on religious adherence to satisfy the legal requirement for religious accommodation. DOD thus views religion as a matter of personnel policy. Contrary to "rumint" (DOD slang for "rumored intelligence"), the U.S. Army, Navy, Air Force, and Marines do not handle religion differently as a consequence of differential recruiting or institutional bias. Public opinion to the contrary, one service is not "more Catholic," "more Evangelical," or "more religious" than any other service. Nor are the services involved in conducting surveys on differences. The Department of Defense does not engage in social or religious engineering.[3]

As Table 9.1 shows, the religious preferences of U.S. military personnel roughly mirror those of the civilian population.[4]

Initially, the military collected religious information to be able to provide appropriate burial services for those killed in combat. The rationale of religious accommodation is a recent addition, proposed in DODD-1300.17 (2009).[5] Because of the nature of military service, U.S. law, instituted by DOD policy, provides a proportionate number of chaplains who serve in the military so that service members can worship according to their personal beliefs when they are not able to attend their home church.

The DOD document *Religion of Active Duty Personnel by Service*, published in 2010, indicates that there are fifty-one formally recognized religions in the DOD.[6] The largest number of adherents in a single category is Roman

TABLE 9.1. *Religious Preferences of the U.S.*
Population and Military Personnel, 2001, Reported
as Percentages of Military Personnel in Comparison
with the General Civilian Population

Religious Preference	Military	Civilians
All preferences	100	100
Protestant	35	45
Catholic/Orthodox	22	26
Other Christian	11	3
Atheist/No religion	21	19
Jewish	< 1	1
Muslim/Islam	< 1	1
Buddhist/Hindu	< 1	2
Other religions	11	3

Catholics. The Protestant numbers are more difficult to assess because of the range of named categories and disputes over theologies. For example, the category of Native American could be Protestant or a completely distinct religion; members of the Church of Christ of Latter Day Saints (LDS) consider themselves Christian and sometimes Protestant, but some Protestants do not consider LDS to be Protestant. To complicate matters further, U.S. military chaplains represent 176 different denominations. By law and policy, all chaplains, regardless of their denomination, must provide religious services to military members of all religious persuasions.

The figures provide little information about accumulative categories, the religious beliefs of individuals, attendance at religious services, perspectives on defense policy, or whether these numbers change when service members are in garrison or deployed. In addition, the percentages of adherents in the U.S. Army, Navy, and Marines offer no identifiable pattern. For example, it cannot be stated on the basis of the numbers available that Catholics tend to join the Marine Corps whereas Adventists tend to prefer the army. Recruiting statistics, especially for the Marine Corps, indicate that the southern states contribute enlistees disproportionately to the U.S. military services. The inference that Catholics and Baptists are significantly represented in these states has led to the conclusion that they are overrepresented in the military. This conclusion is clearly an overreach of available data and is statistically unsupported.

The empirical evidence provides no clear insight into the relationship between the internal profile of the U.S. military and its behavior. It does not reflect whether one religion is more salient than others and thus has a more public presence, whether the religious preferences of senior commanders are similarly distributed, or whether these percentages have shifted significantly over time. The answer to any of these questions would require further investigation of the role of religion in the U.S. defense establishment. Such research is unlikely to be supported at the Pentagon, an organization focused on war fighting and wary of social or religious engineering.

Model I: The Sacred

Many in the United States believe that the United States is a Christian country and that the armed services reflect that fact. The logic and evidence in support of this contention is largely based on an interpretation of history and tradition, the fact that many individuals in the U.S. armed forces are Christian, that just war and justice in war principles are based on Christian principles, and that the United States is a Christian country by numerical percentage. The evidence that the United States is a Christian country by history and tradition seems incontestable. The evidence that the U.S. military has a Christian agenda is more problematic.

Is being a good Christian a necessary qualification for service in the U.S. armed forces? Military commanders invariably avoid this question in favor of another: Is the soldier, marine, or airman a person of good character in terms of ethics and morals, displaying honor, loyalty, and commitment? Religion is neither a sufficient nor a necessary guarantor of these qualities. In an informal survey of twenty-five Marine Corps officers conducted by this author, all reported unanimously that promotion and advancement in the Marine Corps were not related in any way to religious preference. None of the officers had experienced proselytizing. None of the officers believed that it was necessary to be a "good Christian" to be a good officer.[7]

Evidence from the U.S. military seems to further contradict the necessary link between Christian identity, U.S. citizenship, and military service. The military does not preclude the participation of non-Christians in its ranks, nor does it require leaders to take a religious test before assuming command. More than 30,000 noncitizens currently serve in the U.S. military, accounting for approximately 2 percent of active-duty military. For noncitizens, recruitment is not based on religion, but it is a fast-track to citizenship.[8] The rules and responsibilities of the Defense Department do not directly mirror biblical principles; its foreign and defense policies are not held to the rigorous religious standards of Christianity; and it does not assess other countries, cultures, and religions exclusively with regard to religious identity.

Nevertheless, there are those who argue that the United States is a Christian country and that the U.S. military should reflect Christian identity. This advocacy is reflected, but not officially supported, by a number of authors who believe they speak for the DOD. Stephen Mansfield, a civilian with little to no military experience, author of *Faith of the American Soldier* (2005), has exhorted soldiers to follow the example of the Crusaders in their religious devotion. Lt. Gen.

Photo 10 A U.S. Army combat engineer, with Psalm 21 written on his helmet, bows his head as he takes a short rest after securing an important two-lane bridge over the Euphrates River, about 20 kilometers outside Baghdad, April 4, 2003. Photo copyright Reuters/Corbis.

William (Jerry) Boykin, editor of *Shariah: The Threat to America: An Exercise in Competitive Analysis* (2010) defines the enemy in religious terms.[9] Some commentators frame the debate over homosexuals in the military as a religious or moral issue instead of a debate concerning military effectiveness. Presses have recognized the marketability of religion and warfare and have published a large number of books featuring Christian military heroes. Several religious leaders, media figures, and politicians have argued that the U.S. military should be a reflection of the United States' Christian tradition, Christian Constitution, and Christian values. The Pentagon, on the other hand, has discouraged or prohibited such discussions as contrary to good order and discipline.[10]

Is the United States a Christian country? Yes, to the extent that it is part of Western civilization and subscribes to principles of liberal democracy. Is the U.S. military a reflection of, and advocate for, Christianity? Yes, to the extent that many individual soldiers practice Christianity; no, to the extent that members of the armed forces are not required to join a particular faith nor are they evaluated, promoted, or advanced on the basis of their religious adherence. Can U.S. foreign and defense policy be seen as a direct outcome of the Christian faith of a goodly portion of its citizens? No, many other factors play a role, and Christians themselves are deeply divided about foreign and defense policy.

Model II: The Secular

The traditional separation of state and church has worked very well for the United States. The writers of the U.S. Constitution, acknowledging the religious wars of Europe, bowing to practical politics, and respecting the rights of individuals to practice their particular religion, were extremely careful not to establish an official church that would link the power and resources of the government with the power and resources of a religion. Whether the framers meant for the United States to ignore religion entirely and rely on the scientific premises of the liberal state is unknown, but certainly the Constitution is not built around religion or religious institutions.[11] The debate between the secular Constitution and the sacred Constitution will not be settled here, and suffice it to note that the military has had an uneven history in this regard.

Within the services however, religious issues are handled by commanders and settled as military issues rather than as intrinsically religious issues. Although religious diversity has been a reality since 1775, the military has played down religious differences in favor of military discipline throughout the course of U.S. military history. The codification of the accommodation of differing religions was officially institutionalized only in 2009 with a Department of Defense Directive (DODD-1300.17):

Promote an environment free from personal, social, or institutional barriers that prevent Service members from rising to the highest level of responsibility possible. In this environment, Service members shall be evaluated only on individual merit, fitness, and capability. Unlawful discrimination against individuals or groups based on race, color, religion, sex, or national origin is contrary to good order and discipline and counterproductive to combat readiness and mission accomplishment and shall not be condoned.

One of the most publicly contentious situations occurred in the last several years at the U.S. Air Force Academy in Colorado Springs, Colorado, a teaching and training environment (as opposed to an operational environment.) According to the "Cadet and Permanent Party Climate Assessment Survey" released in October 2010, 41 percent of non-Christian cadets, or fifty-one cadets total, reported unwanted proselytizing at the academy at least once during a yearlong period.[12] The superintendent of the academy, Lt Gen. Michael Gould, reacted to the report by increasing the academy's emphasis on freedom of religion and tolerance for religious differences. In so doing, he did not address religious factionalization directly but rather highlighted the premise that unity of command, good order, and discipline should be based on tolerance and respect. Nevertheless, Mikey Weinstein, head of the Military Religious Freedom Foundation, maintained that fundamentalist Christians were trampling on the rights of other religions at the Academy.[13] Instead of the military responding with a theoretical, contextual, and mature theoretical perspective or relying on the established principles of professional military education, the incident became emotionally charged and eventually polarized both students and faculty. This episode demonstrates how a minor situation can be propelled into national attention as a result of the actions of a single individual.[14]

The policies of the DOD may be changing as a result of the Fort Hood shootings. On November 5, 2009, a self-proclaimed religiously motivated U.S. Army major, Nidal Hassan, killed thirteen soldiers and wounded forty-three others. Following an internal investigation, the recommendations tightened the requirements for ecclesiastical endorsement of chaplains and allowed commanders to "distinguish appropriate religious practices."[15] These changes imply that the safety of the troops is not to be compromised by religious activities deemed potentially dangerous. The report also notes that the commander's responsibilities form part of an effort to confront "threats to good order and discipline." The religious awareness implicitly referenced in these recommendations pertains to force protection and is unrelated to the religious preferences of senior command.[16]

It is difficult to assess whether U.S. foreign and defense policy is strictly secular. Several examples of how religion played a role in foreign policy and military activities are illustrative. During the Civil War, Christian principles supported antislavery in the North; in the South, there was a mirror-image emphasis on slaves as property. Preachers and priests served the troops and supported morale on both sides, but they also provided both sides with a religious rationale for fighting. After the war, these differences were played down, but the South remained committed to the "Lost Cause" movement, which was implicitly based on religious principles. The North, now in charge of the military, returned to the principle of separation of religion and military service that has subsequently been the most workable for the United States.[17]

During the administrations of Presidents William McKinley and James Polk, it was alleged that religion played a role in the decision to go to war against the Catholic Spanish, that it was an underlying theme in Manifest Destiny, and that it was a determinative factor in the way the Philippine Insurrection and subsequent occupation were handled.[18] Religion played a role in the Cold War by a conscious policy of adding the word "atheist" to the adjectives associated with the communist regimes.

In sum, advocates of the idea that the United States is a secular state premise their arguments on the Constitution's secular tone, some of the writings of the framers of the Constitution, and the First Amendment's restrictions on the federal government with regard to establishment of an official church and protection of religious freedoms. The Department of Defense generally subscribes to those principles on constitutional grounds and maintains the position that a good military cannot afford religious division within the ranks. Because religion plays a role in all warfare, however – for individuals, institutions, and states – it is arguable that U.S. foreign and defense policy has not always been oblivious to either the religion of the domestic population or the religion of others, particularly in times of war.

Model III: The Separate

The third perspective on the relationship of religion and the U.S. military offers the greatest explanatory power. This position rests on the assumption that citizens vary widely in their religious viewpoints, identities, and beliefs under conditions of free speech, assembly, petition, and religion. The Department of Defense, however, is constrained by law and policy with regard to religious factors both within the services and in relationship to foreign and defense policy. The Constitution protects religion along with speech, petition, and assembly as fundamental to freedom and liberty. Acknowledging the risk inherent in competing power structures, the writers of the Constitution maintained that the institutions of religion and government should be separate and prohibited the establishment of religion. George Washington, in his role as general and then president, set the precedent in supporting religious diversity and pluralism and encouraging good morals among soldiers and citizens without publicly advocating for a specific church or faith tradition.

The people of the United States, the U.S. government, and the Department of Defense have maintained this position since 1793. The influence of religion on the Pentagon is revealed through the moral and ethical principles of the individuals in uniform. Religious influences as found in the Oath of Allegiance and in the military hymns, rituals, and symbols are hidden in plain sight. For an anthropologist or historian, the colors, pendants, insignia, flags, and ribbons are all "color coded." The referenced colors and symbols can be traced to the period of state formation; they are not hidden symbols of religious influence.

The government may fund religious activity to accommodate the religious needs of people who, because of government action, no longer have access to religious resources. This, in effect, requires religious pluralism: the accommodation of all persons who have religious needs. The caveat is that of "military necessity": the religious accommodation cannot impede other official requirements, provide an undue burden on the government, or promote a specific religion. Religion may not assume a formalized role if doing so risks compromising military missions through dissension in the ranks. DOD directives are clear about precluding religious preference in the workplace, providing for individual worship and religious practice only when doing so will not affect the definition of the mission. Religious directives are designed to accommodate individuals, not religious institutions such as churches, synagogues, mosques, or temples. For example, the religious place of worship on a military base, regardless of the particular religion, is technically a "community center" and therefore is nondenominational. Chaplains are recruited from particular denominations but must serve all uniformed personnel regardless of denominational affiliation.

This separation of church and state in the Pentagon is clearly anathema to those who would like to see religion as the dominant force in the U.S. military and in relationship to the deployment of forces in the international arena. Those who believe that the military should be strictly secular are equally convinced that all religious services, accommodation, symbols, and ceremonies should never involve religion in any way, shape, or form. The reality is far more complex than either of these simplistic viewpoints. The DOD can never achieve the delicate balance between too much and too little, as new problems, leaders, understandings, political pressures, and international events conspire to make religious accommodation a work in progress. Nevertheless, both military doctrine and military practice provide clear guidelines for legal behavior within the services.

Conclusion

The U.S. military tends to mirror the rest of the U.S. polity with regard to religious belief. It differs in that military organizations demand a priority of effort during times of war: unity of command, unit morale, ethical behavior, and attention to the Law of Armed Combat are critical to mission success, force protection, and saving lives. These may be derived from religious principles, but they are not denominational or sectarian.

There is as much of a war of ideas within the U.S. military as there is among people of differing faiths or religions in the civilian community. The U.S. military must strive to "prevent, protect, and prevail,"[19] and at the same time protect individual citizen-soldiers whose religious rights are inviolate. With regard to religion in the U.S. military, this research has found that an interpretation of the U.S. military as unduly influenced by Christian radicals is unfounded, just as an interpretation of the U.S. military as strictly secular is naive and unfounded. The U.S. military has instituted policies and practices that recognize individual religious rights while respecting constitutional separation of church and state. There is no evidence that one branch or service in the U.S. military is more "religious" than any other or that promotion and advancement in the military are a reflection of religious adherence.

In international affairs, the Department of Defense presents a model of the institutionalized secular state that recognizes, but understates, the role of religion in warfare. The perception that the U.S. government is therefore "atheistic," however, is wrong. Foreign and defense policies have always been influenced by religiously motivated U.S. citizens, whether in uniform or not. It is harder to argue that defense policy is determined by religious factors. Nevertheless, until the DOD understands the role of religion in warfare, it will be unable to properly assess the role of Islam in the Middle East, Hinduism in India, Buddhism in Tibet, and so on. And until the DOD understands the role of religion in peace, it will be unable to leverage religious power in favor of a more peaceful world.

Notes

1   Fabio Petito and Pavlos Hatzopoulos, *Religion in International Relations: The Return from Exile* (New York: Palgrave Macmillan, 2003).
2   The U.S. military has approximately three million personnel excluding the Reserves, the National Guard, contractors, and civilian support personnel. Any discussion of

the U.S. military and religion and how religion affects the deployment of U.S. military forces is subject to generalization and misrepresentation simply because of size. Moreover, the extent to which religious adherence reflects religious influence is a difficult question to determine without available and credible research.

3 Public information about religious preferences in the U.S. military may reflect reporting biases of public media, news events that may or may not reflect the "norm," and the tendency of DOD not to "report out" after problems have been solved.

4 DOD Defense Manpower Data Center. This information is collected periodically to ensure religious accommodation and is not further officially analyzed. Information about availability can be obtained by contacting the author.

5 DODD-1300.17 can be accessed at www.dtic.mil/why/directives. This directive updated the earlier 1988 version.

6 Data available from the author on request.

7 The twenty-five officers were interviewed at a professional military education facility. They held the ranks of corporal, captain, major, lieutenant colonel, and colonel. The author chose the interviewees by random association and availability. To protect service people from invasion of privacy, DOD requires that full, independent surveys receive official permission and an obligation to abide by the rules and policies of DOD. Such a survey is currently beyond the resources available to this author.

8 Bryan Bender, "A U.S. Military 'At Its Breaking Point' Considers Foreign Recruits," *New York Times*, 26 December 2006.

9 These arguments are reminiscent of the Cold War arguments discussed in Lori Lyn Bogle, *The Pentagon's Battle for the American Mind* (College Station: University of Texas Press, 2004).

10 The exception to this statement is in professional military education where open discussion of any issue related to security is actively encouraged.

11 Isaac Kramnick and R. Laurence Moore take the view that the U.S. Constitution is a strictly secular document. Isaac Kramnick and R. Laurence Moore, *The Godless Constitution: The Case Against Political Correctness* (New York: Norton, 1997).

12 The survey was conducted by the academy: there were 1,470 cadets and a response rate of 47 percent; 1,337 were self-defined as Christian, 128 were non-Christian, and 252 stated no religious preference.

13 Whitney Jones, "The Air Force Academy Cites Progress in Tackling Religious Intolerance," *Christian Century*, 2 November 2010, http://www.christiancentury.org/article/2010-11/air-force-academy-cites-progress.

14 See Martin S. Sheffer, *God and Caesar: Belief, Worship, and Proselytizing under the First Amendment* (New York: State University Press of New York, 1999).

15 See http://www.defense.gov/pubs/pdfs/DOD-ProtectingTheForce-Web_Security_HR_13jan10.pdf.

16 Ibid., findings 2.3 and 2.7, respectively.

17 Randall M. Miller, Harry S. Stout, and Charles Reagan Wilson, eds., *Religion and the American Civil War* (New York: Oxford University Press, 1998).

18 For example, land expropriated from the Catholic Church was distributed by U.S. occupying forces in coordination with business elites.

19 See various statements by Gen. Anthony Zinni and the National Security Strategy of May 2010, http://www.whitehouse.gov/sites/default/files/rss_viewer/national_security_strategy.pdf.

10

Turkey

Ayşegül Komsuoğlu and Gül M. Kurtoğlu Eskişar

The Turkish Republic is a secular country with a Muslim majority. Less than 1 percent of its population consists of non-Muslims. Even though Turkey has been a multiparty democracy since the 1950s, the Turkish Armed Forces (TAF) has traditionally enjoyed a very influential position in Turkish politics.[1] The TAF has proven highly protective of Turkey's secular identity and has intervened in Turkish politics multiple times to block Islamist influence. Despite its thoroughly secular founding principles, however, the TAF routinely employs religious rituals and symbols to increase troop morale, similar to its predecessor, the Ottoman military. Historically, the role and function of religion in the TAF has undergone significant changes, often in response to changing political environments.

This chapter sketches some of the contrasting tendencies that coexist in the TAF. We argue that Islamic symbols and practices in the contemporary military originated during the Ottoman Empire, where they played a central role. Its successor, the Turkish Republic, redefined the space allotted to Islam and chose to maintain an ambiguous relationship with religion.[2] The Republic adopted a strict form of secularism that required the removal of Islam from the new military's official training and institutional structure. Unlike the Ottoman military, the TAF does not retain official chaplains, and it confines the religious practices of troops to the private sphere. At the same time, the TAF routinely employs religious symbols and concepts to boost the combat morale of its soldiers. These include Islamic concepts, such as *shahid* (martyrdom) and *ghazi* (war veteran), which date back to the Ottoman Empire. Islamic symbols are also freely used when they are considered useful for enhancing social cohesion. Finally, the TAF treats its religious staff as temporary, creating their positions in an ad hoc manner for the duration of military campaigns. This further signifies the subordination of religion to the TAF's secular principles.

Second, we argue that, similar to its Ottoman predecessor, the TAF has sought to defend the new state borders while spearheading its modernization efforts. This dual role has posed an increasingly sharp dilemma: How could the army perform the ambitious task of protecting Turkey against all internal and external threats without relying on the very religious symbols that its conscripted soldiers found so meaningful?[3] During the Cold War, Turkey's NATO allies further complicated this dilemma by supporting Islam as an anticommunist ideology. The result of these conflicting tendencies was a tentative equilibrium between secularism and religion in the TAF up to the 1980s.

This equilibrium was challenged in the 1980s, when the Turkish state began incorporating Islamic values into its national ideology, and it was overturned in the 1990s when the TAF declared its explicit opposition to rising Islamist groups in Turkish politics. The end of the Cold War, which changed the West's conception of its enemy, also proved a decisive factor in shifting the role of Islam in Turkish politics. Islamist parties exploited emerging economic and political "opportunity spaces" to rapidly accumulate power.[4] During these years, the widening rift between the Islamists and the TAF translated into an ever-diminishing space for religion in the military. This lacuna had particularly stark implications for officers who openly practiced their religious beliefs, who were known to harbor religious sentiments, or who sympathized with Islamist groups. In the meantime, noncommissioned officers were placed under less scrutiny, given that they were expected to play little if any role in shaping the future of the institution that considers itself the foremost guardian and promoter of secularism in Turkey.

As the chapter shows, there are few formal rules concerning religious practices in the TAF. Therefore, some of the information used here is based on open-ended interviews conducted by the authors with former TAF members, who experienced difficulties during their service or were expelled from the TAF, as well as on published memoirs by former TAF members. Given the high risk of bias in these accounts, this chapter adopts a descriptive instead of an explanatory approach and offers a vignette on the subject.[5]

Historical Background

The complex history of the relations between religion and armed forces of Turkey dates back to the Ottoman Empire, which routinely employed Islamic symbols to justify its use of force. As a result, the role of military clerics was particularly significant during this era. The role of religion as a mobilizing force did not change during the Turkish War of Independence (1919–1923). Troops continued to fight to defend the lands of Islam with moral support from religious leaders. After the establishment of the Turkish Republic in 1923, however, leaders initiated the rapid secularization of state institutions. This bore its mark on the TAF, which had to learn to balance its religious traditions with secular practices. During the Cold War, the TAF sought to balance its role as the protector of secular Turkey with the task of countering the threat of communism, which required relaxing its control over the observance of religious rites among its ranks.

The Ottoman Era

The rulers of the Ottoman Empire employed religion to justify wars and to encourage their soldiers to participate in battle.[6] The non-Muslim population of the empire was exempt from military service. Leaders of religious sects, preachers from mosques, and religious scholars served as chaplains and accompanied the army into war, as did the army's official imams.[7] These practices continued unabated when the Ottoman Army entered a period of modernization in the nineteenth century. Military schools appointed official chaplains and emphasized religious education and daily prayers for soldiers.[8] As the military success of the Ottoman army diminished, the military leadership expanded the number of religious texts for soldiers in an attempt to restore their dampened morale.[9] "All the observers of the Ottoman army between 1850 and 1918 agree, [that] the fighting spirit of the Ottoman troops was to a very high degree religious. Attacks were always carried out to shouts of 'Allah Allah' and 'Allahuekber' [Allah is great]," argues Erik Zürcher. "It would be hard to envisage a religiously mixed army doing the same."[10]

As the Ottoman Empire declined, combat weariness and growing casualties raised the need for the conscription of non-Muslim soldiers. In retrospect, this conscription crisis constitutes one of the main reasons behind the awkward relationship between the TAF and non-Muslim conscripts in contemporary Turkey. As part of the 1839 *Gülhane* reform edict that aimed to transform the subjects of the empire into citizens, Ottoman rulers declared the establishment of an egalitarian system for military recruitment that would include non-Muslims.[11] Starting in 1843, all males had to serve five years in the military and seven more years in the reserves.[12] This requirement posed a host of difficulties, including the absence of religious chaplains for non-Muslims and concerns over lost tax revenue from enlisted non-Muslims.[13] Members of the Greek, Assyrian, and Armenian communities agreed to honor the conscription law in principle but asked to serve in separate units officered by Christians.[14] Young Christian men often rebelled against conscription, fled the towns, or emigrated to Europe or the United States.

During the Balkan Wars, some observers viewed the inclusion of Christians and Jews as undermining the army's religious-moral foundation. Leon Trotsky, who was a war correspondent at the time, remarked that "the inclusion of Christians in the army inevitably destroyed the belief that Islam is the one and only moral bond between the state and the army, thereby introducing the gravest spiritual uncertainty into the mind of the Muslim soldier."[15] Various Christian and Jewish resistances to serving in the ranks of the Ottoman military and the changing structure of the empire during World War I led the government to disarm non-Muslim soldiers.[16] They served in labor battalions performing road repairs or filling labor gaps in agriculture and industry.[17]

For Muslim soldiers from different regions, tribes, and ethnicities, Islam continued to form the most important bond. A German officer who served with the Turkish Army in 1914–1915 described the role of religion in the Ottoman Army as follows:

> The Turkish soldier ... is deeply religious and regards this life as the first stage to a better. In the midst of shelling, shortly before the entry of the battalion into battle, the Imam, or the battalion priest, generally held a short address. The impression left on the onlooker was always curious, particularly when at those points in the address an "Inschallah" (we ask Allah to give it to us) rose over the thirsty plain in earnest but happy tones from hundreds of men's deep voices. ... The Imams were often splendid men with great and good influence on the soldiers, and in the event of all the officers being killed they took control, sometimes taking control of the battalion.[18]

The imams were noteworthy figures in the battalions and played a significant role in encouraging soldiers to continue fighting under the atrocious conditions of the war.[19]

The Birth of the Turkish Republic

Although the military elite led by Mustafa Kemal (Ataturk) sought to establish a modern state in Anatolia, it made extensive use of religion during the Turkish War of Independence (1919–1923). The nationalists realized that the troops engaged in fighting perceived their main goal as saving the lands of Islam from the "infidel." In May 1920, for example, religious leaders allied with the nationalists issued a fatwa that invalidated the sultan's surrender and called on all Muslims to join the struggle for independence. Clerics continued to play a crucial role in encouraging combat in a society exhausted from decades of conflict.[20] Mosques served as recruitment centers and as the public's primary sources of information about the achievements of the nationalist forces.[21]

After the establishment of the Republic in 1923, the new regime rapidly secularized all of the country's bureaucratic and judicial institutions, including the military. The breach with the past, however, was not as complete as is often depicted. The Turkish elite consisted of members of the Ottoman intelligentsia who had served as officers in the Ottoman military, an experience that affected their view of the founding principles of the new military. Although the military entered a path of structural and doctrinal change, political and military leaders of the era continued to promote the use of Islamic symbols to increase the morale of the armed forces. The moral foundation of the military combined Islamic values with nationalist values. To this day, many people still regard the armed forces as the "Hearth of the Prophet" (Peygamber Ocağı) and refer to the Turkish soldier as "Little Muhammad" (Mehmetçik). A wounded soldier is regarded as an Islamic war veteran (*gazi/ghazi*), and a soldier killed in the line of duty is considered a martyr (*şehid/shahid*). As these examples suggest, despite redefining itself as a thoroughly secular institution, the TAF did not completely discard religion.

Chief of Staff (from 1924 to 1944) Fevzi Çakmak, known for his conservative worldview, managed to balance the radical reforms with the religious needs of the military to enable its peaceful secularization. In 1925, Çakmak asked Hamdi Akseki, a well-respected religious cleric and former teacher of religion in the Ottoman Army, to write a religious guide for soldiers.[22] In this text, the ideal soldier is depicted as pious, of good character, morally upright, obedient, attached to his nation and country, and loyal to the welfare of the state. Military discipline involved being a follower of God first, then the Prophet, and finally the rulers of the state.[23]

During these early republican years, officers with a religious educational background were still allowed to serve in the military. Despite the staunchly secular outlook of the new state, however, the TAF remained as suspicious of non-Muslim soldiers as its Ottoman predecessor.[24] Although non-Muslims became full citizens of the Turkish Republic, Islam remained the core identifier for citizens in this secular state. Discrimination against Christians and Jews took both explicit and subtle forms with regard to military service.[25] In 1939, for instance, the government allowed non-Muslim men to pay a fee to shorten their service. As late as 1941, only Muslims were allowed to serve as petty officers. In 1941, the Ministry of Defense decided to conscript all non-Muslim men born between 1896 and 1913. The official reason for the call was the rising German threat, but analysts have suggested that the government was afraid that non-Muslims might collaborate with the enemy. Non-Muslim recruits were prohibited from wearing uniforms or carrying weapons. Most of these recruits were given construction, civil engineering, or mining jobs.[26]

To this day, military service is mandatory for all Turkish male citizens regardless of religion, but in reality promotion to officer status is impossible for non-Muslims. Although all male Turkish citizens have the legal right to apply for an officer's commission, it is common knowledge that non-Muslim citizens are weeded out during the exam stage.

The Cold War

Although it may seem that the internal tensions regarding Islam in the TAF would ultimately result in a crisis, little changed in the 1950s. This persistence of the status quo is curious given the occurrence of two major events that could have redefined the role of religion in the Turkish military yet failed to do so. The first event was the shift to multiparty politics in 1946. In 1950, the Democratic Party (DP) replaced the old Republican People's Party, which had ruled for twenty-eight years. Despite the tendency of the new government to appeal to conservative sentiments, it never attempted to redefine the role of religion in the TAF.

The second event was Turkey's participation in the Korean War, an international event with domestic consequences. The DP legitimized the war as a fight against communism. The Ministry of Religious Affairs emphasized that it was a war between believers and infidels in which the former would emerge victorious. Because Communists were antagonistic to Islam, the ministry pointed out that soldiers who died during the war would be considered martyrs.[27] And as there were not enough official imams in the military to serve the needs of all combat units, they were supplemented by civilian imams, selected by means of an exam in Ankara.[28] The TAF did not hesitate to appoint chaplains for the war, but it also made sure to annul their status once the war was over.

Perhaps the most interesting aspect of the convoluted relationship between the TAF and Islam during these years concerns the missionary work performed by imams serving in Korea. Along with their religious duties in the battalions, these imams performed missionary work. By the end of the war, they had converted fifty-nine Koreans to Islam. The commander of the Turkish brigade, Cemil Uluçevik, received permission from the chief of staff in Ankara to build a mosque for the Korean converts. This mosque, built by Turkish soldiers, is the oldest of its kind in Korea.[29]

Following its participation in the Korean War, Turkey became a member of NATO. Participation in the alliance led to a period of transformation in which Turkey received U.S. military aid and sought to bring TAF regulations into harmony with NATO regulations. Although NATO regulations covered the assignment and duty of army chaplains, the TAF never officially established a chaplaincy unit and quietly skirted the issue. The TAF, however, did permit a number of officers to attend the newly established Faculty of Theology at Ankara University.[30] These officers wore uniforms while studying at the university and resided in TAF dormitories.

Interviews with officers who served alongside theology graduates in the TAF suggest that several of these graduates had the opportunity to serve in the field of religious services. Service consisted of general talks on spiritual and moral values and had little, if any, religious content. The number of officers with a theology background was limited, and they did not provide regular religious services, as would chaplains in other militaries. The position of "religion officer" existed only during active combat.[31] Consequently, they were not regarded as a threat to the secular foundations of the TAF or the Republic at the time.

In the 1970s, the TAF relaxed its control of religion in the ranks in response to perceptions of increasing threat from the Soviet Union. This change dovetailed with U.S. efforts to form a "green belt" of Muslim allies in the Middle East to confront the rise of left-wing movements.[32] An interviewee who joined the Turkish Air Force Academy in 1977, for instance, claims that soldiers had free access to religious literature during those years. He further comments that "while commander [name removed] played billiards in the mess hall, we read *Riyadh as-Saaliheen* [*The Gardens of the Righteous*, a compilation of hadiths by Imam an-Nawawi] in the mess hall. It was a free environment. We used to watch the religious program on TV on Fridays [without any problems]."[33]

Another ex-officer described his years as a petty officer in similar terms: "In 1975–1976 ... all medical military students and students of the petty officer school received military education together. It was summer and Ramadan. When we applied to the head officer for permission to perform *teravih* [a special prayer for Ramadan], we received a very normal [positive] response. ... Our officers never discriminated against us."[34]

The military permitted the construction of mosques on military bases during this era. Anticommunist publications focused on bridging Muslim and secular values to counter the rise of communist values.[35] When the instruction of religion and moral values became mandatory in all Turkish schools in 1974, the TAF followed suit and began offering religious instruction in military academies. These classes were taught by theology graduates who were recruited to serve as officers for this purpose.

These officers also served as religion officers during the Cyprus conflict in 1974, preaching on spiritual subjects as a means of lifting troop morale.[36] Interviews with two religion teachers who served as religion officers in Cyprus imply that this exceptional service situation continued after the end of active combat mainly in response to the international crisis that prolonged their stay on the island. A retired officer who performed this duty explains it as follows:

Cyprus is still in a state of war. That's why there are religion officers serving there. ... Starting in 1981, many officers who were religion teachers in military schools have served as religion officers ... for two year terms. ... I served there from 1987 to 1989. When I arrived [on the island] in 1987, I saw that the service was not very regular, and mostly remained on paper. [Since] providing religious instruction to the soldiers was the main reason that I was sent there in the first place, I decided to take matters into my own hands and set out to build a regular practice. ... I prepared a list of religious subjects that I deemed as necessary for a private to know and asked my superiors to teach them through seminars given every other week. My proposal was accepted. Since we were given two divisions, I shared the task with two petty officers with theology background. ... I prepared the manuscripts. ... Our task was not easy. [While] the troops were always informed earlier about our visits ... when we arrived ... mostly they were out for military exercises or education. ... [Nevertheless,] I never saw a similar regular practice elsewhere.[37]

As the interviews also underline, interpreting the appointment of religion officers during the Cyprus crisis as a permanent shift in the TAF's formal stance toward the explicit display of religious activity among its ranks would be misleading. Instead, it seems to have been congruent with their practice of using Islam and Islamic symbols to increase cohesion among the ranks of what the TAF regarded as its expeditionary forces during these years.

The leaders of the 1980 military coup in Turkey supported the use of Islam as the ideal means for uniting an increasingly polarized society. The government used textbooks to promote the idea of a "nation of soldiers," drawing on Islamic notions of martyrdom and jihad. Schoolchildren were taught to identify with a primordial military ethos, common to all Turks, that was Muslim in essence.[38] An eighth-grade religion textbook argued that "Turks are from birth a nation of soldiers. Islam also commands one to fight for the fatherland all the time. ... Among the [pre-Islamic] settled Turks there were those adepts of the Zoroastrian, Buddhist, Manichean, Jewish, and Christian religions. Yet it is seen that these religions did not conform to the Turks' spirit of warfare."[39]

Interviews reflect that, even after the coup of 1980, the TAF continued its practice of monitoring explicit displays of religion in the ranks. Interviews and memoirs suggest, however, that there was no overt discrimination toward religion.

Contemporary Challenges

After the collapse of the Soviet Union, the communist threat was replaced by the rise of Islamic extremism. In tandem with this new concern, following the 1980 coup d'état, the Turkish state introduced a policy of "the Turkish-Islam synthesis." This policy sought to deflect extremist Islam by emphasizing a moderate and controlled form. Despite these efforts, the Iranian Revolution across the border and the rise of the Islamist Welfare Party under the leadership of Necmettin Erbakan exacerbated TAF fears of threats to the secular foundations of the Turkish Republic. The close ties between the Welfare Party and the religious elite, and Erbakan's Islamist discourse further heightened TAF concerns. It is thus possible to regard the TAF's tight control over its personnel's religious activities as a knee-jerk effort to protect the secular roots of the Turkish state. The election of the Justice and Development Party (JDP) in November 2002 altered this scene significantly. The JDP, which had ties to the old cadres of the political Islamist movements formerly established by Erbakan, gradually diminished the tutelary role of the army in civilian affairs.

Confrontation in the 1990s

In late 1980s, the TAF found itself torn between this Turkish-Muslim synthesis and its efforts to undermine Islamic extremism, a futile struggle that ultimately resulted in increasingly extreme measures. Interviews suggest that the Islamic Revolution in Iran also effected the perception of Islamic sensibilities in the eyes of high-ranking officers.[40] Referring to the higher ranks of the TAF, one of our interviewees voiced this complaint: "Following the revolution in Iran, [the higher-ranking officers in the TAF] confused us with the mullahs there. They could not distinguish the difference between Shiites and Sunnites. [During the 1970s], while the [Necmettin] Erbakan cabinet was in charge, [Erbakan] made some provocative comments. He claimed that they received most of their votes from the military. Such statements shook our place in the establishment."

Interviews and memoirs depict the 1990s as a period of significant shift in the TAF's treatment of Islam.[41] The shift resulted in part from the changing threat perception among NATO countries that diminished the strategic importance of Turkey.[42] NATO redefined its purpose as a peacekeeping force dedicated to eliminating the new dominant threat, namely radical Islam. Consequently, it can be claimed that the TAF sought to reinforce its image as capable of stemming the Islamist threat.[43]

The increasing visibility of Islamic discourse in Turkey's public sphere led to greater sensitivity regarding the overt display of religious affiliation in the TAF. The success of the Welfare Party, which had explicit Islamist leanings, triggered reactions from secular civil-society organizations and the TAF. In their speeches, high-ranking military officers constantly underlined the significance of the secular Kemalist ideology for the preservation of the Turkish state. They held meetings in which they called on civilians to take action against Islamic extremism.

In 1996, an order regulating prayer in the military was leaked to the media, prompting another heated debate.[44] The circular banned TAF personnel from using prayer rooms on military bases and urged them instead to pray in public mosques or at home. The same notice also stated that no call for prayers would be issued in prayer rooms or mosques located on military bases. Those facilities would contain only books and magazines published by the Ministry of Religious Affairs. Additionally, the notice prohibited Arabic inscriptions on the walls of mosques in army bases and banned religious items such as rosaries and skullcaps. Soldiers serving as prayer leaders were prohibited from wearing the attire of a civilian imam, as issued by the Ministry of Religion. Following the leak, the Grand National Assembly called the minister of interior to task for oppressing the religious freedoms of military personnel and the minister, in turn, argued that the order merely sought to remind soldiers of existing institutional rules.[45]

On February 4, 1997, the army took the extreme measure of sending tanks through Sincan, an Islamic neighborhood of Ankara, the Turkish capital, to show its concern about the rise of Islamic discourse.[46] Later that month, the National Security Council (NSC) discussed the topic of escalating Islamism. The meeting had a long-lasting impact on Turkish politics. The NSC repositioned the TAF as the foremost guardian of the state's secular principles. Military representatives met with members of the Constitutional Court, the Supreme Court of Appeals, the Council of State, university rectors, and journalists to emphasize the threat posed by extremist movements. In June 1997, Prime Minister Erbakan resigned in part because of pressure from the military. After these events, known as the "February 28, 1997 Intervention," the Constitutional Court banned both Erbakan and his party from engaging in political activities.

This cataclysmic incident rapidly shifted the role and visibility of Islam among the ranks of the TAF. During the 1990s, military personnel were highly affected by the new political atmosphere. The religious affiliation and activities of TAF personnel became major factors in the evaluation of their performance and in their promotion. Interviews and published memoirs claim that military officers could no longer pray or display religious devotion in public. Officers who used to perform Friday prayers expected to forgo them.[47] An interview suggests that, until these developments, religious education based on *The Soldier's Religion Book* was a part of the night training offered on bases. Conscripted soldiers with a background in theology usually gave these seminars on religion.[48] Following February 1997, however, this practice swiftly came to an end.[49]

The Officer Purge of 1997

During the 1990s, the Supreme Military Council (known by the Turkish acronym YAŞ), which dictates promotions and appointments in the military, expelled an increasing number of officers and cadets who were suspected of engaging in Islamic activities (see Table 10.1).[50] Under Article 125 of the Turkish Constitution expelled officers had no right to appeal this YAŞ decision. They also automatically lost all of their pension rights.

In addition to these expelled officers, many more officers are said to have been forced to resign during this period.[51] The TAF's new policy probably influenced the reluctance of students from Islamic institutions (*İmam-Hatip* schools) to pursue a military career. When asked about their occupational choices after graduation, only 4.2 percent of male students responded with a wish to join the military or become a police officer.[52] In another survey, only 1 percent of the students in these schools stated that they wanted to pursue a military career.[53]

A semimilitary organization called the West Working Group (WWG) is widely regarded as the primary source of information on the religious practices of TAF officers and was held responsible for the purges discussed here. The WWG was tasked with collecting information about the political and religious orientation of institutions and public figures.[54] It advised the National Security Council in religious matters and in March 2001 influenced the NSC's decision to step up the fight against Islamic extremism.[55] According to an expelled general,

[The WWG] was an establishment for identifying those people who did not share their beliefs, and expelling them from the military. They were able to build their own cadres under the claim of purging reactionaries. When the West Working Group stated that "X person harbors extremist tendencies, [so] submit his documents [to our group]," the commander of the troop in question could not refuse the request. A commander refusing to follow such an instruction would prepare his own doom.[56]

Meanwhile, the Islamist press widely publicized the memoirs of expelled officers and cadets. Expelled cadets highlighted efforts to prevent them from performing religious duties such as daily prayers. They also described the pressures placed on pious personnel and emphasized freedom of religion in the military.[57] One officer recalled:

My wife's headscarf and my daily prayers were interpreted as "definite" evidence of my extremist tendencies. They were enough, no more was required. ... First they asked for the pictures of the wives and the children of all officers and petty officers. My wife's picture was with a headscarf, so when I gave it to the secretary, my secretary said, "Sir,

TABLE 10.1. *Officers Expelled as a Result of Suspected Reactionary Beliefs and Behaviors, 1990–2001*

Year	Officers	Petty Officers	Total
1990	47	143	190
1991	19	78	97
1992	13	48	61
1993	13	35	48
1994	16	38	54
1995	18	59	77
1996	46	52	98
1997			297
1998	127	145	272
1999	20	61	81
2000	20	42	62
2001	11	70	81
total			1,418

let us send a picture without a headscarf."... We sent it as it was and that was the day we were blacklisted.[58]

Although the number of expelled students and commissioned and noncommissioned officers has dropped in the last decade, debates on religious freedom in the TAF continue. Secularists and Islamists have exploited these debates to promote their views on governance and their understanding of secularism. The YAŞ expulsions led to a particularly heated debate between supporters, who are perceived as Kemalist secularists, and opponents, who are viewed as Islamist and conservative. In the late 1990s, members of the Welfare Party called for permanent chaplains to be employed by the military, and they questioned the military's grounds for purging devout officers.[59] Although the minister of the defence maintained that prayer, wearing a headscarf, or abstaining from alcohol were not grounds for expulsion, these assurances failed to convince Islamist members of parliament.

In 2002, the rise to power of a party with Islamist sensitivities, the Justice and Development Party (JDP), brought an end to the political process that began in February 1997, as evidenced by the decline in the number of officers expelled because of suspected reactionary behavior (see Table 10.2).[60] The JDP's election victory signaled an end to parliamentary and media debates over religious freedom in the military.

TABLE 10.2. *Officers Expelled Because of Suspected Reactionary Beliefs and Behaviors, 2002–2010*

Year	Total Officers Expelled	Expelled for Suspected Reactionary Behavior
2002	44	44
2003	20	20
2004	20	20
2005	15	15
2006	54	6
2007	61	12
2008	24	5
2009	3	3
2010	0	0
2011	0	0

The Contemporary Status Quo

To this day, the TAF employs no military chaplains. Instead, theology graduates who have been employed as officers serve as instructors for the compulsory Religious Culture and Ethics Course classes in military academies. In case of war – as in Cyprus, Bosnia, Somalia, and Afghanistan – these graduates are expected to perform as temporary chaplains.[61] Instead of addressing the religious needs of soldiers in its ranks permanently, the TAF has adopted a semiformal approach that involves tapping into its conscript pool. The mosques or prayer rooms that exist on many military bases are operated by conscripts who have some background in religious education.[62] These conscripts are expected to lead prayer sessions in addition to their regular duties.[63] Occasionally, with permission from the chief of staff, preachers from the Ministry of Religious Affairs will visit bases to give talks on patriotism and basic Islamic teachings.[64]

Unlike officers, whose religious behavior is kept under close scrutiny, conscripted soldiers are free to perform religious rites. There are no official restrictions on mosque use or prayer by conscripted soldiers, although in some cases officers have been known to encourage conscripts to limit their praying by arguing that military duty is a good substitute. Fasting during Ramadan is an exception to this pattern, presumably because it is the most widely observed Muslim practice in Turkey.[65] Many officers and soldiers fast during Ramadan, and the meal schedule is arranged to facilitate fasting. Interviews suggest, however, that during the 1990s, fasting during Ramadan was highly discouraged in military schools.[66] One interviewee, for instance, explained the conditions during those years as follows: "They used to send us [religion teachers] about fifteen to twenty days before the start of Ramadan, to explain to the cadets that soldiering is also an expression of piety, and that [fasting] would interrupt the training, etc. But, in the end, those who wanted to fast did so, and the *suhoor* meal (the meal consumed early in the morning by Muslims before fasting) was provided before dawn during that month."[67]

An interesting exception to the military's aversion to displays of religion can be observed in the eastern and southeastern regions of Turkey, where the TAF has been engaged in a prolonged conflict with the Kurdistan Worker's Party (PKK), the Kurdish terrorist organization. To foster support among the local religiously conservative population, the army has chosen to promote its image as an institution sensitive to religious symbols and observant of religious rituals. In those particular regions, the army has encouraged its officers to attend public Friday prayers in uniform, and in some cases, it has even asked officers to pray with conscripts to boost their morale.[68]

Under the JDP, Turkey's political environment has been changing rapidly. Recent years have seen a turbulent political debate around limiting the role of the military in Turkish politics. The new political elite, which sought to circumscribe the role of the TAF in politics, was supported in this endeavor by liberal intellectuals who regarded this change as vital for the consolidation of Turkish democracy. Several dramatic events in recent years have polarized opinions about the political influence of the military, leading to acrimonious debates. In the so-called Ergenekon case (2007), the military was alleged to have been involved in illegal activities to prevent Islamist movements from gaining political power.[69] This case and related lawsuits poured hot oil on an already heated discussion and attracted a great deal of attention both domestically and abroad.

Such incidents pose difficult questions about the TAF's role and its position in Turkish politics that fall outside the scope of this study. One lawsuit, however, does pertain directly to religious practices in the TAF given the military's response to the case. To rebut "unconscientious people who make dire accusations against the TAF," the chief of the General Staff, Ilker Basbug, explicitly acknowledged TAF use of Islamic symbols among its ranks:

There are dire claims [directed against the TAF]. We call those documents used in military training "field manuals." When you read the section discussing assaults there, particularly [military] attacks, [it says,] What do we tell our soldiers to chant [when they attack]? We urge them to cry out "Allah Allah." How could the military ever consider bombing God's house [mosque]? This is unconscionable; I curse the people [who make these claims]. The military's Little Mohammed trains to the sounds of "Allah Allah." This is stated in our field manual. Would such people bomb God's houses, and [attack] those people praying there? I curse them![70]

Developments in the last two years suggest the transformation that started in 1997 has reached its conclusion. On March 10, 2011, the Turkish parliament restored the expelled officers' rights for employment and retirement benefits.[71]

In May 2012, a hotly debated ban on religious attire and symbols at officers' clubs and social facilities was changed so that it no longer applied to civilians.[72] The original regulation read:

Aside from those people of advanced age who wear a simple beard due to piety and elderly mothers who wear headscarves without covering their face, it is forbidden for people with the following qualifications to enter the social facilities: a) Beard, religious robe, turban, skullcap, and such nonmodern attire; b) those who do not shave daily, or those who arrive with dirty and/or unironed clothes, and c) foreign nationals.[73]

In June 2012, the Turkish Grand Assembly passed a resolution that removed "the attitudes and behavior of the spouse" as a criterion for evaluating applicants for officer training at the military academy and for commanding officers undergoing promotion exams.[74] This move was interpreted by the Turkish press as a green light for the promotion of officers whose wives wear traditional Muslim attire.[75]

In determining the role of religion in the TAF, the conservative Justice and Development Party may seek to emulate its Ottoman predecessor. Such attempts would be bolstered by alleged deepening rifts in the TAF.[76] While the TAF has never held a monolithic stance on religion, some have argued that officers with a more moderate approach toward religion have gained the upper hand in recent years. At the same time, it seems unlikely that the TAF will radically alter its attitude to accommodate the expectations of the current political regime.

Notes

1   The TAF is the second largest force in NATO after the United States. It consists of Land Forces Command, Naval Forces Command, and Air Forces Command as well as the Gendarme General Command and the Coast Guard Command, which are subordinated to the Ministry of Interior during peacetime.

2   The literature on secularism in Turkey is vast, and summarizing its main debates is beyond the scope of this study. For a comparative analysis that underlines the main characteristics of Turkish secularism, see Ahmet T. Kuru, *Secularism and State Policies toward Religion: The United States, France, and Turkey* (New York: Cambridge University Press, 2009).

3   Metin Heper and Ahmet Evin, eds., *State, Democracy, and the Military: Turkey in the 1980s* (Berlin: Walter de Gruyter, 1988).

4   See M. Hakan Yavuz, *Islamic Political Identity in Turkey* (New York: Oxford University Press, 2003).

5   The term "vignette" is described by Christine Barter and Emma Renold as follows: "Vignettes may be used for three main purposes in social research: to allow actions in context to be explored; to clarify people's judgements; and to provide a less personal and therefore less threatening way of exploring sensitive topics. In qualitative research, vignettes enable participants to define the situation in their own terms." See Christine Barter and Emma Renold, "The Use of Vignettes in Qualitative Research," *Social Research Update* 25, University of Surrey (Summer 1999), http://sru.soc.surrey.ac.uk/SRU25.html.

6   On the role of Islamic ethos in the early Ottoman polity, see, for instance, Knut Mikjel Rio and Olaf H. Smedal, *Hierarchy: Persistence and Transformation in Social Formations* (New York: Berghahn Books, 2009): 185–187.

7   İ. Hakkı Uzunçarşılı, *Osmanlı Tarihi*, vol. 3/1 (Ankara: TTK, 1995): 348–349; Ümit Ekin, "Osmanlı Ordusunda Moral Yükseltici bir Kurum olarak Ordu Şeyhliği," *Sakarya Üniversitesi Fen-Edebiyat Dergisi*, vol. 10, no. 1 (2008): 174–176; İsmail Hakkı Uzunçarşılı, *Osmanlı Devleti Teşkilatından Kapukulu Ocakları, Acemi Ocağı ve Yeniçeri Ocağı*, vol. 1 (Ankara: Türk Tarih Kurumu Yayınları, 1984): 232–233; Kemal Beydilli, *Osmanlı Döneminde İmamlar ve Bir İmamın Günlüğü* (İstanbul: Tarih ve Tabiat Vakfı Yayınları, 2001); Mehmet Zeki Pakalın, "Ordu Şeyhi," *Osmanlı Tarih Deyimleri ve Terimleri Sözlüğü*, vol. 2 (Istanbul: MEB Yayını, 1971): 729.

8   "Alay İmamı," *TDV İslâm Ansiklopedisi, vol.* 2 (Istanbul: Türk Diyanet Vakfı, 1989): 348.

9   İsmail Kara, "Cumhuriyet Devrinde 'Askere Din Dersleri,' İyi Asker İyi Müslüman, İyi Müslüman İyi Asker Olur," *Toplumsal Tarih*, issue 166 (December 2007): 49.

10 Erik Jan Zürcher, "The Ottoman Conscription System in Theory and Practice," *Arming the State* (London: I. B. Tauris, 1999): 88.

11 The English translation of the *Gülhane* edict is available in J. C. Hurewitz, ed., *The Middle East and North Africa in World Politics: A Documentary Record* (New Haven, CT: Yale University Press, 1975).

12 Enver Ziya Karal, *Osmanlı Tarihi*, vol. 6 (Ankara: TTK, 1954): 160.

13 Ibid., Cevdet Paşa, *Maruzat* (Istanbul: Çağrı Yayınları, 1980): s.114; Cevdet Paşa, *Tezakir* (Ankara: TTK, 1986).

14 Erik Jan Zürcher, "Ottoman Labor Battalions in World War I," http://www.hist. net/kieser/aghet/Essays/EssayZurcher.html.

15 Leon Trotsky, *The War Correspondence of Leon Trotsky: The Balkan Wars 1912–13* (New York: Monad Press; Sydney: Pathfinder Press, 1980): 194.

16 See Cengiz Mutlu, *Amele Taburları* (Istanbul: IQ Kültür Sanat Yayıncılık, 2007): 47–49.

17 Ibid., 49; Zürcher, "Ottoman Labor Battalions in World War I". A number of memoirs from the World War I period emphasize the differences between Muslim and non-Muslim soldiers in the Ottoman military. See, for instance, Alexander Aaronsohn, *With the Turks in Palestine* (New York: Cambridge University Press, 1916): 23–24.

18 Hans Kannengiesser, *The Campaign in Gallipoli* (London: Hutchinson, n.d. [although preface is dated 1926]): 146.

19 The commander of 1st Battalion of the 57th Regiment in Gallipoli, Zeki Bey, for instance, notes in his memoirs: "I went first up the right-hand trench, perhaps thirty-five yards up it. There I found not an officer but only the Hoja – the chaplain – of my battalion. It being the 1st Battalion of the regiment, he ranked as Mufti – the 2nd and 3rd would have an Imam. He was a very brave man and kept his head very well. I went up close to him. He said 'You can't go further up here' – there were some dead and wounded. ... The men told me, 'Behind this place there are English.'" Charles Edwin Woodrow Bean, *Gallipoli Mission* (Sydney: ABC Books, 1990): 189.

20 *Türk Silahlı Kuvvetleri Tarihi Türkiye Büyük Millet Meclisi Dönemi* (23 Nisan 1920–29 Ekim 1923), vol. 4, sec. 1 (Ankara: Genelkurmay Basımevi, 1984): 206.

21 Ali Sarıkoyuncu, "Şeyh Edebali ve Milli Mücadele'de Bilecik Müftüsü Mehmet Nuri Efendi," *Diyanet İlmî Dergi*, vol. 30, no. 3 (July, August, September 1994): 15–24.

22 For a list of religious publications for soldiers during the early Republican period, see İsmail Kara, "Cumhuriyet Devrinde Askere Din Dersleri, İyi Asker İyi Müslüman, İyi Müslüman İyi Asker Olur," 53.

23 Ibid., 51.

24 The scarce non-Muslim population in contemporary Turkey consists mostly of Armenians, Greeks, Jews, and Assyrians.

25 For several accounts on the conscription memoirs of non-Muslim soldiers, see Rıfat N. Bali, *Gayrimüslim Mehmetçikler: Hatıralar – Tanıklıklar* (İstanbul: Libra Kitap, 2011).

26 For further details, see Rıfat N. Bali, *Bir Türkleştirme Serüveni (1923–1945): Cumhuriyet Yıllarında Türkiye Yahudileri* (Istanbul: İletişim Yayınları, 1999): 408–423; Rıfat N. Bali *Devletin Yahudileri ve Öteki Yahudi* (Istanbul: İletişim Yayınları, 2004): 301–307.

27 "Süleymaniye Camiinde Şehitler Muazzam Dini Merasimle Anıldı," *Milliyet (Daily)*, 11 December 1950.

28 İbrahim Doğan, "Kore'ye İslamı Türk Askeri götürdü," *Aksiyon*, issue 505, 8 August 2004.

29 Ibid, For other examples of the memoirs of Turkish imams who served in Korea, see Selim Efe Erdem, "Seul'deki Türkler," *Radikal*, 7 September 2005; and http://theseoultimes.com/ST/?url=/ST/db/read.php?idx=2726&PHPSESSID=9cc4079be1daf23817db6e469aa402e7.

30 Retired major, expelled from TAF, interviewed by the authors, June 2010. The memoirs of Lt. Col. Sami Kocaoğlu (ret.), who studied in the faculty of theology from 1956 to 1960, also confirm these details. "NATO belgeleri tercüme edilirken sadece 'din işleri subaylığı' atlandı," *Zaman*, 5 May 2005.

31 Ibid.

32 For details, see Baskın Oran, ed., *Türk Dış Politikası, Kurtuluş Savaşından Bugüne Olgular, Belgeler, Yorumlar*, vol. 1 (Istanbul: İletişim Yayınları, 2001).

33 Retired squadron leader and member of the Association of Justice Defenders (ASDER), a group association run by expelled officers from the TAF, interviewed by the authors, November 2010. The interviewee is referring to the one-hour program on Islam aired on the only television channel available at the time, which was operated by the Turkish state.

34 Resigned major, interviewed by the authors, March 2011.

35 Faik Bulut, *Ordu ve Din* (Istanbul: Berfin Yayınları, 2008): 154–155.

36 Retired major, expelled from the TAF, who served as a religion teacher in (Turkish) military academies, interviewed by the authors, June 2010.

37 Retired major who served as a religion teacher and also served in Cyprus, interviewed by the authors, November 2010.

38 Sam Kaplan, "Din-u Devlet All Over Again? The Politics of Military Secularism and Religious Militarism in Turkey Following the 1980 Coup," *International Journal of Middle East Studies* vol. 34, no. 1 (February 2002): 116.

39 Cihad Tunç, *Ortaokullar için Din Kültürü ve Ahlak Bilgisi 3* (Istanbul: Milli Eğitim Basımevi, 1987): 115, cited in ibid., 120.

40 Two retired squadron leaders interviewed by the authors, November 2010.

41 Several accounts can be found in Turkish dailies. For example, Col. Cengiz Tangören was interviewed by Nuriye Akman on 21 June 2009 in *Zaman*; Maj. Şahin Akdoğan was interviewed by Umut Yavuz in *Yeni Asya* on 7 March 2010; and Prof. Dr. Ahmet Alper was interviewed by Seda Şimşek in *Bugün* on 13 April 2010. An exception to dates in stories of expelled officers is the account by İskender Pala, an expelled officer and prominent academic. In his memoirs, he mentions that he could not use the navy's social facilities in 1987 because his wife wore a headscarf. He also underlines that his experience was one of the earliest incidents of discrimination, given that the headscarf debate was still a minor issue in the 1980s. See İskender Pala, *İki Darbe Arasında* (Istanbul: Kapı Yayınları, 2010): 84–87.

42 Baskın Oran, ed., *Türk Dış Politikası: Kurtuluş Savaşından Bugüne Olgular, Belgeler, Yorumlar*, vol. 2 (Istanbul: İletişim Yayınları, 2001).

43 Retired major, expelled from the TAF, interviewed by the authors, June 2010.

44 "1996 Jandarma Genel Komutanlığı Genelgesi," *Milliyet*, 27 March 1996.

45 The written reply of Meral Akşener, the minister of interior, to the written question of Diyarbakir deputy Yakup Hatipoglu on the practices regarding the military personnel observing religious rites in the TAF [Diyarbakır Milletvekili Yakup Hatipoğlu'nun, dinî vecibelerini yerine getiren ordu mensuplarına yapılan uygulamalara ilişkin sorusu ve İçişleri Bakanı Meral Akşener'in yazılı cevabı] (7/1609); the written reply of Meral Akşener, the Minister of Interior, to the written question of Istanbul deputy Mehmet Ali Şahin on the practices regarding the military personnel observing religious rites in the TAF [İstanbul Milletvekili Mehmet Ali Şahin'in, dinî vecibelerini yerine getiren ordu mensuplarına yapılan uygulamalara ilişkin sorusu ve İçişleri Bakanı Meral Akşener'in yazılı cevabı] (7/1612), T.B.M.M., TUTANAK DERGİSİ, CİLT: 16, 29 uncu Birleşim, 10 December 1996. See also the written reply/response of Mehmet Ağar, the minister of interior, to the question of Gaziantep deputy Mustafa R. Taşar to the prime minister on the allegation of a circular issued to the military troops [Gaziantep Milletvekili Mustafa R. Taşar'ın, askerî birliklere gönderildiği iddia edilen bir genelgeye ilişkin Başbakandan sorusu ve İçişleri Bakanı Mehmet Ağar'ın yazılı cevabı] (7/1168), Dönem 20, Yasama Yılı 2, TBMM Tutanak Dergisi, Cilt 11, 1 inci Birleşim, 1 October 1996.

46 For a chronology of these events, see Svante E. Cornell, "Turkey: Return to Stability?" *Middle Eastern Studies*, vol. 35, no. 4 (October 1999): 209–234.

47 In one instance, the prime minister and the deputy prime minister attended a Friday prayer service during a military maneuver while all military officers stayed behind in their headquarters. Interview with Muhittin Fisunoğlu by Nuriye Akman, *Sabah*, 1 December 1997.

48 Retired major who served as a religion teacher and also served in Cyprus, interviewed by the authors, November 2010.

49 As of 1996, their number was thirty. Figure supplied by retired major, ibid.

50 "TSK'dan 19 yılda bin 657 subay ihraç edildi," *Hurriyet*, 5 December 2009.

51 The Islamist press has claimed that many officers were forced to resign. The expelled general Ahmet Alper has claimed that 10,000 officers were forced to resign. Prof. Dr. Ahmet Alper, interviewed by Seda Şimşek, *Bugün*, 12 April 2010.

52 Survey by Coşkun published in 1999, cited in Ruşen Çakır, İrfan Bozan, and Balkan Talu, *İmam Hatip Liseleri: Efsaneler ve Gerçekler* (Istanbul: TESEV, 2004): 89.

53 Survey by Sarpkaya published in 1998, cited in ibid., 90.

54 Ümit Cizre, "Demythologyzing the National Security Concept: The Case of Turkey," *Middle East Journal*, vol. 57, no. 2 (Spring 2003): 218.

55 Ibid., 219.

56 Interview (part two) with Prof. Dr. Ahmet Alper by Seda Şimşek, *Bugün*, 13 April 2010.

57 Several accounts can be found on ASDER's Web site, http://www.as-der.org.tr. The Web site also collects memoirs published on other Web sites and in printed media interviews.

58 Interview (part two) with Prof. Dr. Ahmet Alper, 13 April 2010.

59 Discussion on Article 42, "4.8.1971 tarihli ve 1462 sayılı Harp Okulları Kanunu yürürlükten kaldırılmıştır," Dönem 21, Cilt 32, Yasama Yılı 2, T. B. M. M. TUTANAK DERGİSİ 93. Birleşim, 11 May 2000. Question on mandatory retired commissioned and noncommissioned officers by the Supreme Military Council asked by Sanliurfa and answered in writing by Minister of National Defense and Vice Prime Minister İsmet Sezgin [Şanlıurfa Milletvekili Abdulkadir Öncel'in, Yüksek Askerî Şûra kararıyla emekliye sevk edilen subay ve astsubaylara ilişkin sorusu ve Millî Savunma Bakanı ve Başbakan Yadımcısı İsmet Sezgin'in yazılı cevabı] (7/4445) Türkiye Büyük Millet Meclisi, Genel Kurul Tutanağı, 20. Dönem 3. Yasama Yılı, 66. Birleşim, 12 March 1998.

60 "TSK'dan 19 yılda bin 657 subay ihraç edildi," *Hurriyet*, 5 December 2009, except data for 2010.

61 Interview with a retired army major who served as a religion teacher at Turkish military academies and who served in Cyprus as a religion officer, November 2010.

62 As an interviewee pointed out, some of the major military academies, including Kuleli Military High School, do not have a mosque on their campuses. Ibid.

63 Ibid.

64 Interview with İsmail Öner by Nuriye Akman, *Sabah*, 19 May 1996.

65 A 2007 survey shows that whereas only 45 percent of subjects said they performed their prayers, 79 percent said they fasted during Ramadan. ANAR Research Company, field survey with 2,224 subjects, 9–22 October 2007.

66 Two retired air force squadron leaders, interviewed by the authors in Istanbul, November 2010.

67 Retired major, interviewed by the authors, November 2010.

68 Bulut, *Ordu ve Din*, 160; and interview with a retired army major who served as a religion teacher at Turkish military academies and who served in Cyprus as a religion officer, November 2010.

69 The case has led to the detention of hundreds of people to date, including a former chief of General Staff, many high-ranking generals, and a large number of civilians (including university professors and journalists). See Gareth H. Jenkins, *Between Fact and Fantasy: Turkey's Ergenekon Investigation* (Washington, DC: Central Asia–Caucasus Institute and Silk Road Studies Program, 2009); and Metin Heper, "Civil-Military Relations in Turkey: Toward a Liberal Model?" *Turkish Studies*, vol. 12, no. 2 (June 2011): 241–252; Ersel Aydinli, "Ergenekon, New Pacts, and the Decline of the Turkish 'Inner State'," *Turkish Studies*, vol, 12, no. 2 (June 2011): 227–239.

70 "Başbuğ'dan Darbe İddialarına Son Nokta," *Hurriyet*, 25 January 2010.

71 See http://www.resmigazete.gov.tr/main.aspx?home=http://www.resmigazete.gov.tr/eskiler/2011/03/20110322-3.htm/20110322.htm&main=http://www.resmigazete.gov.tr/eskiler/2011/03/20110322-3.htm.

72 See Official Gazette of the Republic of Turkey, 17 May 2012, http://www.resmigazete.gov.tr/main.aspx?home=http://www.resmigazete.gov.tr/eskiler/2012/05/20120517.htm&main=http://www.resmigazete.gov.tr/eskiler/2012/05/20120517.htm.

73 "Orduevinde Düğüne Sakal ve Türban İzni," *Sabah*, 18 May 2012.

74 İstanbul Milletvekili Şirin Ünal ve Çankırı Milletvekili Hüseyin Filiz ile 1 Milletvekilinin; Harp Akademileri Kanunu ve Bazı Kanunlarda Değişiklik Yapılmasına Dair Kanun Teklifi ile Milli Savunma Komisyonu Raporu (2/697), Türkiye Büyük Millet Meclisi, Yasama Dönemi 24, Yasama Yılı 2, Sıra Sayısı 300.

75 See, for example, http://www.cnnturk.com/2012/guncel/06/21/esi.basortulu.olan.subaylara.kurmaylik/666046.0/index.html; and http://www.hurriyet.com.tr/gundem/20800628.asp; http://yenisafak.com.tr/Gundem/?t=21.06.2012&i=390238&k=11.

76 Ersel Aydınlı, "A Paradigmatic Shift for the Turkish Generals and an End to the Coup Era in Turkey," *Middle East Journal* 63, no. 4 (Autumn 2009): 581–596.

Conclusion

Promising Themes, Future Approaches

Eric Patterson

In 1963, Gabriel Almond and Sydney Verba published a social science classic, *The Civic Culture: Political Attitudes and Democracy in Five Nations*.[1] That book, a comparison of the political cultures of five countries (Mexico, the United States, the United Kingdom, Italy, and Germany), gave birth to a half-century of comparative and domestic political studies, including recent literature by foremost scholars on topics such as civic trust and social capital. Reading this volume on national militaries – and their institutional as well as supportive national cultures – reminded me of *The Civic Culture* in numerous ways. This book is also a comparative approach to cultures in diverse countries and, similar to *The Civic Culture*, it focuses on political subcultures, a sense of patriotic duty or obligation to participate, political allegiance, organizational membership, and socialization. The volume in your hands might have been written as a military offshoot of that social science milestone, because it clearly focuses on comparative national military cultures. As suggested later in this conclusion, as with *The Civic Culture*, this book's approach should be extended to other countries in a systematic fashion and its findings replicated in these countries a decade hence.

This book is the first, to my knowledge, to compare the religious environment in which specific national militaries function. The chapters provide keen insights into some of the world's most important militaries by any standard: largest militaries (India, Pakistan, the United States, and Turkey); top military spenders (the United States, the United Kingdom, Japan, and India are all in the top ten, and Canada, Turkey, and Israel are in the top twenty); countries with the highest number of deployed United Nations peacekeepers (Pakistan and India); most experienced in recent foreign deployments (the United States and the United Kingdom); not to mention active members of the world's elite alliance – the North Atlantic Treaty Organization (Canada, the United States, the United Kingdom, and Turkey). This chapter introduces the multidimensionality of the religion-conflict nexus, advances a number of summative themes drawn from previous chapters, and suggests several vectors for future research.

Religion, War, and Peace

This book offers a novel angle on an old constellation of issues. War and religion have long been connected in a variety of ways. One such nexus concerns issues of life, death, and the meaning of both – conversations that the violence of war occasions. It may not be entirely true that there are "no atheists in foxholes," but it is true that the imminence of death occasions deep reflection on many facets of morality and mortality.

War also brings to mind issues of justice and moral obligation, both of which religion has something to say about. Protagonists and victims of war often think in terms of justice for those who have suffered: they are "owed" something for past aggression and wrongdoing. Such deep-seated notions of justice are usually rooted in ethical codes, which in turn are based in religion. So, too, conceptions of punishment and restitution are often defined by religiously informed moral categories such as atonement, reparation, and sin.

In addition, religion can reinforce a powerful sense of obligation for protecting society from aggression, righting wrongs, or both. Just war theory, rooted in nearly two millennia of Christian thinking, is a case in point. Just war thinking provides a moral compass for decisions about when to go to war (*jus ad bellum*) and how war is fought (*jus in bello*). Augustine wrote that it was moral for political authorities to prevent evil, punish evildoers, and right wrongs, and his assumptions are rooted in religious thinking: the vocation of political authorities ("legitimate authorities") to stand up against evil, the idea that some causes are just ("just cause"), and an emphasis on the ethical motivations for state violence ("right intent"). Augustine, Aquinas, and others argued that these principles derive directly from the Scripture, particularly Romans 13.[2]

Although there is no precise correlate to just war theory in other religious traditions, other faiths do weigh in on the ethics of war, from Islam's prohibitions on denuding the landscape, which would then make it impossible for civilians and farmers to maintain a livelihood,[3] to postindependence Jewish thinking on religious justifications for national military service, as discussed in Chapter 5 by Stuart Cohen.

Critics argue, however, that the discussion of religion, ethics, and conflict is a smokescreen for the real problem – that religion is the cause of most contemporary warfare. Is this true? Are we in a new period of religious wars? The answer is no: most wars of the past twenty years have not been caused by, or solved through, religion. Indeed, often religion has been rolled into a conflict by those who do not understand the deeper sources of conflict or the war's multidimensionality, which can include economic, ethnic, demographic, cultural, political, and other factors alongside religion. The long-running conflict in Northern Ireland is a case in point. Although the Troubles were ostensibly between Catholics and Protestants, neither side used violence over interpretations of the Bible, over the nature of the Eucharist, over papal authority, over the role of saints and religious symbols, or over any other religious disagreement to which Catholics and Protestants are party. Rather, this was a conflict about justice, rights, long-term discrimination, tit-for-tat for violence, criminality, political power, and economic opportunity. In fact, the leading "Catholic" organizations, the Irish Republican Army (IRA) and its political affiliate, Sinn Féin, have long been critical of the church and Rome for being quietistic and therefore tacitly abetting what was considered to be English oppression. The IRA is explicitly rooted in the left-of-center secular nationalisms found around the globe in the mid-twentieth century; it is philosophically akin to the Basque separate group ETA and the original Palestine Liberation Organization but not al-Qaeda, Hezbollah, or other religiously inspired terrorist organizations.

So, how should one think about religion and war? The starting point is to realize that religion has direct and indirect causal linkages to war and peace.[4] Religious interpretations can directly induce or exacerbate conflict in a number of ways. For example, a religious text or revelation may directly mandate violence. In Uganda, the leadership of the insurgent Lord's Resistance Army (LRA) claims direct divine revelation for its campaign. LRA commander Joseph Kony claims that spirits talk to him and that the LRA is "fighting for Uganda to be a free state governed by the Ten Commandments, a democratic state, and a state with a freely elected president."[5] Alternatively, religion may directly cause conflict when a religious actor claims the authority, based on religion, to prescribe killing. Osama bin Laden claimed the authority as an observant member of the Muslim *ummah* (community) to issue a fatwa to kill Americans and Jews: "The ruling to kill the Americans and their allies – civilians and military – is an individual duty for every Muslim who can do it in any country in which it is possible to do it."[6]

Elsewhere, the perpetrators of violence may justify their actions with religious claims. Some Arabs in the 1990s argued that the presence of Western troops in the land of Mecca and Medina was a desecration of Islam. Similarly, religion may sacralize a tangible thing or place, making it holy and therefore resulting in a perceived obligation to protect it. The violence between Hindus and Muslims over the location of ancient Hindu temple sites is a case in point.

Religion as the primary, direct cause of conflict is actually rare, despite the highly religious nature of many societies. More often, religious factors are important but indirect contributors to conflict. Sometimes religion, regardless of spiritual content, is a critical sociocultural identity marker and therefore the cleavage point for competition and violence. That competition is usually between groups and over political power and material resources, such as among Lebanon's many communities. A change of religious affiliation may result in persecution, as happens to many Evangelical Protestants in southern Mexico and parts of Guatemala. Most of the time, these groups are not fighting over spiritual practice or theology, but they utilize definitions of "us" and "them" that are faith based or religio-cultural and difficult to overcome. In other places, religious symbols have been manipulated for sectarian or mass mobilization as collective action frames. Ayatollah Ruhollah Khomeini vilified the shah's "Persian" regime, in part by employing symbols that redefined citizenship and identity in religio-nationalist terms. In any event, religious actors, themes, and ideas can be powerful – even transcendent – motivators. How else can one explain the self-sacrificial work of a suicide bomber?

At the same time, how can one explain the self-sacrificial work of Mother Theresa? She represented religion as a powerful, positive force for peace. Thus religious factors may directly or indirectly contribute to peace, not just war. A well-documented example is the role that the Community of Sant'Egidio – a Catholic lay organization – played in brokering peace in Mozambique's two-decade civil war. The Community developed relationships with both sides of the conflict over more than a decade and provided the auspices for an ultimate peace deal.

Religious actors for peace include trusted intermediaries who provide social services during and after conflict. Some of these groups have embraced faith-based pacifism, as do Quakers, Baha'is, and Mennonites. They tend to tie their commitments to peace directly to a scriptural or spiritual revelation. The Mennonites are well known for their peacemaking efforts in the midst of intractable conflicts, most notably in Central and South America. Likewise, there are many faith-based organizations that minister to the needs of those suffering in conflict and postconflict settings by providing food, shelter, medical care, counseling, and other services. These are not "force multipliers" of the U.S. government or the United Nations; indeed, they may be critical of specific governmental policies. They are, however, allies in the commitment of Western governments to human rights and flourishing.

Other agents for peace include individuals or groups who report a "calling" to engage in religiously inspired peacemaking, such as Archbishop Desmond Tutu's reconciliation work in South Africa. Recently, the U.S. Agency for International Development partnered with the archbishop in a peace and justice conference in Colombia designed to build trust among communities divided by the long civil war there. This is not the first time that the U.S. government has provided financial support for, or ended up at the same table with, religious peacemakers. Pope John Paul II claimed spiritual authority to act as an agent of peace, and he was clearly identified by President Ronald Reagan as an ally of American ideals, although the pontiff was also critical of some aspects of American society.

Finally, religiously inspired claims can redefine identities to promote reconciliation, transforming opponents to "God's children" and "brothers and sisters." In Mozambique, for example, religious peacemakers motivated states to follow their lead and guarantee the peace. Similarly, faith-inspired forgiveness transcends the often unresolved temporal issues of a conflict, as has happened for some victims of Latin America's military dictatorships and the Rwandan genocide.

In sum, religious actors and impulses infuse contemporary violence and peace building and thus are critical for social scientific study as well as foreign policy consideration. With a few important exceptions, there has simply not been enough work on these issues. Scholars have conducted even less work, however, on the key themes this book addresses: the issues surrounding religion in and around national militaries.

Key Themes in This Volume

Although this book was written by authors from different countries adopting different approaches, there are a number of consistent themes throughout the work. These include questions surrounding religion in the ranks as a mirror of the religiosity of society at large, the prevalence of a customary civil religion in many national militaries, the utility of some form of religious professional within the formal military structure, the differences between classical (secular) armed forces and religionized or ideologically motivated state military entities, debates over the appropriate balance of religion in the national militaries, and the onset of – and possible cognitive dissonance occasioned by – postmodern values in Western militaries.

Religion in the Ranks Mirrors Society at Large

Armed forces are a reflection of the state, particularly in a democratic society. Although those drawn to military service are likely to be distinguished by certain attitudinal predispositions, soldiers, marines, sailors, and airmen are nonetheless likely to reflect many of the same attitudes as their fellow citizens. This is particularly true in countries that maintain a national service requirement, such as Israel.

This volume corroborates this point: the religious sentiments of citizens and soldiers in most of the countries studied seem to correspond. In highly religious societies such as Pakistan (Chapter 4) and India (Chapter 7), a great deal of accommodation is made to allow for or integrate religious observance into the rhythms of military life. In more secular societies such as Japan (Chapter 1) and the United Kingdom (Chapter 3), many of the cultural practices that have lost their significance as acts of religious piety and worship have nonetheless remained as customary practices that enrich military life, such as prayers and visits to shrines.

This question about whether the military mirrors its society is often debated in elite circles in the United States, Canada, and the United Kingdom, where the militaries are voluntary and where – for the past few decades – a tiny percentage of the population has chosen to serve. It is likely that the younger members of the armed services, particularly enlisted personnel who serve only one or two tours of service, resemble their nonmilitary counterparts. However, it is unclear whether careerists – particularly high-ranking noncommissioned and commissioned officers – hold substantively different attitudes and values from the public at large. It is also interesting that, at least in the United States, the military is ranked year after year in surveys as one of the most trusted institutions in American life. Does this have to do with veneration for military service alone, or does it suggest that the average American citizen finds some values set in the military subculture that is attractive? More research is needed on these questions.

A related question has to do with the way that Western societies are changing. As societies secularize, as in the case of Western Europe and Canada, postmodern values may increasingly infuse the normative framework of the military and change the rationale for service. For instance, in the chapter on Canada (Chapter 2), Joanne Benham Rennick reports on an increasing sentiment in favor of compassion and peace building in contrast to historic motivations "For God and King." This suggests that more work is needed to explore the meaning of service in countries such as Canada and the Scandinavian states. How do these changes affect attitudes and justifications for the use of armed force and the way these societies understand their commitments to the international community?

The fact that, in many contexts, religion in the ranks parallels religion in society at large does call for additional research. This book includes no case studies from continental Europe, Africa, the Arab Middle East, or Africa, suggesting that there is a great deal of work yet to be accomplished. How should we understand the role of religion in a country ruled by a religious-minority regime (e.g., Syria and Bahrain)? What about a monolithic Catholic country in Latin America or a highly secularized continental European country? What role does religion play in a country where some clergy were implicated in violence (Rwanda)? What about the lives of clandestine believers serving in antireligious militaries, such as China? More work is needed to broaden our understanding of these issues.

The Role of Civil Religion in Military Culture

The U.S. military counts among its many traditions invocations, benedictions, open chapel programming, edificatory remarks by professional military chaplains, and many rituals associated with death and burial. From the cross at the graveside to prayers for national leaders, victory, and peace, religious symbols are an inherent part of the military environment.

Indeed, military culture tends to be conservative, hierarchical, and highly symbolic. The customs and courtesies of the profession of arms include far more than deference to authority. These customs often reinforce a sense of memory and morality. Warriors remember a long tradition of those before them who defended the homeland in the past and won glory on the battlefield: Washington, Frederick the Great, Napoleon and Wellington, Grant, Foch, Montgomery, De Gaulle, Eisenhower, Patton, and MacArthur. The same holds true for the sea (from Nelson to Nimitz) and more recently the air (von Richenbacher, Doolittle, and the aces of MiG Alley). In most cases, it is not simply the victory but also the broader code of conduct that these men epitomized. It is Washington kneeling in prayer at Valley Forge; Grant embodying Lincoln's determination to win both the war and the peace; Nelson's sacrifice of his health (to malaria), then an eye, then an arm, and ultimately his life in defense of his country; MacArthur's "I will return ..." promise to the Philippines and his valedictory speech, "Duty, Honor, Country" at West Point. There is a morality here, a spiritual code of conduct rooted in sacrifice for country and for comrades.

Today, there is some controversy over these symbols, usually generated by politically liberal elites, either academic or in the policy world. In the United States, the revisionist approach to the Establishment Clause in the U.S. Constitution reinterprets the notion of "no established church" in a highly religious society by seeking to bar religion from the public sphere. It is beyond the parameters of this concluding chapter to weigh in on this culture war in American public life, other than to note that from the founding through the mid-twentieth century, there was no expectation that the United States would become an irreligious or antireligious country. Likewise, as Boston University professor Stephen Prothero records in his writing on "religious literacy," twentieth-century court cases expected religion to remain a part of education and public life, but they ruled that the government could not favor one religion over others or use tax dollars to overtly support one religious creed.[7]

Survey results suggest that Americans remain a religious people, even if they are not deeply interested in theology.[8] Americans also share a support for civil religion: a meaningful, often shallow, Judeo-Christian notion of religion, the sacred, and the role of faith in individual and public life. This approach to religion is characteristic of the vast majority of the American armed forces as well.

This book demonstrates that such is also the case in other countries. The United Kingdom is most similar to the United States among Western countries, given the role of chaplains, prayers, and symbols in its armed forces. Many other countries, however, retain some symbols from a more religious past, including Canada and Japan. According to Aaron Skabelund and Akito Ishikawa (Chapter 1), Japan is particularly interesting, as it is a highly secular populace that nonetheless has retained cultural practices that have religious roots. The Japanese military seems to continue many of these practices in a deeper and more meaningful way, through prayers for the deceased and visits to shrines. This intersection of religious ritual and civil institutions should not be surprising, particularly as regards history and the dead. Militaries look to the past for inspiration from those who went before, and with death an ever-present possibility it is not surprising for members of militaries to pay solemn tribute to the dead and the possibility of the spiritual. In sum, many of the militaries studied herein not only reflect their societies but also maintain within their DNA a civil religion of values, memories, and rituals.

A Role for Religious Professionals

Most of the national militaries discussed in this volume employ religious professionals, be they formal chaplains or other functionaries. By far, the largest and most robust military chaplaincies are those in the Anglophone world: the United States, Canada, the United Kingdom, and South Africa. The U.S. model for chaplains is clear: their essential purpose has always been to provide military members an opportunity to exercise their right to worship under constrained and sometimes dangerous conditions. In religiously diverse countries, most notably Canada and the United States, this has meant that chaplaincies must display some diversity within their corps as well as flexibility in the practice of individual clergy if they are to meet the "free exercise" needs of their congregations.

There are many places around the world, however, where military chaplains represent only a quasi-established, national church. This is typically the case in Catholic countries, such as Latin America, where Catholicism has long enjoyed privileged status. Similarly, although many Muslim countries do not have formal chaplaincies based on the Western model, those that do tend to have monoreligious chaplaincies. For instance, Jordan has a highly professional, entirely Muslim chaplaincy that has seen service in Afghanistan.

This volume suggests several other roles for religious professionals. For instance, in Turkey (Chapter 10) there has never been an established chaplaincy because the military has long prided itself on modernizing (and secularizing) the country. Bowing to the popular religiosity of the enlisted ranks, however, as well as the need for some spiritual guidance in times of conflict, the military has hired theology students and theology graduates to provide religious services for the troops. In some ways this represents an instrumental approach: religion is a lived reality that must be accommodated as an operational necessity whether or not the officer corps approves.

In contrast, revolutionary Iran (Chapter 6) has taken a much different approach to the issue, deploying imams and other religionists with duties far beyond after-hours faith observances. Imams served as recruiters, exhorters, and faith-based justifiers of the regime's policies and military strategies. Indeed, the Islamization of Iran's security apparatus included the type of officials who would have been labeled "apparatchik," "commissar," and "political officer" in a communist country. These individuals watched for reactionary forces, worked to keep a pure Islamist ideology in front of the officers and troops at all times, and vigorously promoted the worldview of Ayatollah Khomeini and his inner circle. These ideologues declared the regime's wars "holy" because the regime itself was an expression of Allah: conflict with the United States and war with Iraq were thus holy wars.

In short, there are a variety of models of religious professionals participating in military service, from chaplains providing religious services to ideologues whipping the troops into a fanatical frenzy. We have read little, however, about how religious professionals might help train the troops in avoiding religious-cultural faux pas. In the final section of this chapter, I discuss the possibility of developing nonclerical religious affairs experts.

Ideological versus Classical Militaries

In her fascinating discussion of Iran, Mahsa Rouhi describes a long-term conflict between the "classical" military and the revolutionary government. The classical military refers to the shah's armed forces, many of whom were trained in modern, Western modes of warfare. The development of the Iranian military, prior to the 1979 revolution, emphasized a secular, technocratic professionalism and allegiance to the state. In contrast, the revolution brought to power ideologues who feared a reactionary military but needed the armed forces to stave off an invasion by Iraq. Over time, the regime developed a set of ideological structures that infused religion into all facets of national security. Tehran did this first by developing parallel military structures that professionalized over time, most notably the Revolutionary Guards. Second, the regime dispersed imams and ideologues through the ranks of the traditional military. Third, it recruited a religious and ideologically motivated population to do their duty and serve in the nation's defense.

In the Iran case, the outcomes were startling. One of Rouhi's findings is that the ideologically driven approach, articulated in religious concepts of service and sacrifice, created an army of would-be martyrs. The logic motivating a legion of "true believers" intent on self-destruction, be they kamikazes or Shi'a revolutionaries, is far different from that of a traditional national army. Many of Iran's neighbors practice conscription, but during the Iran-Iraq War tens of thousands of young men volunteered not simply to serve, but to participate in certain death, such as through human minesweeping.

The Iran case evokes twentieth-century totalitarian regimes more than it does contemporary militaries. Nonetheless, religion-inspired conflicts remain common. The chapters on Pakistan and India (chapters 4 and 7) are suggestive of how fragile some "classical" militaries are, and how factions in these societies would like to see a more religionized, more ideological approach to conflict. Were violent Islamists to take over the military leadership of Pakistan or Hindu nationalists seize the reins of the Indian state, would much change? Rationalists argue that ideologues in power become more "responsible" because they have so much to lose. Cases such as Iran, Cambodia, Nazi Germany, and the early Soviet period suggest that this is not always the case.

Postmodern Ethics

This chapter has pointed to the traditional cluster of military values that emphasizes duty to country and comrades, service, conformity to the group, and sacrifice in a near-religious manner. As the chapter by Benham Rennick (Chapter 2) suggests, however, postmodern values challenge the traditional model of military culture. Particularly in Western Europe and

North America, the diversity of value systems available comes directly into conflict with traditional military expectations of obedience and conformity. Benham Rennick specifically discusses how postmodern conceptions of ethics come into conflict with the martial values on which national militaries typically depend.

What will postmodernity mean for national militaries? How will the existentialism and radical individualism of postmodernity, as well as the practice of questioning authority and the fluidity of morality, affect notions of service, command authority, and political will? To date, we simply do not know, although it is clear that fewer and fewer Westerners are volunteering to take on the rigors of military life as a profession. Here the body of literature generated by *The Civic Culture* may be useful: the second generation of that scholarship, led by Ronald Inglehart's book *Culture Shift in Advanced Industrial Societies*, argued that Western societies were becoming increasingly postmodern and postmaterialistic in their definitions of security and politics.[9] What is missing is extended research on the influence of postmaterialist values on national militaries.

Balancing Religion in the Ranks
Several chapters discussed whether there was too much, or too little, religion in the ranks. In the Iranian case, the ayatollahs were convinced that there was simply too little religion in the ranks, so they empowered a massive system of faith and indoctrination not only for the military but also for the entire country. Some of Pakistan's leaders have likewise been concerned about the mores of the populace and the military and therefore imposed Islamizing programs to inspire religious purity across all sectors of society.

Many authors in this book, however, are more concerned about whether there is too much religion in national militaries. Aaron Skabelund and Akito Ishikawa (Chapter 1) report that there are significant reservations in some quarters of Japan that the Self-Defense Force is excessively entangled with religious practices that venerate Japan's imperial past. Likewise, Martin Cook (Chapter 8) is concerned that actors and organizations are attempting to evangelize the U.S. military from within in ways that violate not only the Establishment Clause but the sentiments of the American public as well. So, too, one must thoughtfully consider the contemporary religious militancy apparent in Pakistan, India, Sri Lanka, and elsewhere.

That said, it is unclear whether there is some general principle to be taken from these cases, other than that a society must judge for itself what the appropriate role for religion is in daily life, and therefore in military life. Militaries that are open and representative of the general public are far more likely to be in accord with national religious sentiments than are those that represent only a minority viewpoint. Indeed, disputes over the role of conscience, religion, and values are a hallmark of a democracy, particularly in so highly religious a democracy as the United States.

Avenues for Future Research

This volume makes an important contribution to the study of the national and institutional environment of religion in some of the world's most important countries. Similar to any good research project, it opens multiple vistas for future research.

The first is deepening the analysis of the countries included in the volume. Even two chapters cannot provide an adequate portrayal of the multidimensionality of issues faced by the U.S. military, especially given the narrow public preoccupation with past troubles at the Air Force Academy and the small U.S. chaplaincy. The U.S. military is large enough and diverse enough within the American political and social landscape to warrant an edited volume of its own. That book could not only look at the training environment of military undergraduates at the three academies but also compare them to other military undergraduates who are the products of ROTC and other commissioning programs as well as the training and students found at later stages of officers' careers (e.g., the Command and Staff College and the War College). Comparisons of attitudes on religion in military households as compared to those of other Americans, examining and controlling for other demographic factors, would be of interest. So would analyses of how religious factors do or do not pervade the political landscape that the U.S. military faces, be it promilitary interest groups (e.g., the Veterans of Foreign Wars, the American Legion, and more recent groups), antiwar activist networks, or the complicated landscape of Congress. Of course, military chaplains, both as pastors and as mediators with religious leaders in host nations, require scholarly attention.

A follow-on volume might include a new constellation of countries for comparison, including those with the largest militaries (e.g., Russia and China) as well as the more active militaries of Western Europe, notably France, Germany, Italy, and Spain. Highly religious countries, such as Bangladesh (always one of the world's top contributors of bodies to UN peacekeeping missions), Brazil, and Poland are also worthy of sustained attention. Further work on the countries examined in this volume might entail more contemporary analysis of past cases (especially the United Kingdom and Iran) as well as a return to all of these countries in the near future to assess changes and trends.

Another vector for future research, largely untouched by this volume, is the topic of world religions training for the military. As national militaries increasingly deploy to highly religious environments, how should military personnel prepare for the cultural and religious land mines attendant in their work? Since the terrorist attacks of September 11, 2001, this has been an area of controversy raised by friendly critics of the U.S. government. The United States and its allies have done little to alter their training regimens to prepare their officers, diplomats, and aid experts on the nexus of religion and world affairs – this, despite the Iranian Revolution and violence across the greater Middle East for three decades, not to mention the religious and cultural overtones of conflagrations in Bosnia, Kosovo, Sudan, East Timor, West Africa, and throughout the global war on terrorism. Indeed, as I and others have noted, there has been an aversion in many government quarters to dealing with these issues. It was only in 2007, six years after the September 11 attacks, that various military programs began their first investments in some form of world religions awareness.[10] This usually takes the form of an in-residence elective course on religion and security at the war college level for the small coterie of military officers who can attend in-residence. In addition, in the past three years, U.S. Central Command and the Air Force's Air University have invested significant resources in understanding and training on religious and cultural issues. These efforts are largely, and rightly for now, directed at the greater Middle East.

Yet, what of Canada, France, Italy, South Korea, Poland, Bulgaria, or Georgia? How are these states preparing their troops for engaging in highly religious environments in central Asia? What about Bangladeshis deployed to Somalia? Catholics deployed as part of the UN observer mission on Cyprus? A comparative look at current policies in this regard would be of immense interest to foreign and national security policy observers, as would ensuing policy recommendations.

A fourth area for research involves religious justifications for "military operations other than war." This phrase, often redacted to its ungainly initials MOOTW, has come to mean the use of the military instrument in situations other than traditional interstate wars, such as counterterrorism, counterinsurgency, and in some cases peacekeeping, peace enforcement, and national reconstruction. One can imagine an entire spectrum of operations that differ from the traditional battle space found at Gettysburg or Midway, from aggressive humanitarian intervention (e.g., East Timor, Kosovo) to counterguerrilla warfare (e.g., Colombia) to coercive diplomacy (e.g., no-fly zones over Iraq). Are there religious justifications for such activities? Are there ethical justifications for such activities?

Benham Rennick's chapter on Canada demonstrates that justifications for military deployment have changed over time, as have the sentiments of people in the ranks who wanted to operate beyond the national interest or mission parameters, narrowly defined, and act on behalf of human compassion to alleviate suffering. Traditionally, notions of just war and realpolitik informed these debates. Religious and secular pacifists tended to abstain from these discussions and reject war altogether. Is a new set of arguments for armed humanitarian intervention and for coercive diplomacy on behalf of human life emerging that is rooted in religious arguments? Furthermore, postwar stabilization and reconstruction operations, which are often nation- and institution-building missions, raise a host of new issues that were absent in "victory-then-exit" operations. What are the religious justifications, if any, for rebuilding war-torn countries? How do these religious justifications vary across religious traditions?

Conclusion

Although many have dreamed of a perpetual peace, and some hoped that the twenty-first century would usher in a new era of security, such has not been the case. At the time these chapters were being written, the United States and its allies were heavily engaged in operations in Afghanistan, Iraq, and Libya, and war-torn societies struggled to find equilibrium in North Africa, West Africa, southern Africa, East Africa, Colombia, the "frozen" Korean Peninsula, various points in central Asia, the jungles of Mindanao, the highlands of Kashmir, and elsewhere. Many of these conflicts – though not all – include religious factors intertwined with issues of economic and political competition, cultural chauvinism, and historic grievance. National militaries engage with a highly religious world on a daily basis, both at home and abroad.

This book does offer numerous hopeful notes. Perhaps the most important of these is that even those armed and trained to kill can learn to live in harmony with others from different faiths. While Indian citizens kill one another over a sacred shrine in India, the Indian military has found ways to maintain esprit de corps and mission focus in its ranks. Likewise, from Pakistan to the United States, highly religious societies produce soldiers, sailors, marines, and airmen who are also highly religious, yet none of the militaries studied herein have imploded into religious violence in the ranks. This is a testimony to their sense of national service and martial cohesion, and perhaps is a signal that societies have something to learn from their militaries.

Notes

1   Gabriel Almond and Sydney Verba, *The Civic Culture: Political Attitudes and Democracy in Five Nations* (Princeton, NJ: Princeton University Press, 1963).

2   Romans 13:1–5 (King James Authorized Version) reads, "Let every soul be subject unto the higher powers. For there is no power but of God: the powers that be are ordained of God. Whosoever therefore resisteth the power, resisteth the ordinance of God: and they that resist shall receive to themselves damnation. For rulers are not a terror to good works, but to the evil. Wilt thou then not be afraid of the power? Do that which is good, and thou shalt have praise of the same. For he [the government official] is the minister of God to thee for good. But if thou do that which is evil, be afraid; for he beareth not the sword in vain: for he is the minister of God, a revenger to execute wrath upon him that doeth evil. Wherefore ye must needs be subject, not only for wrath, but also for conscience sake."

3   James Turner Johnson, "Debates over Just War and Jihad: Ideas, Interpretations, and Implications Across Cultures," in *Debating the War of Ideas*, ed. Eric Patterson and John P. Gallagher (New York: Palgrave Macmillan, 2009). See also John Kelsay, *Arguing Just War in Islam* (Cambridge, MA: Harvard University Press, 2007).

4   For a full treatment of this model, see "The Religious Dynamics of War and Peace" in Eric Patterson, *Politics in a Religious World: Building a Religiously Informed U.S. Foreign Policy* (New York: Continuum, 2011): 73–87.

5 S. Farmar, "I will Use the Ten Commandments to Liberate Uganda," *The Times*, 28 June 2006.

6 Osama Bin Laden, "World Islamic Front Statement: Jihad against Jews and Crusaders," 23 February 1998.

7 Stephen Prothero, *Religious Literacy: What Every American Needs to Know – And Doesn't* (New York: HarperCollins, 2007).

8 For evidence on this, see ibid. as well as the 2007 Pew Global Attitudes Survey, http://religions.pewforum.org/reports#. Historically, this argument can be found in Alexis de Tocqueville, *Democracy in America* (1831).

9 Ronald Inglehart, *Culture Shift in Advanced Industrial Societies* (Princeton, NJ: Princeton University Press, 1989).

10 Patterson, *Politics in a Religious World*, 86–87.

Contributor Biographies

Amit Ahuja is an assistant professor of political science at the University of California, Santa Barbara. He holds a PhD from the University of Michigan and degrees from St. Stephen's College, the University of Delhi, and the School of Oriental and African Studies at the University of London. His work focuses on the participation and mobilization of marginalized ethnic groups. His research interests include ethnic politics, political development, security studies, and South Asia. His current book project, which focuses on Dalit mobilization, seeks to explain the variation in success of Dalit-based parties across four states in India: Bihar, Maharashtra, Tamil Nadu, and Uttar Pradesh.

Joanne Benham Rennick is an assistant professor of contemporary studies, Wilfrid Laurier University. She holds degrees from Wilfrid Laurier University and the University of Waterloo. She is the author of *Religion in the Ranks: Belief and Religious Experience in the Canadian Forces* (2011) and has published widely on religion in the Canadian armed forces as well as on religious diversity and discrimination in North America.

Stuart A. Cohen is professor of politics at Ashkelon Academic College, Israel. His research focuses on the changing relations between Israeli society and the Israel Defense Forces (IDF), IDF force structure, manpower policies, and military strategy. He also specializes in Jewish political tradition and the diplomatic history of the Middle East. He has been Visiting Scholar at Harvard University's Center for Jewish Studies and Visiting Fellow at the University of Cape Town. He is the coauthor of *The Jewish Polity: Jewish Political Organization from Biblical Times to the Present* (with Daniel Elazar, 1985) and the author of *The Three Crowns: Structures of Communal Politics in Early Rabbinic Jewry* (1990); *The Scroll or the Sword? Dilemmas of Religion and Military Service in Israel* (1997), and *Israel and Its Army: From Cohesion to Confusion* (2008).

Martin L. Cook is Admiral James Bond Stockdale Professor of Professional Military Ethics at the U.S. Naval War College. He was Professor of Philosophy and Deputy Department Head at the U.S. Air Force Academy and Professor of Ethics in the Department of Command, Leadership, and Management of the U.S. Army War College in Carlisle, Pennsylvania in 1998. He serves on the editorial boards of *Parameters*, the scholarly journal of the Army War College, and *The Journal of Military Ethics*. His most recent book, *The Moral Warrior: Ethics and Service in the U.S. Military*, was published in 2004.

Stephen Deakin is a senior lecturer at the Royal Military Academy Sandhurst where he teaches leadership to British Army officer trainees and to military leaders worldwide. His primary publishing area is military ethics. He is the author of numerous book chapters and academic papers that examine ethical issues from the perspective of the British military.

Victor Dobbin, CB MBE PhD DD, retired from the British Army in 2000, having been chaplain general (major general) for five and a half years. During his years as chaplain general, he became particularly interested in the development of one aspect of army doctrine – the moral component of fighting power – and was involved with the introduction of a mandatory package of training on values for all British military personnel. On leaving the army, he was awarded a Churchill Fellowship that enabled him to travel to the United States as well as to Holland and Germany to study how ethics is being developed and taught within the military professions in these countries. Since then he has established a charity on leadership and ethics, and he has given lectures at international military conferences in South Korea, Sri Lanka, Switzerland, and elsewhere.

Gül M. Kurtoğlu Eskişar is an associate professor of international relations at Dokuz Eylul University, Izmir, Turkey. After graduating as the valedictorian from Bilkent University with a BA degree in International Relations, she received both her MA degree in International Relations and PhD degree in Political Science from the University of Chicago. While doing her graduate studies at Chicago, she received various prestigious scholarships from the Fulbright Foundation, the University of Chicago, and the Andrew Mellon Foundation. Kurtoğlu Eşkisar is a specialist on political Islam, on which she wrote her dissertation and has published various articles in the *Japanese Journal of Political Science* and the *Romanian Journal of Political Science*, among others, to date. She also coedited, with Ayşegül Komsuoğlu, a book in Turkish on political Islam in different parts of the world. Her current research focuses on the dynamics of state control and the impact of patronage networks on the potential tensions between secular and religious populations in different Middle Eastern countries.

C. Christine Fair is an assistant professor in the Center for Peace and Security Studies, within Georgetown University's Edmund A. Walsh School of Foreign Service. Previously, she served as a senior political scientist with the RAND

Corporation, a political officer to the UN Assistance Mission to Afghanistan in Kabul, and a senior research associate in the Center for Conflict Analysis and Prevention at the United States Institute of Peace. She is also a senior fellow with the Combatting Terrorism Center at West Point. Her research focuses on political and military affairs in South Asia. She has authored, coauthored, or coedited several books, including *Treading Softly on Sacred Ground: Counterinsurgency Operations on Sacred Space* (2008); *The Madrassah Challenge: Militancy and Religious Education in Pakistan* (2008), and *Fortifying Pakistan: The Role of U.S. Internal Security Assistance* (2006).

Ron E. Hassner is an associate professor of political science at the University of California, Berkeley. His research revolves around symbolic and emotive aspects of international security with particular attention to religious violence, Middle Eastern politics, and territorial disputes. His book, *War on Sacred Grounds* (2009) examines the causes and characteristics of disputes over sacred places around the globe and analyzes the conditions under which these conflicts can be managed. He has also published on the topic of religion and conflict in *International Security, International Studies Quarterly, Security Studies,* and *Terrorism and Political Violence,* among other journals, and he has contributed chapters on similar themes to several edited volumes.

Akito Ishikawa is an assistant professor in the Faculty of Letters at Hokkaido University in Sapporo, Japan. His books have examined the meaning of religious art through modern Protestant theology and religious philosophy, and war in relation to religious culture. Akito has taught courses on the history of religion and culture of war. His research interests include religious thought, military thought, and religious terrorism.

Ayşegül Komsuoğlu is an associate professor of political science at Istanbul University, Turkey. She received both her MA degree on Balkan, Middle East and Central Asia Studies and PhD degree on International Relations from Istanbul University. She was a visiting scholar at Emory University (2003–2004) and at U.C. Berkeley (2009–2010). Komsuoğlu has published articles in *Gender, Place and Culture* and in *Nationalism and Ethnic Politics,* among others. She is the author of a book on political leadership in Turkey. She edited a book on political opposition in Turkey and also coedited, with Gül Kurtoğlu, a book in Turkish on political Islam in different parts of the world. She has taught political science and modern Turkish history at several universities. Her recent research interests are clientelist relations in Turkish politics and political Islam in Turkey.

Pauletta Otis is a professor of security studies at the Command and Staff College, Marine Corps University. Before assuming a position as Senior Researcher for Religion and International Affairs at Pew Forum (2005–2006), she held the position of Professor of Strategic Studies at the Joint Military Intelligence College (1997–1998, 2002–2004). She was a tenured professor of political science and international studies and chairman of the Political Science Department at Colorado State University–Pueblo from 1989 to 2004, and continues to teach extended studies classes for the Colorado Consortium. She has also worked in the military security community as a subject matter expert in the areas of terrorism, counterterrorism, and religious violence.

Eric Patterson is dean of the School of Government at Regent University in Virginia Beach, VA, and Senior Research Fellow at the Berkley Center for Religion, Peace, and World Affairs, Georgetown University. His public speaking, research, and teaching focuses on ethics and international affairs, religion and contemporary statecraft, and just war theory in the context of ongoing conflict. He is the author or editor of seven books, including, most recently, *Ending Wars Well: Order, Justice and Conciliation in Contemporary Post-Conflict* (2012), *Ethics Beyond War's End* (2012), *Politics in a Religious World: Building a Religiously Literate U.S. Foreign Policy* (2011), and, with John Gallagher, *Debating the War of Ideas* (2009). Prior to going to Georgetown, Patterson spent three years working for the federal government. He served as a White House Fellow and before that was William C. Foster Fellow in the State Department's Bureau of Political and Military Affairs.

Mahsa Rouhi is a PhD candidate in international relations at the University of Cambridge and a research associate at the Center for International Studies at Massachusetts Institute of Technology. She is also a nuclear security predoctoral Fellow at the Belfer Center for Science and International Affairs at Harvard University. She received her bachelor's degree in economics from Shahid Beheshty University and a master's degree in political theory from the University of Sheffield. Her dissertation focuses on Iran's foreign and security policy making, with a special focus on Iran's nuclear-related policy making.

Aaron Skabelund is an assistant professor of history at Brigham Young University. He completed a PhD in modern Japanese history at Columbia University and a postdoctoral fellowship with the Japan Society for the Promotion of Science at Hokkaido University. His first book, *Empire of Dogs: Canines, Japan, and the Making of the Modern Imperial World* (2011), examines the history of empire – Western and Japanese, human and canine – by analyzing the actual actions and metaphorical deployment of dogs. He is currently working on a social and cultural history of Japan's postwar military, the Self-Defense Forces.

Index